SHATTERED DREAMS OF REVOLUTION

SHATTERED DREAMS OF REVOLUTION

From Liberty to Violence
in the Late Ottoman Empire

BEDROSS DER MATOSSIAN

STANFORD UNIVERSITY PRESS
STANFORD, CALIFORNIA

Stanford University Press
Stanford, California

Printed and bound by CPI Group (UK) Ltd, Croydon, CR0 4YY

Library of Congress Cataloging-in-Publication Data

Der Matossian, Bedross, 1978- author.
 Shattered dreams of revolution : from liberty to violence in the late Ottoman Empire / Bedross Der Matossian.
     pages cm
 Includes bibliographical references and index.
 ISBN 978-0-8047-9147-2 (cloth : alk. paper)--ISBN 978-0-8047-9263-9 (pbk. : alk. paper)
 1. Turkey--History--Revolution, 1908. 2. Turkey--Politics and government--1909-1918.
 3. Turkey--Ethnic relations--History--20th century. 4. Turkey--History--Ottoman Empire, 1288-1918. I. Title.
 DR584.5.D47 2014
 956'.02--dc23

                              2014018282

 ISBN 978-0-8047-9270-7 (electronic)

Typeset by Bruce Lundquist in 10/14 Minion

To my parents,
Vartan and Haiganush,
and beloved aunt,
Osanna Der Matossian

CONTENTS

CONTENTS

ACKNOWLEDGMENTS

In the course of my writing this book, many friends, scholars, colleagues, mentors, and organizations played an important role. I am indebted to all of them.

First and foremost, my deepest appreciation and gratitude go to three people whose mentorship and invaluable guidance have contributed immensely to the realization of this project. Through his patience and expertise, Rashid Khalidi was indispensable for the writing of this book. While I was at Columbia University, he infused in me the interest to explore interethnic relationships in the Middle East. Nader Sohrabi has been guiding me through the different stages of writing by broadening my horizons in understanding late Ottoman history. Our fascination with the Young Turks period resulted in fruitful exchanges of ideas and contributed to the crystallization of this book. Karen Barkey has been a great mentor and a source of support during the past decade. Her guidance in critically understanding the framework of empires and ethnic groups was crucial in shaping the direction of this book.

I express my sincere gratitude to Richard Hovannisian, who ignited in me the desire to pursue modern Armenian history and has been a parental figure during my academic career. I am especially grateful to Philip Khoury and Craig Wilder at the Massachusetts Institute of Technology for their constant support and encouragement at very difficult times.

This project would not have been possible without the support of Stanford University Press editor-in-chief Kate Wahl. Her comments and insights during the various stages of writing were instrumental to the successful completion of the book. Frances Malcolm, associate editor, played an important role during the submission of this project. Mariana Raykov, the production editor, facilitated the production phase for this book. Special thanks go to Cynthia Lindlof for doing a superb job in copyediting the manuscript in a rigorous way. I also thank the two anonymous reviewers for their outstanding feedback on earlier versions of this book; their thoughtful comments brought the book to a new level. Thanks also to Eyal Ginio and Ronald Grigor Suny for reading and commenting on earlier drafts. Andrea Jones's close reading and comments on the manuscript were extremely useful. On a personal level I would like to thank my friend and colleague Ari Ariel for patiently reading and commenting on earlier drafts of this manuscript. His constant encouragement, positive attitude, and support contributed immensely to the realization of this project.

I benefited from scholarships and fellowships that enabled me to research and write this book. I would like to thank the Department of History and its chair, William Thomas, at the University of Nebraska–Lincoln (UNL) for their support of this project. I also thank the Harris Center for Judaic Studies at UNL and its director, Jean Cahan, for their research support. The support of the Department of Middle East, South Asian, and African studies at Columbia University has been instrumental during my graduate school years. In particular I thank the Clara and Krikor Zohrab Fellowship and the Gorvetzian Family Fund for their constant financial support. The Armenian National Institute, the Armenian General Benevolent Union, the Gulbenkian Foundation, the GSAS Summer Fellowship, the Middle East Institute summer fellowships, and Union of Marash Armenians Scholarship have all contributed immensely to this project through their travel and research grants.

Research for this project has been done in different institutes, archives, and libraries. The assistance given by the staff of these institutions has made the research for this book possible. First and foremost, I thank my longtime friend Rev. Father Norayr Kazazian, director of Gulbenkian Library in Jerusalem, who has made available most of the Armenian primary sources for this book. His constant support and friendship all these years have made a great difference. I also thank Hayfa al-Khalidi from the Khalidiye Library (Jerusalem), Khader Salamah from al-Aqsa Library (Jerusalem), Mustafa al-Safadi from the Islamic Heritage Institute archives (Jerusalem), the staff of the Jewish National Library (Jerusalem), the Central Archives for the History of the Jewish People (Jerusalem), and the Central Zionist Archives (Jerusalem). I thank the National Association for Armenian Studies and Research (Belmont, MA) for its support, as well as Ara Sanjian and Gerald Ottenbreit Jr. from the Armenian Research Center (University of Michigan–Dearborn), Kavous Barghi from the Hoover Institution (Stanford University), the staff at the Weidner Library (Harvard University), Firestone Library (Princeton University), and New York Public Library. Finally, I would like to thank the staff of Butler Library at Columbia University for their indispensable help and assistance in providing me with most of the sources that I needed for this research.

Sebouh Aslanian, Marc Mamigonian, Uğur Umit Üngör, and Raffi Yezegelian have been great friends in the past decade, providing much-needed intellectual and emotional support. Their friendship truly made a great difference. Heartfelt thanks to Levon Altiparmakian, the late Paersa Marianne Altiparmakian, Tamar Boyadjian, Mabel Chin, Mary Hoogasian, Vartiter Hovannisian, Antoine Karamanlian, Sergio and Malina La Porta, Tsolin Nalbantian, Katia Peltekian, Boghos Shahinian, Salim Tamari, and Keith and Heghnar Watenpaugh. The following individuals have been particularly helpful throughout my academic journey: Taner Akçam, Reuven Amitai, Sossie Andezian, Aram Arkun, Arman Artuç, Lala Demirdjian-Attarian, Anny Bakalian, Kevork Bardakjian, Yuval Ben-Bassat, Houri Berberian, Michael Bobelian, Barbara Bullington, David Cahan, Julia Phillips Cohen, Hamid Dabashi, Assaf David, Daniel DeAngelo, Rina Djernazian, Edma Dumanian, Howard Eissenstat, Lerna Ekmekcioglu, Ayda Erbal, Roberta Ervine, James Garza, Aret Gıcır, Gloria Hachikian, Martin Haroutunian, George Hintlian, Abigail Jacobson, Elizabeth Johnston, Jeanette Jones, Banu Karaca, Raffi and Nanor Karagozian, Shant Karakashian, Aylin and Ara Koçunyan, Asbed Kotchikian, Lori Maness, Vartan Matiossian, Bob Matoush, Mark Mazower, Brinkley Messick, Anahid Mikirditsian, Garabet Moumdjian, Barlow Der Mugrdechian, Marc Nichanian, Seta Ohannesian, Nayire Ohannesyan, Ceren Ozgul, Cenk Palaz, Razmik Panossian, Sandra Pershing, Christine Philliou, Mehmet Polatel, Hamid Rezai, George Saliba, Ara Sarkissian, Linda Sayed, Andrea Scott, Bob Scott, Hovann Simonian, Joseph Simonian, Edward and Silva Siyahaian, Gerald Steinacher, Michael Stone, Lena Takvorian, Kadir Üstün, Alexander Vazansky, Kenneth J. Winkle, and Salem Zway. I would like to thank İsa Akbaş, Lorans Tanatar Baruh, and Edhem Eldem for providing me with the images for this book. During my seven years in New York City I was fortunate to have had Marianne Olmsted as my room-mate. Her constant support and positive attitude influenced immensely the course of my studies in general.

Last but not least, none of this would have been possible without my family. I am indebted to my father and mother, Vartan and Haiganush, who put all their effort to raising me. My "second mother," Aunt Osanna, made my (and my siblings') education her life's goal, and to that end she overcame many obstacles. My sister Victoria's care, compassion, and prayers have been instrumental in the past years. My brother and sister-in-law, Mihran and Naira, along with their daughters, Talar and Kohar, have been a source of cheerful energy, encouragement, and support. I am also indebted to my aunts Salwa Kafity, Berjouhi Kafity, Lucy and Antoine Abboud, Elizabeth, Lucine, Margo, Mary, Teresa Karamanlian, and my late aunts Araksi Ghazarian and Mary Karakashian. In the past few years new members entered into my family and supported me on a very rocky road. I thank my father-in-law and mother in-law, Jerair and Shakeh Siyahian, for genuinely embracing me like a son and providing love, support, and encouragement when I needed them the most. My sisters-in-law, Ani and Aida, warmly embraced me as a brother and have been cheering me on since.

Finally, I do not know how I would have written this book without my wife, Arpi Siyahian. Words would not express my gratitude to her love, commitment, dedication, and sacrifice in accompanying me through my journey on the tempestuous seas to the safe land. Her critical approach to history and her wisdom in life made it possible to write every single page of this book. Eternally I am indebted to her.

SHATTERED DREAMS
OF REVOLUTION

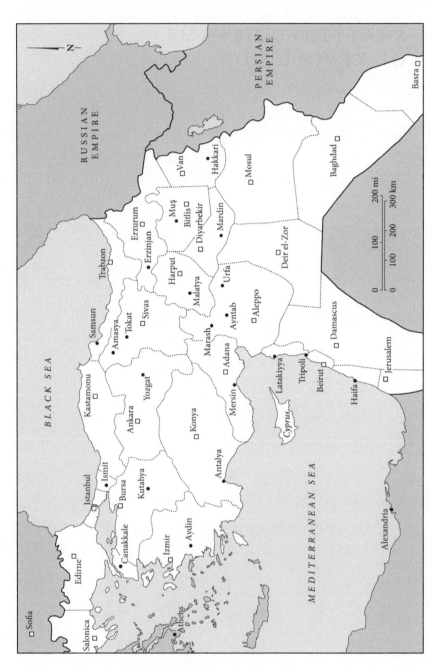

The Ottoman Empire at the end of the nineteenth century

INTRODUCTION

ON AUGUST 30, 1908, more than one hundred years ago, a major ceremony took place in the Armenian Apostolic Church of St. Gregory the Illuminator (Surb Grigor Lusavorichʻ) in Cairo, celebrating the Young Turk Revolution of July 24, 1908. The celebration, which was organized by the Armenian Revolutionary Society, was attended by important Muslim and Christian figures from a range of ethnic backgrounds. The event, led by the Armenian bishop Mguerdich Aghavnuni, was attended by important dignitaries such as Rashid Rida, the famous Islamic jurist and scholar, and Dr. Faris Nimr, editor of the pro-British *Al-Muqaṭṭam* (named after the mountain overlooking the city). During the event, Bishop Aghavnuni invited Nimr to the altar,[1] and Nimr commenced his speech:

> My Ottoman brothers:
> Ladies and gentlemen, I am addressing you as my Ottoman brothers, devoid of epithets and titles and stripped of veneration and glorification, as I do not find a sweeter expression on the Ottoman ear than this simple phrase, and there is no expression more desirable to the Ottoman and dearer to his heart than this simple phrase after we tasted the sweetness of Ottoman freedom and made the commitment to brotherhood and equality under the patronage of our empire.[2]

Nimr continued his speech by emphasizing that Muslims and Christians living in the empire were equals. After listening to other similar speeches, the Muslim crowd became enthusiastic. Several audience members lifted Rashid

Rida onto their shoulders and carried him to the altar to embrace the Armenian bishop.[3] This symbolic move was made for the practical implementation of one of the Revolution's major ideals: brotherhood.

There is no doubt that the Revolution of 1908 was affected by the regional and global waves of revolutions and constitutional movements that emerged in France (1789), Japan (1868), Russia (1905), and Iran (1905–1911).[4] All of these revolutions had in common that they believed the predicaments of their states and societies should be solved through the kind of political reform that had transformed the West into a successful entity: constitutionalism and parliamentary rule vehicles to curb the power of the monarchy. The revolutionaries of this period saw these political mechanisms as the only sure way to guarantee the demise of older, absolutist political systems.

The French Revolution of 1789, with its aura of success, as well as its slogans, symbolism, and language, became the master template for the revolutions of this period, an ahistoric model that traveled from one context to another.[5] In some cases, the revolutions failed to achieve their goals because of internal and external factors that hindered the endurance of their ideals.[6] In other cases, constitutionalism was used as a means to strengthen, centralize, and preserve the integrity of the national territory.

Much has been written on the causes and initial implementation of Middle Eastern revolutions during the early twentieth century. There is, however, a paucity of material that appropriately addresses their complexity and their impact on the *Weltanschauung* of the different ethno-religious groups in the postrevolutionary era. Existing scholarship on the impact of the Young Turk Revolution is divided into two groups. One views the Revolution as a factor that led to a decline of interethnic relations that culminated in the rise of ethnic nationalism, while the other romanticizes the period as the beginning of a positive project that was interrupted by World War I and the collapse of the empire.[7] Both approaches fail to adequately problematize the Revolution and demonstrate its complexities. In fact, the revolutionaries' uncritical adaptation, acceptance, and implementation of constitutionalism became counterproductive in an era in which it proved impossible to forge a unified nation and preserve the integrity of the Ottoman Empire. Thus, romanticizing the period and arguing that the different ethno-religious groups within the empire tried to see themselves as part of an Ottoman nation under the label "civic nationalism" is rather misleading.[8] The reality is that constitutionalism failed to create a new understanding of Ottoman citizenship, grant equal rights to all citizens, bring them under one roof in a legislative assembly, and finally resuscitate Ottomanism from the ashes of the Hamidian regime.

Achieving these goals became impossible due to the ambiguities and contradictions of the Revolution's goals and the reluctance of both the leaders of the Revolution and the majority of the empire's ethnic groups to come to a compromise regarding the new political framework of the empire. That the revolutionary ideals were obscure was particularly evident in the prerevolutionary period, when, as Nader Sohrabi states, constitutionalism that satisfied everyone was multivocal, and "multivocality spelled ambiguity." This multivocality was "a catalyst for consensus and coalition building among groups with contradictory and conflicting interests."[9] But the expectations raised by the Revolution for the formation of a new, constitutional nation under the label "Ottomanism" soon proved to be illusory. The major reason was that the Young Turks were not wholeheartedly committed to constitutionalism. For them, constitutionalism was only a means to an end: to maintain the integrity of a centralized Ottoman Empire. In fact, the Young Turks were determined to preserve the empire even if that meant violating the spirit of constitutionalism itself, as they demonstrated in their coup d'état of January 23, 1913, during the Balkan Wars. The Young Turks pursued all available means of consolidating their power within the empire, including interference in administrative affairs, the ouster of state and military personnel, vast purges of political opponents in the provinces, and most important, rigid enforcement of their own vision of reforms. That vision completely contradicted the *Weltanschauung* of the nondominant groups in the new era in which they wanted to preserve their ethno-religious/ethnic identities and privileges in tandem with the new, ambiguous project of Ottomanism.

This book tells the story of the shattered dreams of Arabs, Armenians, and Jews, three diversified ethnic groups representing vast geographic areas, as well as a wide range of interest groups, religions, classes, political parties, and factions. I would like to clarify an important point: my choice to use the concept of "ethnic group" rather than "national group." Ethnic group denotes a population "sharing common cultural characteristics and/or seeing itself as being of common descent or sharing a common historical experience."[10] In addition, by using the terms "Armenians," "Arabs," and "Jews" in the framework of ethnic groups, I do not intend to essentialize them and represent them as consistent or static in both time and space. The ideas of nations and nationalism were confined to only the intelligentsia and political activists who became the harbingers of cultural and political nationalism that emerged in the empire in the second half of the nineteenth and the beginning of the twentieth centuries. In the nineteenth century, the majority of the Ottoman Empire's constituent groups did not see themselves as part of a nation but rather as part of an ethno-religious community. Their identities meshed in an array of overlapping identities, highlighted by religious, linguistic, and cultural diversity, on the one hand, and regional and local loyalties, on the other. For example, the identity of an Iraqi Jew whose first language was Arabic, but who grew up in Baghdad, was not the same as that of a Salonican Jew living in Salonica whose first language was Ladino (Judeo-Spanish). Similarly, the identity of an Armenian living in Sivas who spoke the local Ottoman Turkish dialect was not the same as that of an Armenian from Istanbul who spoke fluent Armenian and identified with the Armenian bourgeois class. Despite this diversity in terms of language, culture, religion, locality, region, and class, the various groups falling within the bloc of an ethnic group still had an important common bond in their ethnic boundaries.

Ethnic boundaries, a concept I borrow from the social anthropologist Fredrik Barth, "are best understood as cognitive or mental boundaries situated in the minds of people and are the result of collective efforts of construction and maintenance."[11] Barth provides two vital explanations of the nature of ethnic boundaries in general that apply equally well to the particulars of the Ottoman Empire at the turn of the twentieth century. First, he argues that despite the flow of people from one group to another, ethnic boundaries persist. For Barth, ethnic distinctions are not based on a lack of mobility, contact, and information among these groups but instead "entail social processes of exclusion and incorporation whereby discrete categories are maintained despite changing participation and membership in the course of individual life histories." Second, he asserts that "stable, persisting, and often vitally important social relations are maintained across such boundaries and are frequently based precisely on the dichotomized ethnic statuses." In other words, he emphasizes the fact that ethnic distinctions are not based on the absence of social interaction; rather, they are the very foundations on which embracing social systems are built.[12] Thus, the ethnic boundaries between "Armenians," "Arabs," and "Jews," as well as other ethnic groups that constituted the larger Ottoman conglomerate, persisted not as a result of the absence of interaction but, conversely, as a result of the extensive interaction among them. This interaction was a key factor that distinguished one group from another. Thus, in this spatial and temporal scene, in which identities of groups were vague and overlapping, ethnic boundaries persisted, albeit in a fluid form.

In addition to this more theoretical reason for employing the term "ethnicity" to refer to these groups, I also use such qualifiers as "Kurds," "Turks," "Armenians," "Jews," "Arabs," or "Albanians" in order to adhere to the spirit of the newspapers published around and after the time of the Revolution, all of which referred to ethnic groups by using these qualifiers. Whether they intended to represent these groups as national, ethnic, or religious categories or as a combination of the categories is hard to tell, mainly because such usage depended on the historical and political context of each newspaper and each article. I have also based my own toponomic conventions on contemporary newspaper practice. For example, most of the ethnic presses used the term "Turkey" and "Ottoman Empire" interchangeably, as we will see throughout the text.

The book examines the ways in which the Revolution and constitutionalism raised these groups' expectations amid the postrevolutionary turmoil and how they internalized the Revolution, negotiating their space and identity within the rapidly changing political landscape of the period. Finally, it relates how the euphoric feelings of the postrevolutionary festivities gave way to a dramatic rise in ethnic tensions and pessimism among the nondominant groups. As a result, their faith in the Revolution and constitutionalism as vehicles for the realization of their dreams began to fade. Understanding the impact of revolutions from the perspective of nondominant groups and synthesizing that understanding with the known perspectives of the ruling elite are vital to comprehending their real complexities. However, this project does not provide decisive conclusions about the impact of the Revolution on all of the Ottoman Empire's nondominant groups. Linguistic restraints and the scope of this study make including all these groups—including Greeks, Albanians, Kurds, Bulgarians, Assyrians, and Macedonians—in order to provide a single solution to the major historiographical issues of the period overly ambitious. This project is not, however, a microhistorical study. It does not concentrate on a single region and attempt to extrapolate major conclusions; rather, it takes a macrohistorical approach that includes different regions of the empire, ranging from central to peripheral areas. The aim of this book is to elucidate the complexities of revolutions through a comparative, inter- and intracommunal, cross-cultural analysis and initiate further dialogue among scholars in studies in a variety of disciplines. In doing so, it will also add to the substantial scholarship on this subject undertaken during the past few years.[13]

The Revolution of 1908 is a study in contradictions; to be understood, it must be considered from two apparently incompatible perspectives. On the one hand, it should be understood as a positive manifestation of modernity, since the authors of the movement originally intended to reinstate constitutional and parliamentary rule in order to address the empire's predicaments. On the other hand, the Revolution should be viewed as a negative event that shook the empire's traditional, fundamental structures and substructures, disrupting its finely tuned internal balance and opening a Pandora's box of ethnic, religious, and political conflicts. Understanding the frictions, tensions, and negotiations between modernity and tradition is essential to an accurate view of the postrevolutionary period. This perspective also has wider implications, since such stresses were not exclusive to the Ottoman case but had both regional and global ramifications. The other multiethnic empires of the period, the Austro-Hungarian and Russian Empires, were also contending with such enormous challenges and vertiginous complexities.[14]

The Young Turks' reluctance to sincerely accommodate the political aspirations of ethnic groups put an end to the ideals of the Revolution, which despite their ambiguity were adhered to by the different ethnic groups. The principles of the Revolution remained unrealized due to the lack of a sincere negotiation process between the ruling elite and the nondominant groups concerning the empire's political systems, the emergence of ethnic politics in tandem with the consolidation of national identities, and international pressure on the Ottoman state, all of which became serious challenges to the amalgamation of modernity and tradition and hampered healthy political development.

The book ends with a discussion of the Counterrevolution of 1909, which became an important juncture in the history of the Second Constitutional Period (1908–1918). For the Armenians, who suffered a huge massacre in the province of Adana in southeastern Anatolia during that period, the Counterrevolution became a turning point that shook their trust in the Young Turks and the ideals of the Revolution by demonstrating the incompetency and insincerity of the new regime. For some of the Arab notables, this juncture resulted in an inability to reclaim their previous status, leading some to cooperate with the new regime while others began looking for alternative ways to express their grievances—through, for example, proto-nationalism that later crystallized into Arabism. For the Jews, the Young Turks' reaction to the Counterrevolution highlighted the fragility of empire and served to warn Zionists that the Young Turks would not tolerate the national aspirations of any group. Finally, for the Young Turks themselves, this period demonstrated the vulnerabilities of a constitutional regime and convinced them that granting too much freedom to ethnic groups under the rubric of constitutionalism would undermine their attempts to secure the empire's stability and its territorial integrity. The major result of these shifts among the Young Turks was a serious violation of the spirit of constitutionalism and an increased hostility in the attitude of the dominant toward the nondominant groups. Hence, an examination of this period is critical, since it provides a context for further developments in the region. The most important of these is how different ethnic groups, political parties, religious entities, factions, and both dominant and nondominant groups negotiate and redefine their positions by adapting themselves to and navigating through the new, unstable political framework achieved by the Revolution.

Although the 1908 Revolution opened new opportunities for minority ethnic groups, it also created serious challenges both for them and for the authors of the Revolution. The postrevolutionary period became a litmus test for the endurance of the main principle of the Revolution: the creation of an Ottoman citizenry based in equality, fraternity, and liberty whose allegiance would be to the empire. The realization of this goal was extremely difficult, since the empire's various ethnic groups each had their own perceptions of what it meant to be an Ottoman citizen. While the Young Turks' version of Ottomanism entailed the assimilation of ethnic difference, Ottoman Turkish as the main language, a centralized administrative system, and the abandonment of ethno-religious privileges, the ethnic groups perceived Ottomanism as a framework for promoting their identities, languages, and ethno-religious privileges, as well as an empire based on administrative decentralization. What followed was a tense battle between the Young Turks' main political party, the Committee of Union and Progress (İttihad ve Terraki, or CUP), and the various ethnic groups concerning the future of the empire and their role in it. Through this battle of ideas, the ethnic groups did negotiate their places in the empire, but they did so through ethnic politics, contradicting the unified political system that the Revolution strove to achieve. While the supreme ideal of the Revolution was the creation of a political system in which individuals would participate as citizens of the empire rather than as members of disparate ethnic blocs, in reality, many people continued to prioritize their ethnic identities over their Ottoman citizenship.

A brief overview of the major transformations that Armenians, Jews, and Arabs experienced during the nineteenth-century Ottoman Empire is necessary to a full understanding of the impact the Young Turk Revolution had on these three nondominant groups and how the Revolution changed the dynamics of power among them.

Reforms in the Nineteenth-Century Ottoman Empire
and the Rise of the Young Turks

During the nineteenth century, the Ottoman Empire, along with the semiautonomous Ottoman provinces of Egypt and Tunisia and, to a lesser extent, Iran, initiated a series of reforms to strengthen their political power and preserve the integrity of their territories. This defensive developmentalism, which was most successful in Egypt and somewhat successful in the Ottoman Empire, aimed at strengthening the state internally through centralization, radical military reform, and the introduction of rationalized legal norms along Western lines.[15] The strategies were also intended to improve global standing at a time when the power of these political entities was dwindling both locally and internationally. This resulted in a vast array of radical reforms in the fields of politics, economy, society, and religion.

In the case of the Ottoman Empire, the reform era can be divided into three periods: the reigns of Sultan Selim III and Mahmud II (1789–1839), the era of the Tanzimat (reordering) reforms (1839–1876), and the Hamidian period (1876–1909). Although these reforms affected different aspects of society in the empire and in Iran, they nonetheless managed to partially attain their primary goal. However, the Tanzimat era had a profound impact on non-Muslim groups in the empire, especially through the two royal decrees of Hatt-ı Şerif of Gülhane in 1839 and Hatt-ı Hümayun in 1856. The former pledged to extend reforms to all Ottoman subjects, regardless of creed or religious affiliation, while the latter promised equality among the empire's subjects, Muslims and non-Muslims alike. The Gülhane edict also gave rise to the concept of being an Ottoman subject, something more explicitly defined in the Nationality Law of 1869.[16]

Both decrees were intended to secure the loyalty of the empire's Christian subjects at a time when nationalist agitations were rising in its European section. Consequently, they tried to mold the notion of Ottomanism by breaking down the religious and cultural autonomy of the *millet*s (religious communities). Despite failing to attain this goal, these reforms made substantial changes in the dynamics of power among the non-Muslims. This was especially true in the case of the 1856 edict, which was intended to reform the communal administration of non-Muslim elements.[17]

These nineteenth-century reforms also led to a constitutional movement in the Ottoman Empire that arose between 1865 and 1878, primarily represented by a group of intellectuals calling themselves the Young Ottomans.[18] Despite being the by-product of the Tanzimat, this group was extremely critical of those reforms, viewing them as a superficial imitation of Western tendencies implemented by autocratic Ottoman statesmen without taking into consideration the Islamic values of Ottoman society. In addition to advocating for a genuine new identity of Ottomanism, they demanded the adoption of such liberal concepts as citizenship and some individual rights. The Ottoman society they envisioned would be a synthesis of Western modes of governance and Islamic Ottoman traditions. Despite encountering numerous obstacles, they were able to implement constitutionalism in the Ottoman Empire, although for only a very short time.[19]

This First Constitutional Period (1876–1878) was disrupted when Sultan Abdülhamid II (1876–1909) prorogued the Parliament, suspended the constitution, and established a despotic rule that lasted three decades.[20] The Young Ottomans' legacy was, nevertheless, carried on by another influential group—one that would play a dominant political role at the end of the nineteenth century and the beginning of the twentieth. This group, calling itself the Young Turk movement, emerged in the Ottoman Empire and its expatriate communities at the end of the nineteenth century. Their main political party, the CUP, became the dominant force within the movement. The Young Turks were influenced by the political currents raging in Europe at this time. Most important of these were positivism and scientific materialism, which became a molding force in their intellectual development.[21] After three decades of relentless efforts and political activism, this group staged the Young Turk Revolution of 1908, reinstating the Ottoman constitution and opening the Parliament. Thus, they launched what came to be known as the Second Constitutional Period (1908–1918), which ended with the Ottoman defeat at the end of World War I.[22] The goal of the CUP's constitutionalism was to transform the Ottoman Empire into a new system in which meritocracy was going to play a dominant role in reforming the political system. This system would serve as a platform for the CUP in strengthening its grip over the empire.

Armenians in the Nineteenth-Century Ottoman Empire

Armenians living in the Ottoman Empire experienced four major transformations during the nineteenth century: emergence of cultural nationalism as a result of the Armenian Renaissance (Zart'ōnk'); change in the power dynamics within the Armenian community after the introduction of the Armenian National Constitution (1863) and the formation of the Armenian National Assembly; rise of the Armenian merchant class; and deterioration of the political situation of Armenians in the eastern provinces in Anatolia that led to the emergence of Armenian revolutionary movements.[23]

In the Ottoman administrative system, Armenians, as well as Greeks and Jews, were organized in *millets*, which were semiautonomous bodies.[24] Under the *millet* system, these groups enjoyed a wide array of religious and cultural freedom, in addition to substantial legal, fiscal, and administrative autonomy. For example, the Armenian patriarch enjoyed complete jurisdiction over his *millet's* spiritual administration, charitable organizations, and religious institutions. He was supported in these efforts by influential Armenian magnates in Istanbul called Amiras who exerted immense influence over the Patriarchate and the community through their strong ties to the Ottoman ruling elite.[25] Amiras played the role of mediators between the Ottoman ruling institutions and the Armenian *millet* in a way that recalls the work of Arab notables (*ayan*) in Syria and Palestine during the second half of the nineteenth century.[26] As a result of both political shifts within the Armenian community in Istanbul and Tanzimat reforms, the Amiras' importance declined in the latter part of the nineteenth century.[27] They were supplanted by the rising Armenian bourgeoisie, represented by the middle class, Armenian guilds (*esnafs*), and Armenian merchants.[28]

In the first half of the nineteenth century, these new groups, in cooperation with the similarly rising Armenian intelligentsia, constituted the core of the Armenian constitutional movement, whose aim was to curb traditional authority and run the affairs of the community through a constitution and a national assembly.[29] Two important factors helped them realize their goal: the Tanzimat reforms and the personal connections that members of the constitutional movement, employed in the Ottoman bureaucracy, had with liberal Ottoman statesmen.[30]

After a long struggle between the conservative and liberal elements and with the intervention of the Ottoman government, an Armenian National Constitution was unanimously approved by the Armenian National Assembly on May 24, 1860, and ratified by the Ottoman government, after a long delay, on March 17, 1863.[31] The National Assembly became a kind of mini-Parliament, the empire's first nontraditional institution in which conventional politics were exercised, including elections, voting, hearings, debates, the exchange of ideas, and decision-making processes. It is, however, important to mention that the constitution was implemented unevenly in the eastern provinces.[32] What truly facilitated the development of Armenian political thinking in the empire was the creation of an internal public sphere in which the Armenian press played a dominant role.[33] The press became the medium through which Armenian interest groups expounded their views regarding political and administrative reforms. In the years between 1855 and 1876, some one hundred newspapers in Armenian and Armeno-Turkish were published in Istanbul, and thirteen were published in Izmir. Other such papers appeared in Erzurum, Bitlis, Izmit, and Sivas.[34]

By the promulgation of the Armenian National Constitution, an educational council was formed to spread, through the schools that proliferated in the provinces, the Armenian language among Armenians who did not speak the language. These educational enterprises would not have been realized without the direct support of the rising middle class, represented by the merchants, and the backing of liberal elements in the Armenian community. Some of these institutions played a dominant role in the spread of cultural nationalism among Armenians residing in coastal and major cities in the empire during the second half of the nineteenth century. External groups, most important of which was the Catholic Armenian Mekhitarist Congregation located in Venice, followed by Catholic and Protestant missionaries, played a part in the introduction of modern education.[35] Through their eminent colleges in Aintab (1874), Merzifon (1886), Tarsus (1888), Harput (1852), Kayseri (1871), Izmir (1878), and Istanbul (1863), the Protestant missionaries expounded the political ideals of the West to their students.

As the earlier formation of the Armenian National Assembly indicates, the First Constitutional Period was not the Armenians' first encounter with parliamentary politics. During this period, however, Armenian deputies were elected to both of the empire's representative houses: the House of Deputies (Meclis-i Mebusan) and the Senate (Meclis-i Ayan).[36] This situation ended when Sultan Abdülhamid II took drastic measures to prorogue the Parliament and suspend the constitution amid the deteriorating situation in the Balkans; the Russo-Turkish War of 1877–1878; and the twin Treaties of San Stefano and Berlin, both of which were regarded as disasters for the Ottomans.[37] He subsequently established an absolute monarchical rule that lasted the next thirty years. As part of this process, the sultan cracked down on liberal intellectuals, many of whom escaped to Europe and Egypt, where they formed exilic public spheres.[38] In these radicalized groups, exiled members of the empire's minority ethnic groups interacted with one another and attempted to mobilize their host governments against the sultan through the media, public gatherings, and congresses.

The 1878 Treaty of Berlin, which aimed at finding a new solution to the "Eastern Question," greatly modified the terms of the Treaty of San Stefano but did not nullify its major provisions. It also gave rise to the "Armenian Question" in the international arena.[39] Both demographic changes in Anatolia that resulted from the immigration of Muslims from the Balkans and the Caucasus and tensions in the Balkans had an important impact on the deteriorating situation in the eastern provinces. In a span of twenty years, from 1862 to 1882, immigration of the Muslim population from the Balkans and Russia increased the Ottoman Muslim population of Anatolia by at least 40 percent.[40] A good number of these immigrants moved to the eastern provinces, to areas where Armenians lived, the majority of whom were peasants, thus creating a population imbalance and friction between the locals and the immigrants. The overall result was an intensification of agrarian tensions.[41] It is noteworthy that the situation in some parts of the Anatolian provinces had already been deteriorating. Not only these agrarian tensions but also frequent attacks by Kurdish tribes on Armenian peasants, heavy taxation, friction with the influx of Muslims from the Caucasus, administrative corruption, and failure of Armenian efforts to solve these problems diplomatically led to the emergence of Armenian revolutionary groups.[42]

It seems that a major ideological shift took place within the Armenian political activists of Anatolia between 1878 and 1880, since the revolutionary movement emerged in the provinces only after that time. In 1885, Mguerdich Portukalian founded the Armenakan Party in Van (eastern Anatolia), which became the first party to be openly engaged in revolutionary activities.[43] The Armenakan Party was followed by the Social Democratic Hunchakian Party (Sōtsʻialistakan Dēmokratakan Hunchʻakean Kusaktsʻutʻiwn, or SDHP), founded in Geneva, Switzerland, in August 1887 after their journal, Hunchʻak (Bell), was established. The Hunchakian Party, also known as the Hunchaks, became the first socialist party in the Ottoman Empire.[44] Its platform focused primarily on the injustices taking place in the Armenian provinces and asserted that achieving freedom for the masses required establishing a new order based on humanitarian and socialist principles.[45] The Hunchaks saw revolution achieved through propaganda, agitation, terror, and organization, and peasant and worker action as the means to that end. However, an internal crisis within the party resulted in the emergence of a new faction that came to be known as the Reformed Hunchaks. The two primary reasons for this splintering were socialism and party tactics. This faction believed that the European powers abandoned the Armenian Question because of the socialist doctrines of the party. Hence, they demanded the elimination of socialism from the party's doctrine and called for changes in tactics and administration. In 1898, this faction named itself the Reformed Hunchakian Party (Verakazmyal Hunchʻakean Kusaktsʻutʻiwn).[46]

In 1890, the Armenian revolutionary groups felt the need to unite under one banner, which eventually led to the establishment of the Federation of Armenian Revolutionaries (Hay Heghap'okhakanneri Dashnakts'ut'iwn, or FAR) in Russian Tbilisi, the first merger of various Armenian groups, primarily in Russia, into a single party. By 1892, the organization had already been recast and consolidated as the Armenian Revolutionary Federation (Hay Heghap'okhakan Dashnakts'ut'iwn), otherwise known as the ARF, Dashnak, or Dashnakts'ut'iwn, with *Droshak* (Flag) as its official organ.[47] In the fall of 1892, the ARF held its First Congress in Tbilisi, where it ratified a platform that outlined a decentralized organizational structure with the goal of political and economic freedom in Turkish Armenia (T'rk'ayastan).[48] This would be accomplished through propaganda, arming of the population, and violent acts against corrupt government officers.[49] By the end of the nineteenth century, clandestine ARF branches were active in Trabzon, Erzurum, Erzincan, Van, Muş, Bitlis, and Hınıs.

While the ARF program aspired to freedom and autonomy within the framework of the empire, the Hunchak program aspired to the complete separation and independence of Turkish Armenia. Consequently, these groups used different tactics to achieve their goals. For example, in order to quickly bring European attention to the Armenian Question, the Hunchaks staged mass demonstrations. Their most notable activities were the Kum Kapu demonstration of July 27, 1890;[50] the placards (*yafta*) incident in Anatolia in 1893;[51] and the Sassun Rebellion of August 1894 against the nomadic Kurdish tribes and government tax collectors.

What finally focused European attention on the Armenians' plight was not, however, any of these actions but rather Sultan Abdülhamid II's reaction to domestic unrest. The sultan's reprisals for the Armenian uprising used the newly established Hamidiye Regiments and led to the massacres of Sassun (1894).[52] News of the horrors of the massacres aroused Great Britain, France, and Russia, who sent a joint Inquiry Commission to the area to investigate. On May 11, 1895, these powers sent a memorandum to the sultan urging him to make reforms in the six Turkish Armenian provinces.[53] The sultan's refusal to implement such reforms led to the Demonstration of Bab-ı Ali (Sublime Porte) in Istanbul on September 18, 1895, as well as the accompanying massacre in Istanbul, which continued until October 3. This second sequence of events led the European powers to pressure the sultan to sign the Armenian Reform Program as the massacres drew to a close. This did not, however, bring peace

to the Armenians of the eastern provinces. Between 1895 and 1896, the Hamidian regime prosecuted a series of massacres in Trabzon, Erzincan, Erzurum,
Gümüşhane, Baiburt, Urfa, and Bitlis. Approximately two hundred thousand
Armenians were killed, while hundreds of town quarters and villages were
looted, and thousands of acres of Armenian land and properties were seized by
the Kurdish beys and the Hamidiye chieftains.[54] Madteos II Izmirlian, patriarch
of Istanbul, who strongly criticized the regime for the bloodshed, was deposed
and banished to Jerusalem by Sultan Abdülhamid II on August 26, 1896. He
was replaced by Patriarch Maghakia Ormanian, who reigned until the Young
Turk Revolution of 1908.

Although it shared some aims with the Hunchaks, ARF avoided using
mass demonstrations, concentrating instead on targeted operations and as-
sassinations. In this, they were influenced by Russian secret societies such as
the Narodnaya Volya (The People's Freedom) and Zemlya i Volya (Land and
Freedom). ARF's major operations during this period were the seizure of Bank
Ottoman on August 26, 1896, which was intended to focus European attention
on the plight of Armenians in the provinces, and the attempt on the sultan's
life July 21, 1905, after the Friday prayer ceremony (Selamlık).[55] The mission to
assassinate the sultan failed because he had been delayed by conversing with
Şeyh-ül İslam.[56] The incident was, nevertheless, hailed by Şura-yı Ümmet (The
council of the nation),[57] the Young Turk organ in exile.[58]

Armenians were distinguished from other minority groups in the empire
by their close relationship with the Young Turk movement in exile—an association based on the two groups' shared interest in the reinstatement of the constitution and overthrow of the Hamidian regime.[59] In 1902, ARF, represented
by Avedis Aharonian and the Reformed Hunchaks, participated in the Paris
Congress of the Ottoman Liberals.[60] Representatives of the two groups could
not come to an agreement because the Young Turks were opposed not only to
revolutionary tactics but also to recognition that Armenian rights were guaranteed by international treaties, something that all the Armenian delegates insisted upon.[61] As a result, the Armenian delegates declared that they would not
support the decisions of the congress and would give a concomitant declaration
to the congress instead. In that statement, the Armenians primarily argued in
favor of a federal system, whereas the Young Turks inclined toward centralization and the prevention of foreign intervention. After this declaration, the Armenian delegates considered their duty done and left, deeming their presence
at the congress not beneficial.[62]

After this first congress, the Young Turk press in exile became extremely critical of Armenian activities in Europe—particularly Armenian congresses aimed at courting European public opinion and Armenian revolutionary activities within the empire.[63] Much of this criticism stemmed from the Young Turks' total opposition to the use of violence and foreign intervention as means for social change.

Between 1905 and 1907, however, the relationship between the Young Turks and ARF improved due to the efforts of Prince Sabahaddin Bey, a nephew of the sultan and an ideologue of the Liberals.[64] ARF's decision to cooperate with the Young Turks occurred during its Fourth Congress in 1907.[65] This led ARF to participate in the Second Congress of Ottoman Opposition Parties in Paris in 1907. The congress adopted armed resistance as a means of realizing the Revolution.[66] Despite a generally positive attitude regarding Armeno-Turkish cooperation, both groups harbored skepticism derived from their ideological discrepancies. While Armenians believed in revolution as a means to change, the Young Turks advocated a more diplomatic approach. Furthermore, as we have stated, the majority of the Young Turks opposed decentralization, autonomy, foreign intervention, and implementation of internationally guaranteed treaties, arguing that these eventually would lead to the disintegration of the empire. Thus, between 1905 and 1908 a cautious rapprochement began between the Armenian Revolutionary Federation and the Young Turks on both a political and practical level. Practical cooperation was manifested in the eastern provinces of Van and Erzurum.[67]

Jews in the Nineteenth-Century Ottoman Empire

Jewish communities in the empire, like Armenian communities, experienced structural transformation with the introduction of a constitution and the emergence of new interest groups represented by the Francos (Jews of Italian origin), the Alliance Israélite Universelle (AIU), and the Zionists, who were mostly in Palestine. These shifts, which led to the emergence of Jewish progressive movements within the empire, also were heavily influenced by the Tanzimat reforms, which constituted a dramatic change in the Jewish *millet*, just as they did within the Armenian and Greek ones.[68]

Unlike the Armenians and Greeks, the empire's Jews had lost political power during the nineteenth century, mainly due to political and economic changes taking place at that time.[69] Like the other *millet*s, the Jewish community was run according to its own law (*halakhah*), enjoying considerable internal autonomy.

Despite having autonomous ethno-religious status, however, the Jews did not have a major religious leader, as did the Armenians or Greeks, to oversee their affairs. This situation led the Jewish community to appoint Abraham Levi as chief rabbi (*hahambaşı*) in 1835.[70] His position was recognized by the Ottoman government, making him both the temporal and spiritual leader of the Jewish community. The Tanzimat reforms, particularly the edict of 1856, encouraged non-Muslim communities to establish assemblies constituted of religious and nonreligious elements that would conduct their affairs.[71] These reforms culminated in the Jewish Constitution of 1865.[72]

Reforms in the administrative, educational, and legal areas opened new horizons for the empire's non-Muslim populations. While the empire's Jews were experiencing the impact of the Tanzimat reforms, the Jews of Europe were experiencing important transformations under the influence of European Enlightenment. From 1750 to 1850, western European Jewry engaged in a Jewish enlightenment called *Haskalah*.[73] Members of this movement perceived the eastern Jews as culturally inferior to the European Jews and believed that the only way to elevate eastern Jewry from its dire condition was to civilize it, elevating it to the level of the emancipated European Jewry. Thus, the "Jewish Eastern Question" was born.[74]

The interest of European Jewry in the Ottoman Jews began, in fact, as a result of a series of incidents in the empire, the most important of which was the Damascus Affair of 1840, triggered by the disappearance of Father Tomaso, an Italian monk, in the Jewish Quarter of Damascus on the eve of Passover.[75] The city's governor immediately ordered the arrest of several Jews accused of murdering Father Tomaso to obtain human blood for ritual practices. Eventually, with the intervention of European Jewry, the prisoners were released and proclamations were obtained declaring their innocence. The Damascus Affair gave great impetus to the development of the press as a medium through which the Jewish communities of Europe discussed the situation of their coreligionists in the East.[76]

In accordance with the intellectual stance of the *Haskalah*, it became imperative for European Jewry to solve the Jewish Eastern Question, using education as the means. This objective would not, however, have been realized without the direct involvement and support of the Francos, a group of Jews of Italian origin who constituted significant elements of the Jewish leadership in Istanbul, Salonica, and Izmir.[77] Though education became an important channel for the dissemination of progressive ideals, it also became a source of conflict between traditional and progressive elements.

The progressive current within the Jewish community got a boost in 1860 with the election of Rabbi Ya'kov Avigdor to the post of chief rabbi.⁷⁸ Assisted by the Jewish Franco notable Abraham Camondo, Avigdor formed a temporal council (*meclis-i cismani*), of which Camondo was elected president. The council arranged for the collection of taxes, as well as creation of commissions to examine the accounts of each synagogue and fight corruption in the religious courts.⁷⁹ It was, however, under the leadership of Chief Rabbi Yakir Geron that the Rabbinical Constitution (*Hahamname Nizamnamesi*) was drafted. Approved by the state in 1865, the constitution confined the power of the chief rabbi, giving full executive power to the lay council.⁸⁰ Thus, the Jewish constitution aimed at reducing the power of the rabbinate in much the same way that the authority of the Armenian and the Greek patriarchs had been abridged.

In the case of the Jews, however, these reforms were not as successful in accomplishing that goal as they had been for the Armenians and Greeks. The crisis following the 1856 Edict of Reform caused severe paralysis of communal affairs, resulting in tensions among different factions within the community. Furthermore, the conservative elements gained more power with Moshe Halevi's appointment as locum tenens in 1872.⁸¹ Halevi did not hold elections until he was forced to do so by the pressures of the Young Turk Revolution, a fact that proved his conservative attitudes.⁸² Thus, any source of fundamental change had to come from outside. The AIU, established in Paris in 1860 with a branch founded in the coastal port city of Volos in the Ottoman Empire in 1865, would play this role.⁸³ The AIU's activities of propagating liberal and political ideologies caused much anxiety for Moshe Halevi and his adherents. From its inception, the organization focused on the needs of Jews living under Islamic rule. Its success in establishing schools and higher educational institutions in the Ottoman Empire was partly due to the cooperation of both the Francos and European Jewry.⁸⁴

During the First Constitutional Period, Jewish participation in Parliament was minimal, with only four representatives.⁸⁵ Their participation in the Young Turk movement was also minimal. Albert Fua, the most important Jewish representative in the Young Turk movement, did, however, make a significant contribution to the revolutionary cause. He was a columnist for the French supplement of *Meşveret* (Consultation), CUP's central organ in Paris. He also participated in the first Young Turk Congress of 1902. Fua, who represented the minority bloc, spoke against foreign intervention in a move intended to demonstrate that even a non-Turk opposed such interference.⁸⁶

Another important factor affecting the empire's Jews at the end of the nine-teenth century was Zionism.[87] Political Zionism, based on nationalism that focused on Palestine as the rightful Jewish homeland, led to a wave of immi-gration from Russia and Romania to Palestine. In the 1890s, some Zionist or-ganizations began to emerge, calling for a solution to the Jewish Question.[88] When Theodor Herzl began working to create a coherent, international Zion-ist movement, he did not neglect the Ottoman Empire.[89] Although Herzl was unsuccessful in his attempt to strike a deal with the Ottoman government to support a Zionist project in Palestine,[90] the Zionists continued their activities in Palestine under the auspices of the Jewish Colonial Trust.[91]

Herzl's efforts did, however, lead to the First Zionist Congress, which took place in Basel in 1897. The congress approved a program that outlined the movement's goal: "Zionism seeks to establish a home for the Jewish people in Palestine secured under public law."[92] Jewish purchases of lands from absen-tee landlords led to the dispossession and eviction of hundreds of Palestin-ian peasant families, as well as the expansion of the Jewish Yishuv (colony) in Palestine. Eventually, the Palestinian peasantry reacted, particularly in two sets of conflicts following land purchases: one in Petah Tiqva in 1886 and another in Tibereas from 1901 to 1904.[93] Muslim notables of Jerusalem sent petitions demanding the prohibition of land purchase by Jews and restrictions on their immigration into Palestine.[94] Thus, despite the regulations of the Ottoman gov-ernment, Jewish immigration to Palestine continued. On the eve of the Young Turk Revolution, the number of Jews in Palestine rose to seventy thousand, which was three times more than in 1882. Jewish land acquisition had grown to about 400,000 *dunams* (about 98,842 acres) of land and twenty-six colonies.[95]

Arabs in the Nineteenth-Century Ottoman Empire

The nineteenth-century Ottoman reforms did not have an immediate impact on the areas inhabited by Arabs but began to be felt in the second half of the century.[96] When their effects did become apparent in the Arab communities, these reforms had less impact than they had on the Armenians or Jews, pri-marily because of the political status of Muslim Arabs and the advantage that Armenians and Jews had in relation to the reforms. For instance, because of the *millet* framework, Armenians and Jews were already living in ethno-religious, semiautonomous entities in the empire. Because they constituted a majority in the Arab provinces, Arab Muslims had not been recognized as a separate, au-tonomous group. In the second half of the century, however, some segments of the population in the Arab provinces began to develop a sense of identity based on either religion or ethnicity, emphasizing autonomy as the ultimate tool for improving the condition of their communities. This process began with a cultural renaissance (al-Nahḍah) that originated among the Arab Christians and culminated in Arab political movements in the provinces of Syria, Lebanon, Iraq, and Palestine, which gained momentum in the postrevolutionary period.

The promulgation of the 1856 Edict of Reform caused decisive changes in relations between Muslims and Christians in the Arab provinces. Reactions in Syria and Palestine were generally negative, primarily because of the wider privileges that local Christians enjoyed under the reforms, whereas Syrian Christians welcomed it. Thus, the new reforms aggravated intercommunal relations not only between Muslims and Christians but also between Christians and Jews.[97] Gradually, this led to advances in both the intellectual activity and the socioeconomic status of Arab Christians.[98] The tensions resulting from the Christians' improved status led to the emergence of ethnic conflicts that resulted in the riots of Nablus and culminated in the Damascus massacres of 1860.[99]

The Damascus massacres, in turn, led to an intervention by the European powers that gave special status to Lebanon. On June 9, 1861, the Sublime Porte signed the Règlement Organique for Lebanon, which had been formulated in Istanbul and according to which Mount Lebanon would be organized into a special Ottoman governorate (mutasarrifiyyah). This governorate was to be administered by a Christian district governor appointed by the Porte. A term of three years was fixed for the first governor, Davud Paşa.[100] At the end of the nineteenth century, the emerging Christian merchant class played a dominant role in shaping political orientation toward the Hamidian regime and the Young Turks. In contrast, the Muslim merchants, though they were involved in a similar trade relationship with the West, were more inclined to favor the administration of the Ottoman Empire and saw the Arab-Turkish relationship as a union against the threat of foreign intervention.

Like their Armenian counterparts, the Arab Christians were influenced by Protestant and Catholic missionary activities in Syria, Lebanon, and Palestine. Eventually, this resulted in the emergence of a literary renaissance in the Arab provinces that was implemented through education and the press. This period witnessed the rise of such important figures as Butrus al-Bustani (1819–1883) and Nasif al-Yaziji (1800–1871), who exemplified the Arab cultural awakening (al-Nahḍah).[101] Despite being influenced by Western ideas, intellectuals in this movement defended Eastern civilization.[102] Another, simultaneous trend emerged in the Arab provinces with an emphasis on Islamic culture. This trend, embodied in Jamal al-Din al-Afghani (1839–1897)—and later in his disciples, Muhammad 'Abdu (1849–1905) and Rashid Rida (1865–1935)—championed the accommodation of European achievements in science and technology within the framework of Islam.

During the First Constitutional Period, the Parliament became an important forum for Arab deputies to discuss issues pertaining to their communities. Of 232 deputies during the two terms of the period, 32 were Arabs, representing the Arab provinces of Aleppo, Syria, Baghdad, Basra, and Tripolitania. When Abdülhamid II prorogued the Parliament and suspended the constitution, most of these intellectuals and political activists moved to Egypt, which then became a hub for exiled Arab thinkers, especially Syrians, who contributed immensely to the development of journalism and the proliferation of political ideas in their adopted country.[103] Led by Rashid Rida and Muhammad Rafiq al-'Azm, these intellectuals established the Ottoman Consultative Society (Jam'iyat al-Shūrah al-'Uthmāniyyah) and published the journal Al-Manār (The lighthouse). The society, composed of Turks, Arabs, Armenians, Greeks, and Kurds, intended to unite the Ottoman nationalities in order to transform the Ottoman government into a constitutional regime and prevent the empire's collapse.[104]

Motivated by fear that an Arab opposition movement might consolidate, and in order to gain the loyalty of the Arabs, especially after losing hope in the Balkans, Abdülhamid attracted the Arab notables to his rule.[105] The sultan's new regime was characterized by an emphasis on Islam and his role as the caliph. In addition, he chose the most conservative Arab Muslims as his advisers.[106] Accordingly, during this portion of his reign, Arab provinces like Syria and Hidjaz gained importance in the palace.[107] This political shift drew the criticism of the Young Turks' press and created tensions among palace factions.[108]

Abdülhamid also began to build his relationships with Arab notables in the provinces, who had long played the traditional role of mediators between the central government and the local population. This led to an increase of power and influence for influential local families. For example, in Damascus, the nonscholarly, landowning bureaucrats played a dominant role in local politics during the Hamidian period. Because these families achieved their political power by cooperating with Istanbul, they closely associated the state ideology of Ottomanism with the advancement of their interests.[109] This meant that any change in the status of the Hamidian regime ultimately would have negative consequences for Arab notables in the provinces, especially in Syria, and explains why notables there were not enthusiastic about the Revolution of 1908. Despite this investment in the fate of the sultan's regime, Arabs did participate in the two major congresses of the opposition groups. Unlike the Armenians, however, they were not an influential partner with the Young Turks: before 1908, the relationship between provincial Arab leaders and the revolutionaries was minimal.

The waves of transformation in the nineteenth-century Ottoman Empire had substantial, but varying degrees of impact on the different elements of the empire. The transformations as part and parcel of the defensive modernization/ westernization/reforms initiated by the Ottoman state influenced these various groups in ways ranging from changes in the dynamics of power within the communities, their relations toward the state, center-periphery relations, and interethnic relations, to the metamorphosis of overlapping vague identities. As demonstrated in this chapter, external factors also played an important role in these transformations. However, in other cases these transformations proved to be counterproductive in achieving their goals—for example, the Ottoman state's attempt to mold a unified Ottoman identity under the vague label "Ottomanism" in the second half of the nineteenth century. It is also important to note that the impact of these transformations was to a certain extent limited only to the elites in the central and coastal cities of the empire and did not encompass the majority of the population living in the periphery. For example, the majority of the Armenians in the provinces were peasantry preoccupied with farming and harvesting. European ideas of liberalism, constitutionalism, or nationalism were alien to them. They were more interested in the application of the concept of justice as part of finding a solution to the agrarian question that had lingered for decades.

Within this complex context of political and socioeconomic upheavals the Revolution became a decisive and fateful moment in the history of the empire. As the following chapters demonstrate, the Revolution became a double-edged sword. On the one hand, it gave hope to the revolutionaries and the disgruntled elements within the empire, promising a new beginning and a better future; on the other hand, it moved the empire into the abyss of disillusionment and disenchantment.

1 THE EUPHORIA
OF THE REVOLUTION

ON JULY 25, 1908, the population of the Ottoman capital, Istanbul, began rejoicing at the reinstatement of the constitution. Thousands of traders, industrialists, and other professionals of all the confessions—Muslims, Greeks, Armenians, and Jews—participated in the procession. The *Levant Herald* described the reaction in Istanbul: "It would be impossible to give and accurately convey the enthusiasm which has seized our population in the past days. . . . The population of the capital took 24 hours to grasp all the scope, all the magnitude of the act of his Majesty the Sultan whose name will be handed down to posterity along with those of the famous reformers."[1] The population of the capital waved flags "and in all the places HIS MAJESTY the Sultan's name was glorified."[2]

The celebrations continued on July 26. A large meeting attended by deputations of the different guilds took place in the square where the Ministry of War was located. From there, the crowd proceeded to Yıldız Palace, where they presented addresses.[3] One of the most important events that took place in Istanbul was the Mass held on August 13, 1908, in Pera's Holy Trinity Armenian Church (Surb Errordut'iwn) at Balık Pazarı (Figure 1). Five days before the event, an announcement was made in the local Armenian press and invitations were sent to Ottoman officials and dignitaries. The streets leading to the church were decorated with flags. Ottoman officials, dignitaries, and representatives of all the religious denominations attended the ceremony, including the şeyh ül-İslam.[4] The ceremony was officiated by the locum tenens of the Armenian patriarch, Bishop Yeghishe Tourian, who gave a patriotic speech.[5] The crowd then pro-

FIGURE 1. Revolutionary festivities in Pera's Holy Trinity Armenian Church at Balık Pazarı. From *Resimli Kitab*, September 1908, 60.

ceeded to Taksim Garden, where the celebrations reached their peak. Representatives of various ethnic groups gave enthusiastic speeches, and thousands of people gathered in the garden to celebrate "Turkish-Armenian brotherhood."

The jubilation and revolutionary festivities that took place in Istanbul are testimony to the postrevolutionary euphoria that descended upon the different cities and ethnic groups of the Ottoman Empire. They also mark the beginnings of the public sphere that emerged from the Revolution that employed both local print culture and local ritual in a way that allowed the new nation's varied ethnic and religious groups to participate in—and incrementally define—the culture of the new Ottoman nation. This process was not always a cooperative one: the new public sphere became the contested terrain in which ethnic groups struggled and competed to create a national political culture.

The celebrations and festivities of the successful Revolution inaugurated a new era and announced the demise of the ancien régime.[6] This required the adoption of new categories of social and political definitions, new symbols, and an attempt to adopt a consensus among all the ethnic groups. As part of this process, there was an attempt to create a "civic religion" that would provide social solidarity for the ethnic groups and emphasize oneness rather than distinction. What were the postrevolutionary celebrations about? Who participated in these celebrations and festivities? What was the anatomy of these celebrations?

Revolutionary Festivities in the Provinces

Parades and public ceremonies in postrevolutionary periods are an extremely important aspect of cultural history that asserts the priority of symbol making, language deployment, discourse construction, and perception of these symbols.[7] In recent years, intriguing research has been undertaken on the celebration of revolution in other postrevolutionary societies.[8] According to one scholar of public festivities, parades are public dramas of social relations in which social actors decide what subjects and ideas are available for communication and consideration.[9]

The newspapers of the Ottoman Empire's different ethnic groups provide a rich source of data regarding celebrations in the immediate postrevolutionary period.[10] Celebrations, parades, and festivities of the Revolution took place in the public sphere and required both participants and audiences. The newspaper accounts reveal that these events involved negotiations between rulers and ruled, as well as participants and audiences.[11] Analysis of these events reveals a strong, collective expression of solidarity with the new regime, although it is a "solidarity" that highlighted diversity—and thus contradicted the revolutionary ideal. In addition, by printing these accounts in their newspapers, the ethnic groups contributed to a greatly enlarged sense of audience. Sharing information about the celebrations of the Revolution facilitated the emergence of a common national language of ritual activity among the ethnic groups, and these public rituals became the sphere in which different ethnic groups interacted.

In addition to legitimizing the emerging new regime and delegitimizing the ancien régime, rituals facilitated popular solidarity where consensus was absent. In the midst of radical political shifts, rituals played a crucial role in supporting the new institutional order.[12] In fact, as Mona Ozouf observed in her study of the French Revolution, revolutionary festivals prosper as long as patriotism is in danger, and it evanesces once patriotism is reassured.[13] In other words, the extensive participation of the nondominant groups in the revolutionary festivities demonstrated their loyalty to the new regime.

As news about the proclamation of the constitution spread to the provinces, similar celebrations began to spring up outside Istanbul. As soon as freedom was declared, the people of Adana and Mersin began decorating all the streets and houses there. Immediately, the inhabitants began visiting each other, and masses were held in honor of the sultan and the Ottoman nation.[14] On August 2, 1908, a delegation of three hundred notables and dignitaries arrived in Mersin from Adana on a train decorated with the royal coat of arms and the imperial monogram (tuğra). The train was received by a huge crowd hailing freedom and the constitution. The crowd, accompanied by live music, then moved to the government building, where they were received by the mutasarrif (administrative governor of a sancak, or district) and many officers. A reception held by the CUP in Mersin concluded the event. On their way back to Adana, the group stopped in Tarsus, where they were received by a huge crowd shouting, "Long live the sultan! Long live freedom!" Upon its return to Adana, the delegation was received by more than four thousand people. Immediately afterward, the crowd moved to the municipal garden, where it was received by the governor and the provincial functionaries. Ihsan Fikri Efendi, leader of the local CUP, gave an enthusiastic speech about the new political order.

On August 7, members of the Tarsus CUP paid a similar visit to Mersin to revive the covenant of brotherhood.[15] A huge crowd and dignitaries greeted the train on its arrival at Mersin. Led by a band of musicians, the crowd of thousands moved toward the municipality, where speeches—many of them by military figures—were given in Ottoman Turkish, Armenian, Arabic, and French.[16]

Such provincial celebrations were, however, not universally immediate. In Van, for example, the telegram of the Imperial Order on the implementation of the Ottoman constitution arrived on July 25. The governor (vali) of the province, Ali Riza, refused to inform the people about the telegram out of loyalty to the sultan. While all the other provinces were celebrating the proclamation of freedom, Van was out of communication. On July 28, a telegram conveying a general pardon of revolutionaries arrived. The governor acted indifferently to this issue, arguing that the pardon was meant only for those who were exiled and stating that he had asked for clarification from the central government.[17] Not until August 11 or 12 did he implement these orders and release the prisoners.[18] Celebrations for the constitution began immediately afterward on August 14, 15, and 16 and continued into September. On September 6, the Armenian Church of St. Mary (Surb Astvatsatsin) held a Mass commemorating Armenian and Turkish martyrs. A huge crowd of at least two thousand, and perhaps as many as three thousand, Armenians and Turks headed to the church. The entrance was decorated with flags, as was a large stage in front of the church, which was draped in red, black, and white flags symbolizing blood, mourning, and freedom. Ottoman officers and other government officials attended a requiem service held after the Mass by the deputy of the patriarch. Afterward, the crowd moved to the Armenian cemetery, where the attendees put wreaths on the tombs of Armenian martyrs. A stage was built in the cemetery for a commemorative event attended by a dozen Ottoman officers, as well as other Turkish and Armenian dignitaries. Numerous speeches were delivered, exalting the names of Niyazi and Enver Bey, the heroes of the Revolution. Later, the procession visited the house of Khrimian "Hayrik" and then the houses of other martyrs.[19]

In Izmir (Smyrna), the news of the proclamation of the constitution was received with great joy and enthusiasm.[20] Bands were stationed all over the decorated town, playing the "Hamidiye March,"[21] the "Marseillaise," and the British and Hellenic anthems.[22] The Jewish Youth Association held a huge celebration. An announcement published a day before the event invited all ethnic groups to participate: "Thus, dear brothers! Leave your occupations; leave your business; you too manifest with happiness the sentiments. . . . Decorate the facades of your cities, shops and boutiques."[23] The procession went on for five hours, with about two thousand Jews walking toward the governmental palace. Ottoman dignitaries marched with them, and all were shouting, "Long live the sultan! Long live the fatherland! Long live liberty!"[24] A large carriage decorated with flowers headed the procession and carried six young girls dressed as angels, who waved Ottoman flags and scarves dyed in the national colors. Later, around five hundred young Jews joined the procession, carrying red and white scarves, the emblem of the Jewish-Turkish Committee, and canes with flags and lamps (lights) at the tips of the canes. Christians and Muslims also joined the procession, with the Muslims shouting, "Bravo! Our Jewish compatriots!" The procession moved to the governor's palace, chanting, "Long live the nation!" and "Long live the sultan!" before touring all the neighborhoods of the city.[25]

Like the Jews, the Armenians and Greeks also held large demonstrations in Izmir.[26] On August 1, Armenian dignitaries gave a huge banquet in Izmir in honor of the Ottoman army. Ottoman officers and politicians arrived at Kramer Palace in Izmir, accompanied by the band of the imperial garrison, and embraced their Armenian brothers.[27] Governor Faik Bey then made his entrance, and the crowd moved into the halls. More than three hundred people attended the banquet, including the leader of the Ottoman Federation of Smyrna, Major Tahir Bey, and many other political and military figures. Dinner was followed by warm and enthusiastic speeches delivered by Armenians and Ottoman military and civil officials.[28]

In Beirut, there were no immediate manifestations of the promulgation of the constitution. As attested in a letter sent by the consular agent of France in Latakiyya to the consul general of France in Beirut, rumors and the uncertainty of the situation created confusion, which precluded such celebrations.[29] It took a couple of days for the official news of the Revolution's success to reach Beirut, after which the celebration took place on July 31 in the Hamidian Garden. A government band roamed the streets, playing music. The streets were decorated with flags, and verses were written in large script on the entrances of the shops, hotels, and houses: "Long live the freedom granter and the constitution donor," and "The constitution is the life of the nation, and long live the sultan who gave the nation its life."[30] Verses from the Quran and the Bible appeared side by side: "Help from God, victory is very near" (Quran 61:13), and "The fear of the Lord is the beginning of wisdom" (Proverbs 9:10). Others more explicitly emphasized Muslim-Christian amity in the context of the new government: "Long live Moslem-Christian brotherhood," and below it "Long live liberty."[31] Local print culture commented on these dramatic declarations and their physical manifestations: "It was almost impossible to believe our ears and our eyes," explained the *Levant Herald* correspondent. "Then at many places and many times during the day, when the people caught sight of a Christian priest and turbaned Moslem in proximity to each other, they were pushed into each other's arms and made to kiss each other!"[32]

The celebrations of July 31 reached their apex with an event that took place in the Hamidian Garden, attended by about two thousand people from different religious backgrounds, during which a group of Armenians followed the procession of soldiers and kissed their rifles in a demonstration of Ottoman loyalty.[33] The sense of solidarity in diversity continued on Sunday, August 1, with a huge demonstration in Beirut's Armenian Church, attended by the commander of the troops, army officers, and the military band. The Armenian bishop, priests, and Muslim dignitaries delivered fraternal speeches in which, according to the *Levant Herald*, "all bewailed the awful events of the present reign in Armenia, and welcomed the new era, in which there was to be liberty, equality, and fraternity ending the so-called Armenian question forever."[34]

In Damascus, news of the reinstatement of the constitution arrived on July 24 and was received by the local population with skepticism. The Damascenes, however, quickly "surrendered to the evidence of the fact. It gave them free course to the immense happiness that jutted out from all the hearts."[35] Five official celebrations took place in Damascus, one in the Quwwatli coffeehouse in the Sanjaka, and the other four in the Garden of the Defterdar.[36]

The festivities began on July 30, when the military (*harbiye*) students and about thirty army officers headed toward the house of the military commander and released Fuad Paşa, who had been imprisoned for seven years on the pretext that he was a political criminal. The next day, Fuad Paşa joined in the Friday prayer in the Ummayad Mosque. While leaving the mosque, he was cheered by thousands of people, who gathered around him, shouting, "Long live freedom; long live the constitution; long live Fuad Paşa!"[37] That same evening, the CUP held a ceremony in the Garden of the Defterdar attended by spiritual leaders, military and civil officers, and a huge crowd of about fifty thousand onlookers. Numerous speeches were given on the advantages of freedom and justice, the disadvantages of fanaticism and separation among the people of the nation, and the necessity of confining religion to the mosques and churches. And the sky filled with the voices: "Long live freedom, and long live the army!"

The last festivities took place on Friday, August 7, in the Garden of the Defterdar and were attended by the governor, Muslim and Christian spiritual leaders, and military and civil officers. CUP members received the attendees, who were wearing badges on their chests that read, "freedom, equality, and fraternity." Many enthusiastic speeches dealt with the baleful acts of the ancien régime and the benefits of the new regime. Sheikh 'Abdul al-Qadir al-Khatib al-Mughrabi compared the despotic regime with the constitutional regime, underscoring the differences between the two through an act of physical connection that reached across ethnic and religious lines. Shaking the hand of a Greek Catholic bishop, he shouted: "Long live fraternity, and long live the homeland, and let every fanatic and ignorant person die."[38]

In Jerusalem, people were not aware of the reinstatement of the constitution until two weeks after its promulgation.[39] A reporter for the Ladino-language newspaper *El Tiempo* described the situation in Jerusalem during the first week after the promulgation of the constitution in Istanbul, indicating that no one knew the significance of the constitution: "Everyone understood the word in a different way; while some said that the government is no longer going to take the *bedel-i askeri*, others understood it that everyone is free to do whatever they wanted."[40] The quote demonstrates the skepticism and the suspense that existed in some of the provinces in relation to the news of the Revolution. On August 6, the crier announced that everyone from all ethnic groups should gather in front of the military barrack (*kışla*) on Saturday, August 8, at 6:00 p.m., when the imperial decree (*firman*) would be read.[41] The announcement was also published in the newspapers. Streets, buildings, and vehicles were decorated with branches, festoons, and flags, and at night the city was illuminated.[42] Celebrations began on Friday evening. On Saturday, thousands gathered, from all corners, in the vast square in front of the *kışla* adjoining David's Tower to listen to the decree read by Governor Ali Ekrem Bey.[43] The celebrations in Jerusalem were also marked by unity in diversity. Part of the Sts. James Brotherhood and about two hundred other Armenian community members formed a group in front of the Armenian Quarter, where they were immediately received by a military band. They then moved toward the *kışla*, where they joined the Jewish and Greek groups.[44] Thousands of Sephardic Jews arrived at the *kışla* after going to the temple.[45] Because it was Saturday, the Ashkenazi Jews did not participate in the celebrations. Furthermore, they criticized the Sephardic Jews "who desecrated the Sabbath in public."[46] The Ashkenazi Jews, however, did participate in the celebrations on Sunday and Monday.

In the evening the square was filled with thousands of people, and a stage was erected for the delivery of speeches. Governor Ali Ekrem Bey gave a speech and greeted the public with "Long live our sultan" (*Padişahımız çok yaşa*) before reading the edict. Meanwhile, a military band played the "Hamidiye March." The Greeks, numbering around two thousand, also rejoiced with music, flags, and speeches.[47] Six or seven government officials gave speeches, as did 'Abd al-Salam Efendi, editor of the newspaper *Al-Quds al-Sharīf* (Noble Jerusalem). Later the group moved to the municipal garden, where Setrak Minassian, an Armenian, gave a speech in Arabic. The Armenians who had gathered in front of their quarter arrived at Jaffa Gate square, where there were about six thousand people waiting. In front of the city gate, the municipality erected a huge arch and decorated it with flags, flowers, and a big banner, which read, "Long live the sultan, long live the army, long live freedom. Freedom, equality, and fraternity." Similar small flags were carried by the paşa, the commander of the army, and all the officials and people of the government.[48] Here, the crowd, an immense ocean of people, was composed of Jews, Muslims, and Christians.

The speeches were given from the balcony of the Postal Telegram Bureau. A student from the Armenian seminary spoke in Ottoman Turkish and explained the significance of the constitution. After this speech, which was warmly applauded, an Arab man spoke and read a poem in Arabic. The speeches were concluded with a reading from the prophet Isaiah, recited by a Jewish child: "The wolf will live with the lamb, the leopard will lie down with the goat . . .

THE EUPHORIA OF THE REVOLUTION   31

and they will not learn war anymore" (Isaiah 2:4). Afterward, the multitudes raised their hands and chanted in Hebrew: "Long live the king; long live freedom; long live justice and equality; long live fraternity"; in Arabic: "May God illuminate the sultan"; and in Ottoman Turkish: "Long live our sultan."[49] After the festivities, some forty thousand Muslims, Jews, and Christians gathered in front of the army palace, where the paşa of the army welcomed them before distributing lemonade, coffee, and cigarettes.[50]

Later on, the groups returned to their neighborhoods to continue the celebrations. The Jewish masses went to the Jewish neighborhood carrying a Torah covered with gilt embroidery, flags of the government, and the flag of Zion with the Star of David on it.[51] Many Jewish figures gave speeches, including the locum tenens of the Chief Rabbinate of Jerusalem, Elyahu Panigel, who addressed the crowds, and a young rabbi, Nissim Danon, who gave a speech in Hebrew on the verse "The people going in darkness saw the light" (Isaiah 9:2).[52] The Armenian group returned to the Armenian Quarter, where Archbishop Izmirlian gave an enthusiastic speech. The courtyard of the Armenian convent was decorated with colorful lamps, and a German band came to play in honor of the Armenians. There was also a speech given in German in front of the convent that applauded the role and efforts of the Armenians in "this salvation work." The celebrations in Jerusalem continued for ten to fifteen days.[53]

Celebrations also took place in other parts of Palestine, such as Jaffa, Safad, and Haifa. In Jaffa, on August 6, the crier announced that the imperial decree was going to be read that day and that it was a national holiday. Flags of the state were put up throughout the city. Thousands of people gathered in the square located between the government and military buildings. Speeches were delivered by different ethnic groups.[54] On August 15, the Jewish community of Jaffa also organized a demonstration in support of the promulgation of the constitution.[55] Hundreds of horsemen from the Jewish colonies of Petah Tikva, Rishon Letziyon, Rehovot, Ekron, and Kastinje (Beer-Tobiah), joined by the sheikhs of the villages and accompanied by Jewish musicians from the colonies, arrived in Jaffa. The entourage moved toward the government building, where it was received by the governor's lieutenant (*kaymakam*) and functionaries. The *kaymakam* also visited the hut erected by the Jews in Neve Shalom. He was accompanied by a military band and surrounded by flags of state, which read, "Long live the sultan, long live the army, and long live freedom." More than ten thousand spectators of all confessions showed up to view this procession, and speeches were given by Muslims and Jews alike.[56]

Three Exemplary Individuals of the Revolution
In addition to the role of these ceremonies in the provinces, the role of revolutionary heroes is vital to a deconstruction of the revolutionary rituals. A
revolutionary ritual cannot be imagined without the glorification of individual
heroes, who play an important role within postrevolutionary societies. These
people become the cult figures that connect diverse groups in an attempt to
create a new, overarching identity. Examining these heroes elucidates how ethnic groups saw themselves being integrated into a larger postrevolutionary society by their heroes.

In the case of the Ottomans, the preeminent heroes of the Young Turk Revolution were Niyazi and Enver Bey. These individuals crossed not only religious
and ethnic boundaries but also the geographic boundaries of the empire to
become popular icons personifying the victory of the Revolution and demise of
the ancien régime. Nondominant ethnic groups also venerated heroes that represented their own suppressed communities. Most of these heroes were either
in exile or in jail as the Revolution ended, so their release and return became a
significant component of public rituals in postrevolutionary manifestations of
the public sphere.

By symbolizing the demise of the ancien régime and the beginning of the
new era, these figures transcended their ethnicity to become Ottoman national heroes. Thus, their return was the completion of the victorious act of the
Revolution. The rituals that marked these moments of reintegration required
a physical manifestation of the hero in front of the public. This manifestation
was multilocal, in that it moved from one province to another before arriving in Istanbul. This aspect of the ritual was particularly important, since the
heroes' reception by people of different provinces and from different ethnic
backgrounds represented the consecration of the new era.

Much has been written about Niyazi and Enver, but much less has been
written from the perspective of Armenians, Arabs, and Jews. For these groups,
three important figures became national heroes and consecrated the beginning
of the new era: Archbishop Izmirlian, Fuad Paşa, and Prince Sabahaddin.

Patriarch Madteos II Izmirlian
Madteos II Izmirlian, the Armenian patriarch of Constantinople (1894–1896),
was deposed and banished to Jerusalem by Sultan Abdülhamid II on August 26,
1896, for boldly denouncing the Hamidian massacres of 1896 (Figure 2).[57] For
twelve years he stayed in the Armenian Cathedral of Sts. James in Jerusalem,

FIGURE 2. Patriarch Madteos II Izmirlian. From *Arewelk'*, October 23, 1908, no. 6931, 1.

where "a policeman was guarding him until came the day of freedom."[58] When news of the proclamation arrived in Jerusalem, Governor Ekrem Bey initially refused to declare the reinstatement of the constitution and prevented Archbishop Izmirlian from traveling. However, after a few days, freedom was declared in Jerusalem, and Izmirlian was allowed to return to Istanbul. About two hundred telegrams from different parts of the empire reached Izmirlian, congratulating him on his freedom.[59] Before he left Jerusalem, he ordered that all his belongings be sold and the money given to the poor of Jerusalem.[60]

After leaving Jerusalem, Izmirlian's entourage traveled to Jaffa, accompanied by CUP branch members from Jerusalem, who gave him a wreath to be placed in the Armenian cemetery of Şişli in Istanbul in memory of the Armenian martyrs.[61] In Jaffa, where the city was decorated with flags in his honor, Izmirlian was received by local Arabs and a military band.[62] From there, the entourage moved to Beirut, where it was received by local Turks and Arabs. The company then headed to Izmir.

On Monday, August 24, four ferries, accompanied by musicians, left the bay of Izmir, displaying flags that read, "Long live Izmirlian," "Long live the constitution," and "Long live freedom." The Armenian National Administration of Izmir, Armenian clergy, and a delegation of the CUP were aboard the *Osmaniye*, one of these ferries. Around 4:00 p.m. that day, Izmirlian's ship arrived. When the crowd saw Izmirlian, it began singing a song especially composed for him, "The Supreme Hero of Freedom; Eternally Long Live Izmirlian."[63] From the ship, Izmirlian himself gave an enthusiastic speech in reply.

A carriage awaited Izmirlian at the bay of Izmir, and about forty other carriages joined the procession, along with the band. The people standing by were shouting, "Long live the soldier, long live the army, and long live Izmirlian."[64] Armenian medals were printed and distributed as the procession came in from the bay. The medal displayed an effigy of Izmirlian on one side and the words "Long live the Constitution" in Armenian and "Long live freedom" in Ottoman Turkish on the other, including a reference to the day of the Revolution: July 11 [24], 1908.[65] The procession moved toward the Armenian Quarter of Izmir, which was decorated for the occasion, before traveling to the Armenian Church of St. Stephen's (Surb Step'anos). Descending from the carriage and entering the church, Izmirlian moved down the aisle under a canopy carried by six young people, three of whom were Ottoman generals.[66] The church was full of both Armenians and Turks. Izmirlian gave a sermon, in which he emphasized unity:

> Freedom is as necessary for a man as breathing air. During the despotic period, the people were deprived of this goodness, but now let us be thankful to God, because with divine intervention he gave it to us. Let us know the value of this goodness, and let us show certainly that we are worthy of it. Let us live in harmony with all our compatriots. Let us especially value the sacrifices carried by our Turkish compatriots and the providential activity of the strong-hearted Ottoman army.[67]

The next day, Izmirlian traveled to Istanbul by ship. About twenty-five ferries came out of the port of Galata to receive him. When his ship approached the port, about one hundred thousand Armenians and Turks were waiting for him.[68] The crowd extended from Tophane to the bridge and from Galata to the Armenian Patriarchate in Kum Kapu.[69] The procession moved to the main Armenian church, and an important ceremony took place in the Armenian cemetery in Şişli in the memory of the martyrs who fell for the cause of freedom.

General Fuad Paşa: The Hero of Elena
Fuad Paşa (1835–1931), a Circassian born in Egypt, was a commander during the Russo-Turkish War of 1877–1878. Nicknamed "Deli" (crazy) for his courageous acts, he was commander of the Ottoman troops during the Battle of Elena during which Ottoman troops defeated the Russians. Consequently, he became known as the "Hero of Elena" (*Elena Kahramanı*) and was promoted by Sultan Abdülhamid II to the position of marshal (*müşir*). In 1902, he was accused of plotting against the sultan and was banished to Damascus. When news of the proclamation of the constitution reached Damascus, the military school students and thirty officers from the army moved toward the house of the commander of the army in Damascus, demanding the release of General Fuad Paşa, who had been imprisoned for seven years on the pretext that he was a political criminal.[70] The commander argued that he needed twenty-four hours to clarify the issue with the central government. The officers refused to grant him this extra time and went to the prison, where they released Fuad Paşa. The next day, Fuad Paşa prayed in the Ummayad Mosque in Damascus. While leaving the mosque, he was greeted by the thousands of people who gathered around him.[71] That evening, the CUP held a ceremony in the Garden of the Defterdar that was attended by spiritual leaders, military and civil officers, and a crowd of about fifty thousand people.

A similar reception for Fuad Paşa was held in Beirut on August 6, 1908. Thousands of people moved toward the train station.[72] At around 3:00 p.m., a military band accompanied by military horsemen arrived. About an hour later, young people arrived, carrying flags and banners and singing songs composed for Fuad Paşa. Upon arriving, "the sea [of people] began to rage" anxiously for the hero's approach. When he arrived, the band began to play the "Hamidiye March," and people began to shout, "Long live Fuad Paşa!" A carriage was waiting to take him to the barracks to greet military officers there. Among them was Riza Bey, head of the CUP. Later, the paşa proceeded to the house of Jurji Bey Sursuq, where the

Masonic delegation received him. On the morning of August 8, a farewell party was held in the Cortina Inn. There, the paşa was again received by soldiers and a military band playing the "Hamidiye March." Afterward, members of the Armenian Society of Beirut approached him, carrying the Ottoman flag and wearing badges on their chests that read, "freedom, justice, and fraternity." They gave the paşa a bunch of flowers as "a proof of their Ottomanism."[73]

As in the case of Patriarch Izmirlian, the paşa's procession ended in the capital. On August 12, Fuad Paşa arrived in Istanbul on the ship *Sakhalin*.[74] Several ferries moved to the sea to receive him, and he thanked the population for all the preparations made for him.[75]

Prince Sabahaddin

For all the ethnic groups, but especially for Armenians, Prince Sabahaddin was the most important personality after the end of the Young Turk Revolution,[76] mainly because of his vision that administrative decentralization was the only panacea for the ongoing ethnic tensions that were jeopardizing the integrity of the Ottoman Empire.[77]

Before his arrival, Sabahaddin, the "main champion of the Armenian cause," stopped in Izmir, where he was received by the Armenians, the ARF, and the CUP in Kramer Palace.[78] In Istanbul, Turks and Armenians began making preparations for the reception of Prince Sabahaddin days before his arrival on September 2, 1908.[79] The prince brought with him the relics of his father, Mahmud Damad Paşa.[80] A detailed program for his reception had been prepared by the CUP. At 4:00 a.m., six ferries decorated with Ottoman flags left Sirkeci bay and went to receive him. The Hunchaks rented a ferry that carried their party members. The official delegation represented by the Ottoman Constitutional Club also rented a ferry, as did about three hundred intellectuals, merchants, lawyers, doctors, and members of the clergy. In honor of Prince Sabahaddin, the ferries were decorated with flags of white and red ribbons provided by the Ottoman Club, which read "Long live freedom and justice" in both Armenian and Ottoman Turkish. Various lectures and speeches dealing with Sabahaddin, his decentralization program, and the reexamination of the Ottoman constitution were given at sea by the people on the ships. In addition, the Armenian bishops and priests held a requiem service for the Muslim martyrs who fell in the Sea of Marmara.

When Sabahaddin's ship, *Principessa Maria*, arrived at Aya Stefano at around 11:00 a.m., seven or eight other ferries were waiting near the docks.

The Greeks had rented a ferry, and the Jews of Haidar-Paşa had rented a ferry that they decorated with flags and a huge banner, which read in Ladino, "The Jewish Youth."[81] At about the same time, the ship arrived with Sabahaddin and the relics of Mahmud Damad Paşa aboard. All the ferries immediately surrounded the ship amid cries of "Long live Sabahaddin!" The ship İzzeddin carried Sabahaddin's brother and members of the CUP to the *Principessa Maria*. All the ships then returned to Galata, where a huge crowd was waiting. Sabahaddin gave his first public address on September 16 in Varyete Theatre.[82]

Analysis of the Revolutionary Rituals:
Space, Symbolism, and Language

Although some of the revolutionary festivals were spontaneous, they all entailed a certain level of organization and planning. Finding an appropriate public space for the celebration was an important aspect of the celebration process. In this space, public enjoyment must be able to manifest repeatedly without any obstacles or impediments. In addition, this space would be the meeting place of all Ottoman citizens, regardless of their ethnic background, who had one thing in common on that day: celebration of freedom and the constitution. In Ozouf's words, what was needed was a "festive space that could contain endless, irrepressible, and peaceful movement like the rise of tidal waters."[83] Thus, the celebration's first requirement was an open-air space whose biggest advantage was that it was a space without memories, allowing it to symbolize entry into the new era. In particular, three important spaces were used for the revolutionary festivities and rituals: gardens, cemeteries, and religious edifices. In some cases, these three types of spaces were used consecutively and therefore contradicted the ideal rituals of revolutionary celebration.

Gardens and open spaces provided the ideal places for revolutionary festivities. They contained three major prerequisites for this type of celebration: they were open air, with no interruptions or obstacles; they were spaces without memories; and they were natural places that symbolized entry into the new order. Thus, they served as ideal places for creating new memories. These new memories were consecrated by the participation of the different ethnic groups. Taksim Garden (Istanbul), Municipal Garden (Adana), Hamidian Garden (Beirut), the Garden of the Defterdar (Damascus), and the Municipal Garden (Jerusalem) were all open spaces in which revolutionary festivities reached their apex. Thousands poured into these gardens and open spaces, creating a sea of people. Interestingly, most of these areas were not decorated, because they lacked any memories: decorations were necessary only in places where memory was evident, where they played the role of transforming the old place into a new one. In the case of gardens, nature was the decorator.

In most cases, although they ended in gardens, revolutionary festivities began in churches, external sections of mosques and synagogues, and municipal buildings. Examples of these are the festivities that took place in Istanbul, Adana, Damascus, and Jerusalem. Although such physical entities, in which memories were omnipotent, contradicted the ideal celebration of the Revolution, they nevertheless served as sources of legitimacy. The revolutionary festivities needed that legitimacy in order to create a new memory.

Churches were the major centers of the revolutionary festival. Housing a multiplicity of obstacles, as well as the strong presence of memory, they contradicted the ideal revolutionary celebration. Referring to the French Revolution, Ozouf argues that the revolutionary festivities in the churches "completely ignored the distribution of the interior space and seemed unaware of its emotional resources." Ozouf's analysis is extremely important and relevant to our case. The interior space of the Armenian churches had lost all meaning because "the pillars were an obstruction to the view, the vault spread its false sky over the celebrant, the architecture seemed to rival the ceremony. The church was badly planned, inconvenient theatre, an artistic illusion that did not even achieve its object."[84] Pera's Holy Trinity Armenian Church at Balık Pazarı, the Armenian Church of St. Mary in Van, the Armenian Church of St. Stephen's in Izmir, the Armenian Church of Beirut, and the Armenian Church of Cairo, all served as important spaces for the revolutionary festivities. However, these churches had to be converted and transformed into new spaces to perform that function. This transformation was achieved through the use of decorations that created a new "secular space" accessible to all ethnic groups, regardless of their religious backgrounds. Decorations in the churches also covered old memories, though they were unable to entirely erase the echoes of the past. For example, during the festivites, all the entrances and streets leading to these churches were decorated with Ottoman flags and banners, upon which revolutionary slogans were written in different languages. In some cases, the interiors of churches were also decorated.

Interestingly, the same could not be said in the case of mosques or synagogues.[85] Neither mosques nor synagogues were converted or transformed into "secular spaces." Hence, they were not accessible to all ethnic or religious groups. They served only as centers of gathering for the coreligionists, for prayer, and for Friday sermons. The celebrations of the Revolution took place in the exterior sections of these religious edifices. This raises important questions: Why would only churches be transformed inside and out? Why are mosques and synagogues transformed only on the outside? Does this phenomenon point out incipient fractures in the unity proclaimed by the postrevolutionary rituals?

Cemeteries were important spaces for one particular dimension of revolutionary rituals: mourning and requiem services. These services paid tribute to those who fell for the cause and for those "Turkish and Armenian Ottoman Brothers who were martyred for the cause of Freedom." In the spatial grammar of postrevolutionary celebrations, cemeteries are a middle ground between religious spaces and gardens. As seminatural, open-space "gardens" devoid of obstacles or interruptions, they have more in common with gardens than with churches. Despite the lack of pillars to obstruct one's view, however, cemeteries still hold a great deal of (literally) buried memory. Moreover, the memory housed in cemeteries had more significance for all the ethnic groups than the memory contained in religious edifices. This memory, after all, related directly to people from many backgrounds who sacrificed their lives for the realization of the new era. It is a crucial part of the revolutionary rituals of mourning, and it is through the idea of mourning that a new history begins.[86]

The Armenian National Cemetery of Şişli and the Armenian cemeteries of Erzincan, Ordu, and Van all served this purpose. In Van, for example, a requiem service took place in the Church of St. Mary on September 6, 1908. After the service, which was headed by the deputy of Patriarch Fr. Zaven and attended by Ottoman generals and officials, the crowd moved to the cemetery, where people put wreaths on the tombs of the Armenian martyrs. A stage was built in the cemetery for a commemorative event. A dozen Ottoman generals and numerous Turkish and Armenian dignitaries, among them the local leaders of ARF, attended the ceremony.[87] In Erzincan, at the initiative of the Young Turks, numerous officers and civil notables, accompanied by a military band, visited the Armenian cemetery and gave speeches expressing regret for the past. One of the speakers said, "O brave Armenians, may your pure blood and our sincere teardrop be sufficient to erase the black past." The following day, the soldiers also paid a visit to the cemetery.[88]

Likewise, when Archbishop Izmirlian arrived in Istanbul on August 25, an important ceremony took place in the Armenian National Cemetery of Şişli. Archbishop Izmirlian, Turkish dignitaries, and a huge crowd moved to the cemetery. A bailiff headed the procession, carrying the Ottoman flag and the wreath that the CUP of Jerusalem had given Archbishop Izmirlian to honor the Armenian victims who fell during the massacres of Istanbul.[89] The procession moved toward the martyrs' hill. To the accompaniment of religious hymns and verses, Archbishop Izmirlian placed the wreath on the tomb of the martyrs before giving a speech.[90]

Symbolism and Language

Government cannot exist without rituals and symbols, because both are crucial to exercising power.[91] Political symbols and rituals are means and ends of power itself. Governing cannot take place without language, signs, and symbols that "convey and reaffirm the legitimacy of governing in thousands of unspoken ways." To that extent, legitimacy is "the general agreement on signs and symbols."[92] Symbolism and language during the revolutionary festivities played an important role in defining the *Weltanschauung* of the different ethnic groups of the empire. Prior to the Revolution (during the Hamidian period), the deployment of symbols was a state initiative aimed at pursuing legitimacy.[93] In the postrevolutionary period, however, this function was thrown into the public domain. The public spheres of the postrevolutionary period seized symbolism from the monopoly of the state and the sovereign, appropriating it in an attempt to create a unified and overarching identity that itself became counterproductive.

Undoubtedly, the organizers of revolutionary festivities consciously or unconsciously manipulated visual representations during revolutionary rituals in order to have a wider impact on the participants. Ritual is an action created by a web of socially standardized and repetitive symbolic elements. On the other hand, actions that do not include symbolism are not rituals; rather, they are customs and habits. It is the presence of symbolism that distinguishes ritual from other actions. Furthermore, the nature of these symbols and the way in which they are employed tells us more about their impact on society.[94] Symbolism was not, however, used in isolation in these rituals. Instead, it usually was accompanied by verbal explanations in Ottoman Turkish, Armenian, Arabic, Greek, Hebrew, and Ladino to provide immediate clarification to the newly evolving symbolism of the Revolution.[95] In addition to clarifying the meaning of these new symbols and expressing the need for social solidarity, multilingualism served the function of national integration.[96]

In all the revolutionary rituals, the flag became the main symbol under which people of varying ethnic groups and religious backgrounds gathered. Essentially, it became the embodiment of the Ottoman nation. Furthermore, as its meanings

THE EUPHORIA OF THE REVOLUTION 41

became the property of the public sphere, the multiple uses of the flag and other bannerlike symbols became a challenge to the official monopoly of the state.[97]

During the festivities of 1908, most flags were inscribed with revolutionary mottos and were sold to be waved at demonstrations. The ethnic press reported on the massive use of flags in the postrevolutionary rituals, noting the important role they played in Istanbul, Izmir, Adana, Trabzon, Beirut, Damascus, Van, and Jerusalem. Mementos from the period also bear witness to the phenomenon: for example, on a postcard from the constitutional period, almost all people in the picture are holding the Ottoman flag high above their heads (Figure 3). Sultan Abdülhamid appears in the center of the postcard, placed among the clouds. He hovers above the people and below a source of apparently divine light. On either side, however, the Ottoman flags surmount him, denoting their symbolic supremacy. In keeping with the role of language as part of the new state's emerging symbolism, the card includes text in five languages: Armenian, Greek, Ottoman Turkish, French, and Ladino. Similarly, another postcard from the period shows the Ottoman army beneath a huge flag reading "Nizâm (Ordre), Adâlet (Justice), Usûl (Discipline), and Yaşasın Kânûn-ı Esâsî (Vive la Constitution!)" in both Ottoman Turkish and French (Figure 4).

FIGURE 3. Postcard from 1908 celebrating the proclamation of the constitution. From İsa Akbaş collection, in Edhem Eldem, *Pride and Privilege: A History of Ottoman Orders, Medals and Decorations* (Istanbul: Ottoman Bank and Archive Research Center, 2004), 135.

FIGURE 4. "Discipline, Justice, Order—Long Live the Constitution!" 1908 postcard.
From İsa Akbaş collection, in Eldem, *Pride and Privilege*, 367.

It is important to note that in addition to Ottoman flags, the flags of local
ethnic groups were also evident in these celebrations. For example, some of the
boats that went out to receive Prince Sabahaddin were decorated with CUP and
ARF flags. In Jerusalem, the Jews celebrating the festivities were carrying flags
of Zion that depicted the Star of David. In Van, a stage was erected near the Armenian church on which red, black, and white flags were situated symbolizing
blood, mourning, and freedom, respectively.

Red and white flags, which symbolized freedom, were also common in
these festivities. In addition, banners, bands, ribbons, and badges—also usually white and red—were widespread during the revolutionary celebrations.
An example of these is the constitutional cockade bearing the inscription
"Kânûn-ı Esâsî'nin Yâdigâri 1326" (Souvenir of the constitution, 1326/1908;
Figure 5). After the proclamation of the constitution in Istanbul, hundreds
of street peddlers began selling red bands containing the inscription "liberty, equality, and justice." People wore these bands on their arms or on their
fezzes. During the revolutionary festivities in Damascus, CUP members received the processions wearing badges on their chests that read "freedom,
equality, and fraternity."

If decorations on physical edifices were meant to transform the space into the representation of a new era by covering the memories manifested in that space, these flags, bands, and strips were meant to represent transformation of the physical body of the Armenian, Arab, Turk, Jew, and Greek into a new entity and identity called Ottomanism.

If flags were meant to exert symbolic influence on the people, the aim of banners was to provide verbal explanations of the new and changing symbolism of the postrevolutionary period. While discussing the content of these banners, one must remember that the French revolutionary rhetoric was evident in the Ottoman revolutionary slogans.[98] The most important of these impacts was the slogan "liberté, fraternité, égalité" (*hürriyet, uhuvvet, müsâvât*), which became endemic to postrevolutionary rituals of the different ethnic groups. There was, however, an important addition to the revolutionary slogan's triad: the Ottoman concept of justice (*adâlet*). This new revolutionary slogan was translated into all the languages of the new nation. An example of this is the postcard of the proclamation of the constitution, on which the slogan appeared in Armenian, Greek, Ottoman Turkish, French, and Ladino, making it easier for everyone to imprint the principles of the Revolution on their minds (see Figure 3). In other instances, the word "fraternity" was replaced with the word

FIGURE 5. Constitutional cockade. From İsa Akbaş collection, in Eldem, *Pride and Privilege*, 368.

"justice," producing the slogan "Long live the constitution, freedom, equality, and justice."

Along with variants of "liberty, fraternity, equality, and justice," variants of the slogan "Long live our king" were used extensively on banners.[99] The sultan was exalted on the banners because he was the one who donated the constitution to his nation, and his primacy was indicated, over and over, by the order of the words. When it came to glorifying the new era, the sultan came first, followed by the army and freedom. For example, in Jaffa and Jerusalem, banners appeared that read, "Long live the sultan, long live the army, and long live freedom."[100]

Other types of banners dealt with the theme of plurality and aimed to strengthen bonds among the different ethnic groups and religions of the empire. Brotherhood became one of the key subjects in depicting the "new" Ottoman nation; for example, a postcard depicts the Ottoman nation, in which the different ethnic groups appear, each wearing their national garb. An Arab, a Turk, a Circassian, a Greek, and an Armenian priest are each represented. In the center of the postcard, uniting them all, is the key figure: the Ottoman soldier, who carries a large flag upon which is written: "Unis pour la patrie, Vatanın-Ağorına İttihad" (United for the fatherland) in both French and Ottoman Turkish (Figure 6). It is no surprise that the Ottoman soldier, the main agent of the Revolution, is carrying the flag. The theme of brotherhood was also widespread in banners posted throughout the provinces. For example, a banner on the Armenian Church of Pera in Istanbul was dedicated to "the immortal memory of Turkish and Armenian Ottoman Brothers who were martyred for the cause of Freedom, July 31, 1908."[101]

In many cases, the messages woven into the banners were tinged with religious fervor. The new social contract in the Ottoman case needed an analogy with religious covenants because thanks to divine intervention, the sultan decided to reinstate the constitution. Although this theme was obvious in speeches and other orations during the rituals, it also became manifest in banners. A correspondent for the *Levant Herald* reported that during the festivities in Beirut, he saw a large inscription that "voiced the new spirit in a verse from the Koran and side by side with a verse from the Bible." Specifically, the verses read: "The beginning is from God, victory is near," and "The fear of the Lord is the beginning of wisdom."[102]

There is no doubt that most of the revolutionary rituals were verbose. If spaces, symbols, and slogans characterized the symbolic aspect of the revo-

FIGURE 6. "United for the Fatherland." 1908 postcard. From İsa Akbaş collection, in Eldem, *Pride and Privilege*, 367.

lutionary festivities and rituals, speeches represented the final verdict, the concluding section of these celebrations. A revolutionary ritual cannot be imagined without a series of speeches that puts the day in proper context, commenting on the ancien régime and presenting the new era. If symbols build the body of the new nation, speeches give spirit to these bodies. As with many uses of language in the public sphere following the Revolution, most of the speeches in Ottoman revolutionary rituals were multilingual in order to secure the allegiance of all ethnic groups living in the empire.[103] By using different languages, however, speakers fractured understanding and contradicted the main principle of the Revolution, which was the creation of unity. The collective aim of these speeches was a paradoxical unity based in diversity.

The limitations of this enterprise were not lost on contemporary observers. For example, when Faris Nimr, editor of *Al-Muqaṭṭam*, delivered a speech in the Armenian Church of Cairo, many of the Armenian attendees did not understand him. The Armenian daily in Istanbul, *Biwzandion*, reported, "It is a pity that many of the attendees did not understand the high ascending phrases of that inexhaustible language [i.e., Arabic]."[104] This issue was also raised by Nimr in a speech celebrating the Revolution in Cairo: "And I would like to see that all these elements and communities complete this exalted gathering by talking to each other in one language instead of different languages. I hope to live and see, by the will of God, that day when the people of my nation speak one language at their public festivals, and that is the [Ottoman] Turkish language, the official language of our government."[105]

Envisioning a better future entailed a discussion of the situation in the past. Indeed, most of the revolutionary speeches contained lengthy discussions of the past. As in the slogans that decorated many of the banners used in revolutionary celebrations, these speeches were influenced by French revolutionary rhetoric. In particular, the past was characterized by the concept of ancien régime. In fact, direct comparisons with the French Revolution were made during these speeches. For example, in Egypt during a festivity in the Britannia Theatre, Dr. Sharaf al-Din Bey opened the ceremony with a speech in Ottoman Turkish:

> Ladies and gentlemen and dear citizens, July 26 [24][106] is a national day for the Ottomans as July 14 is for the French. On July 14 the French demolished the fences of the Bastille prison, and they destroyed the chains of despotism, and on July 24, 150,000 soldiers rose in Macedonia . . . and demanded the return of the constitution and freedom for the nation. And because of this the Turk, the Arab, the Armenian, the Circassian, the Greek, and the Israelite [Jews] consider this day their biggest holiday.[107]

That day, Rafiq Bey al-'Azm, one of the leading Damascene intellectuals of the time, also gave a speech in which he reflected on the past, saying that this was not the first time freedom had been celebrated in the empire. Similar celebrations, he noted, also took place during the First Constitutional Period. He argued that the reason that the sultan abrogated the Parliament was not because the empire was composed of diverse nations and races, as some claim, but because the nation was not yet ready to accept parliamentary rule. Al-'Azm maintained that the drafters of the constitution resorted to the constitution in order to show their power and abused freedom; thus, the sultan punished them.[108]

Most speeches suggested that the constitution was reinstated by divine intervention. Thus, a religious justification of the act of revolution was necessary. For example, Faris Nimr declared in another speech in Cairo on August 31, "We feel that these pains have gone, and it is done with the will of God. He will not return them. We feel that we have found all our national rights, generally, partially, publicly, and privately in one group."[109] In the Armenian Church of Izmir, Archbishop Izmirlian's sermon about freedom and divine intervention contained the assertion that "during the despotic period the people were deprived of this [freedom's] goodness, but now let us be thankful to God because with divine intervention he gave it to us."[110] In some speeches, as in a number of the slogans that appeared on banners throughout the new nation, verses from religious covenants connected the revolutionary event to the divine project.

Undoubtedly, the main theme of these speeches was the concept of fraternity. Forging a sense of unity was, after all, the main focus of these gatherings. Speakers repeatedly attempted to show how the Revolution had changed inter-ethnic relationships by creating a plurality. One example of this tendency is the speech delivered by Bishop Moushegh Seropian, the prelate of Adana, to close the great celebration in the Garden of Taksim on August 13, 1908. After maintaining that despotism and injustice were the main cause of the emergence of revolutionary groups, he continued, "Now that despotism has ended, the injustice is gone thanks to the blood spilled by the Armenian and Turkish martyrs, and thanks to the support of the army . . . we can now become Ottomans with a new fraternity, gathered around a healthy state body [*petakan marmin*]. Freedom and justice are the children of a healthy body and at the same time their mentors. Let us preserve them and guard them."[111] That same day, the theme of brotherhood was echoed in an Ottoman Turkish speech delivered by Krikor Zohrab, who maintained that "before we struck the covenant of brotherhood, the Muslim martyrs and the self-sacrificing Armenians who sacrificed their lives for the homeland had already embraced each other in their tombs."[112]

Usually, these speeches addressing the issue of brotherhood and fraternity included an important symbolic component that consecrated the covenant of brotherhood. Generally, the speeches ended with hand shaking and hugging between spiritual leaders of different ethnic groups. This symbolic move was a practical implementation of the principle discussed in the speeches. At one of the celebrations in Damascus, Sheikh 'Abd al-Qadir al-Khatib al-Mughrabi made this connection particularly explicit. After comparing the despotic regime with the constitutional regime and defying fanaticism, he shook the hand of the Greek Catholic bishop.[113]

Conclusion

One of the most important outcomes of the Young Turk Revolution was the creation of multiple, competing public spheres. Different ethnic groups, scattered throughout the empire, demonstrate the reaction of nondominant groups to the Revolution. Examining symbolism, space, language, speeches, and revolutionary figures in the public rituals of the 1908 Revolution provides a new understanding of the festivals, which were crucial aspects of creating a new Ottoman patriotism. With their condensation of meaning and multivocality, symbols demonstrated the existence of an ambiguous common symbolic culture aimed at uniting all ethnic groups under one identity: Ottomanism. Loyalty to the nation had to transcend ethnic-religious allegiances. Nonetheless, beyond the attempt at national unity, dynamics that contradicted the revolutionary ideal— including confessional divisions, language differences, factionalism, and assertions of separate identity—were evident in these postrevolutionary rituals. In fact, the identity of the different ethnic groups was partly formed and revised in the public sphere through their participation in the revolutionary celebrations.

The postrevolutionary euphoric feelings manifested through the political culture molded by the Revolution are endemic to all societies that experience these types of pinnacle transformations. In the case of the Young Turk Revolution, however, those euphoric feelings were particularly connected to the participation of subordinate groups as a legitimizing force for the Revolution and a consecration of the new era. Their participation provided a temporary relief from the hardships they had endured during the absolutist period and an opportunity to air grievances that had been suppressed for decades. The participation of the Ottoman Empire's multiethnic and multireligious population in this process also made the politics of the 1908 Revolution particularly paradoxical. The contradictory attempts to forge a new Ottoman nation through revolutionary rituals are one dimension of this paradox. The other dimension manifested itself in the political discourse that preceded those contradictory rituals.

2 DEBATING THE
FUTURE OF THE EMPIRE

THE 1908 REVOLUTION created a disjunctive break and an opportunity for opening a new page in the history of the empire. The political discourse in the postrevolutionary period took advantage of this break by creating its own ambiguous rationale and defined the new era by rejecting the established political beliefs of the ancien régime. The issues that nondominant ethnic groups discussed in the immediate aftermath of the Young Turk Revolution were not unique to the postrevolutionary period.[1] Rather, as mentioned earlier, these subjects had been discussed in the exilic public spheres, in Cairo, Tbilisi, Moscow, Geneva, Paris, London, and Boston, by exiled intellectuals and activists. After the Revolution, the discussion of these subjects in the Ottoman Empire became more robust.[2]

There is no doubt that the ideology of the French Revolution, with its aura of success, had a tremendous impact on the constitutional debate in the Ottoman Empire.[3] It left its legacy of the *idée-force*, especially the trinity of ideals—liberty, fraternity, and equality—which found a strong echo among the various ethnic groups and their presses.[4] The issues debated among the ethnic groups after the postrevolutionary period were essential in determining their policy, identity, and space in the Ottoman Empire. In keeping with the French influence, freedom, equality, and fraternity; the ancien régime; and the desired political system were the main contested themes in the political discourse. However, it is important to note that the struggles to define these themes were not monolithic. In other words, one cannot argue that Armenians, Arabs, Jews, and Turks each thought differently about these themes. Such an analysis would be too simplistic and superficial. In a testimony to the ambiguity, fluidity, and complexity of the postrevolutionary period, there were no clear-cut lines separating these ethnic discourses. Ambiguity in this period was no longer "a catalyst for consensus and coalition building among groups with contradictory and conflicting interests";[5] rather, it became a major catalyst for the debilitation of negotiations among the different elements of the empire. The political discourse came to demonstrate one of the biggest challenges of the Revolution: finding consensus among the different political forces, dominant and nondominant alike, in the attempt to create a political plan that would satisfy everyone and upon which the political framework of the empire would proceed.

The columns and articles in the newspapers of the ethnic groups provide us with a rich mine of data for analyzing political discourse in different geographic areas of the empire. In addition to constructing and molding discourses, the press played the role of mediator between politicians and the public, connecting the masses with politics. It also assumed the role of educating and disciplining the public during the fragile postrevolutionary period, in which collective anxiety and confusion were expansive in all sectors of society.[6]

Freedom

The first reaction of the ethnic press to the Revolution was the printing of the Ottoman Constitution of 1876, which was suspended by Sultan Abdülhamid II in 1878. Almost all of the newspapers printed the articles of the constitution. The near universality of this response makes sense. The gap in legitimate political authority created by the Revolution had to be filled. Although the sultan had been the sole source of political legitimacy in the prerevolutionary period, the Revolution changed this status quo by reinstating the constitution as another source of legitimacy. Accordingly, both sultan and constitution became integral to the political discourse during the immediate aftermath of the 1908 Revolution. As one journalist described the situation in the Armenian newspaper *Biwzandion*: "In all the places HIS MAJESTY the Sultan's name was glorified because HIS MAJESTY consented to reinstate the CONSTITUTION of the Ottoman state that was established in the beginning of his glorious reign."[7] This sentiment was echoed in most of the ethnic presses.

In reality, however, the Revolution caused a radical breach in the traditional source of legitimacy. Power became vested in the constitution, which, by extension, meant Parliament and the nation as a whole. Nonetheless, because the sultan and his will were traditionally established authorities, they were vital to the implementation of the constitution. Consequently, the ethnic press throughout the empire marginalized the role of the Young Turks, despite their being key agents in the reinstatement of the constitution. In turn, the army became a symbolic front for the Young Turks. As a result of these negotiations, freedom was regarded as being dependent upon the combination of three important elements: the sultan, the constitution, and the army.

The concept of freedom became simultaneously one of the most important in the lexicon of the Revolution and a major source of ambiguity. Defining the concept of freedom, as well as understanding its privileges and limitations, became the main task of the newspapers in their journey to educate and discipline the public. This process of education and discipline was undertaken primarily to avoid the abuse of freedom. Articles from a variety of newspapers and journals published in Beirut testify to this process.[8] One writer for the Arabic newspaper *Lisān al-Ḥāl* said that the newspaper chose to define and explain the concept of freedom "in order to avoid bad behavior,"[9] whereas *Al-Ittiḥād al-'Uthmānī* (Ottoman union) warned people about the dangers of the post-revolutionary situation:[10] "Yes, the period of the revolution might lead to some disturbances; however, if the force of ignorance beats the force of reason, chaos will prevail, and this is what we are afraid of."[11] Other newspapers noted that while the revolutionary festivities generated much euphoric feeling, they also highlighted a widespread sense of ambiguity regarding the freedom brought by the Revolution. A correspondent for the Egyptian newspaper *Al-Muqaṭṭam* argued that the freedom resulting from the Revolution "does not have the right to intoxicate our minds with the wine of celebration and distract us from examining its true structure." The author further argued that the euphoric feelings of celebration did not reflect the deep animosities that existed in Beirut and other parts of the empire.[12]

Jewish newspapers also addressed these issues. In Palestine, the Zionist newspaper *Ha-Po'el ha-Tza'ir* addressed the ambiguity of freedom: "In one word life has changed . . . and matters are changed, and in all the tongues only the word freedom was heard, which is being translated into various meanings and interpretations from the lack of understanding."[13] The ambivalence to freedom has been also highlighted by other Jewish newspapers. In the Hebrew periodical *Ha-Shiloach*,[14] Ya'kov Rabbinovitz, a Jewish journalist and author, argued—albeit in a classically orientalist way—that Arabs in the Arab provinces did not care much about freedom; rather, what they wanted were justice and law.[15] To prove this, he cites the example of Jaffa, where Arabs did not show any signs of interest concerning the successful Revolution for a week. "Furthermore," he argued, "they continued to be preoccupied with their debates, to drink coffee . . . and to smoke their *nargile* [water pipe] in peace."[16]

The main concern of the different ethnic newspapers was to prevent lawless behavior by their readers. They were afraid that the gap in political authority created by the Revolution, coupled with the common understanding that citizens were free to do as they saw fit, might lead to an immediate escalation of ethnic tensions. Most of the articles and editorials that dealt with the concept of freedom began with questions such as, "What is freedom?," "What is meant by freedom?," or "How should we use freedom?" Three days after the Revolution, an Armenian author wrote an article in the widely circulated, Istanbul-based Armenian daily *Biwzandion*:

> Freedom is the greatest goodness for humanity if it knows how to use it, but when the nation accepting freedom considers it a toy, in that situation freedom will yield the most unsuccessful results. History is a witness. Freedom does not mean unlawfulness or anarchy. Freedom is willing submission to law that protects us against the barbarism that sleeps in each of us.[17]

As these examples indicate, most newspaper articles went beyond emphasizing the positive aspects of freedom, highlighting its negative dimensions in order to warn the masses. Freedom as a motto, as a way of thinking, needed to be tamed, and the uses, as well as the abuses, of freedom had to be defined.[18] In many instances, these articles were influenced by postrevolutionary French writings. For example, Puzant Kechian, editor of *Biwzandion*, wrote an editorial addressing extremism as one of the main abuses of freedom. The subtitle of his editorial was a quote from the prominent French statesman Charles-Maurice de Talleyrand-Perigord, who had been an active participant in the French Revolution: "Pas trop de zèle, surtout pas de zèle" (not too much zeal, particularly not zeal).[19] Kechian argued that the Liberals should not move toward extremism, representing the nation as a drunken person who was unaware of what he was doing. "Our nation, in this moment, is drunk from the nectar of political freedom," said Kechian. "We congratulate it for this joy, but we ask that it does not get drunk a lot, since the next day after drunkenness might not be that pleasant."[20] He warned Armenians not to be dragged into separatist tendencies and advised them to sacrifice in order to reform and develop all parts of Turkey.[21] Extremism as a result of freedom was a concern echoed in other newspapers. One reporter for *Lisān al-Ḥāl* wrote that moderation is an obligation in everything—in demonstrations, speeches, publications, and even unity—whereas extremism "is bad in everything except in loving the homeland."[22]

Disciplining chaos through the law was another dimension in the ethnic press's political discourse on freedom. The consensus was that freedom had to abide by the existing laws; otherwise, it would lead to chaos. From the first day of freedom, this issue of legality was emphasized in different ethnic newspapers. Puzant Kechian argued in *Biwzandion* that the glory of a free nation is achieved by obeying the law. "Thus, in a constitutional nation that does not live under tyranny," he declared, "no one has the right to take the law into his hands and use it according to his will. . . . The glory of a free nation is in its abiding by the law. By respecting the assigned law, a free nation establishes itself to assign law, to declare law."[23] It is evident through examining these newspapers that some discourses struggled with defining the concept of freedom; others highlighted its uses and abuses; whereas a third group dealt with its legality, which indicates that during this fragile period, ethnic groups expressed anxiety about the abuses of freedom not only by their adversaries but also by members of their own communities.

Equality and Fraternity

As noted in the previous chapter, the aim of the revolutionary festivities was to create an Ottoman identity that united the different ethnic groups under one banner. But because this was a paradoxical unity based in diversity, Ottoman revolutionary festivities contradicted their own ideals. The next attempt at creating an Ottoman identity was made through the press. Was the ethnic press successful in creating a unified identity? How did groups reconcile their ethnic identities with the newly evolving Ottoman identity? It is important to note that within the ethnic press there were several conflicting discourses, each striving to dominate the definitions of "equality," "fraternity," and "nation." This is an extremely important point demonstrating that conflicting discourses were evident in both interethnic and intraethnic presses.

From day one, the struggle between particularism and universalism was evident in the ethnic press. For example, in an interview with Archbishop Madteos Izmirlian before his election as Armenian patriarch of Istanbul, he was asked by the Armenian daily newspaper *Zhamanak* (Time) whether he believed in the Ottoman nation as the melting pot of all nations.[24] He answered,

"I believe an Ottoman nation with one soul and one heart can exist, but the different elements constituting that nation cannot become identical. Each one of them should bring its peculiarities."[25] Furthermore, poems on brotherhood and equality were printed on the front pages of ethnic newspapers. The following poem by Alexander Panossian, written on July 31, 1908, summarizes the aim of brotherhood by propagating Ottomanism.[26]

Ottoman

We are brothers, one heart, one will, one soul.
In our love we do not yield to anyone.
Under the flag of freedom that is praised by light
We have the same feeling, demand, and dialect.
Ottoman—our name that all the world envies.

We are brothers by the covenant of freedom
We want always to live hand in hand near each other
Always honest, straight, duteous
We will be an example to all the Fraternity.
Ottoman—we do not need another glory or treasure.

We are brothers of tears, pain
We are attached to each other in such a way with holy cement
Where, Turk and Armenian, in consent or against fortune
We will stay together, always inseparable.
Ottoman—it is our name as the name of one person.

We are brothers; heaven and earth tremble
If all the powers, nations come together,
By crying "Freedom, Justice, and Law"
We will always love each other.
Ottoman—let the gossiping tongue be silenced.

The poem argues that it is as a result of freedom that all of the Ottomans became brothers. It is, however, interesting that brotherhood refers only to brotherhood between Armenians and Turks. This perception is very much evident in the Armenian press. In part, this seems to be based on the idea that fraternity is possible only if it includes the dominant group. Another reason for the prevalence of this idea was the constant conflict between the Armenians and Turks. Brotherhood was understood to dissolve this conflict, making a new beginning possible. One article in *Biwzandion* summarized the fate of the two peoples in this way:

> Those who spilled their blood were mainly those two elements who have lived so closely with each other, who have witnessed the amalgamation of their fate during the centuries. Those are the Armenians and the Turks, who have sacrificed for the cause of the reform of the whole empire, as did the Greeks and the Bulgarians for the salvation of Macedonia. Now that freedom has saved their tongues and pens from the chains, our Turkish compatriots are admitting that it is through the spilling of the blood of thousands of Armenian martyrs that the efforts of the Young Turks were realized and freedom was established. . . . These bloody events greatly energized the Armenians and the Turks, and their fraternal ties have been strengthened with the bonds of blood and dedication.[27]

Constant reaffirmations of loyalty to the Ottoman state were made by the Armenian press, especially in the Armenian daily *Arewelk'*, indicating that Armenians had no separatist political tendencies and that they desired true Turkish-Armenian brotherhood.[28] How did the Ottoman Turkish press react to the calls of fraternity by the Armenians? An article in *Tanin*, the CUP organ, refers to the Armenians, for whom, it asserts, freedom has carried the biggest sacrifices:

> It is true that among them appeared those who followed extremist ideas of getting detached completely from the Ottomans. But the majority, having sound opinion, was always convinced that an independent Armenian country cannot be established and remain strong. The Armenian demand has been justice. And here, they became owners of justice and equality. Thus, we are sure that the Armenians are going to embrace these rights with us in one spirit and one place and that they are not going to have ambitions other than to work with us for the collective welfare of our country. Our compatriot Armenians know well that the modern current of human society is pushing the world not to the subdivision of small states but rather to the formation of a conglomeration of huge empires.[29]

Underscoring this apparent unity of purpose, an article published the next day in *Biwzandion* agreed with *Tanin*'s approach, arguing that Armenians wanted autonomous administration rather than independence. In fact, the article asserted, Armenians would wholeheartedly accept conscription into the army, knowing that "equality cannot prevail until every subject equally participates in the defense of the empire."[30]

Despite these moments of concord, a crisis point in the discourse between the Armenians and the Turks took place when the editor of *Tanin*, Hüssein Cahid, published an article in which he propagated the concept of *millet-i hâkime* (the ruling nation) and asserted the superiority of the Turkish element in the empire as the ruling elite.[31] Cahid argued that if authority were handed to the non-Muslim elements of the empire, Ottoman interests would not be the top priority in their acts and deeds. He maintained that Muslim elements, if they wanted to preserve their way of life, should "maintain the authority and the influence" in their hands and not let others seize it.[32]

The Armenian press reacted vehemently to Cahid's views.[33] One such article written by H. M. Shahe in *Zhamanak*, "Turkey for the Turks," argued that one of the main factors that had turned Turkey into a place of unending injustice and agitation was the question of nationalities.[34] According to the author, peace would never prevail in Turkey unless the question of nationality was solved. In fact, he predicted that these tensions were going to increase and might even be the reason for the dissolution of the empire. For him, the dreams of the Revolution had been shattered by the stance that Cahid and other writers for Ottoman Turkish newspapers had taken toward the Armenians. Shahe criticized the attitudes of the Ottoman Turkish newspapers toward the non-Muslim population, arguing that they did not want to accept Armenians as Armenians and Greeks as Greeks. In addition, they wanted to strip these ethnic groups from their national privileges and eliminate proportional representation for the parliamentary elections. The author concluded his article in an angry tone: "We have not sacrificed hundreds of thousands for a constitution perceived that way. We have suffered for years, and if this is our achievement, we will also start looking for the old regime."[35]

As other authors pointed out, equality also meant that non-Muslims would lose privileges they had enjoyed for a long time. For example, one article in the Arab press analyzed the Ottoman constitution from the perspective of dominant and nondominant groups. It argued that in the beginning the empire was divided into two main populations: Muslims and non-Muslims. The Turks had greater privileges than others because they were the conquerors. "However," according to the author, "the constitution removed the differences legally, and everyone became an Ottoman, owner of one's rights." He argued that one of the major changes that occurred during the Second Constitutional Period was the abolition of the reasons for privileges among non-Muslim groups. He maintained that all the nations would become truly Ottoman if the new Ottomanism, with its diversity, were implemented intelligently.[36]

Ancien Régime

The discussion about the ancien régime as it existed both before and after the Revolution, in both its past and present form, was endemic to all the ethnic presses. During the first days of the postrevolutionary period, while the festivities were at their height, newspapers warned people to be vigilant about the fragility of the new regime and wary of former officials of the ancien régime. Indeed, some writers even hinted that because the Young Turk Revolution was bloodless, the ancien régime had not been uprooted. One Armenian author argued that freedom should have been received through bloodshed on the scale of that of the French Revolution.[37]

Similarly, a Hebrew newspaper pointed out that without huge disruptions, without shedding of blood, and without huge sacrifices, the people of Turkey were able to obtain the most valuable thing for a nation: a parliament.[38] The article noted that this was a precarious state of affairs, since many figures from the ancien régime either had fled the country or still functioned in their positions. In other words, the major players in the old government "who deceived the sultan for thirty years" had not been arrested after the Revolution and posed a serious threat to the new nation.[39]

Only after the downfall of Grand Vizier Said Paşa's cabinet on August 6, 1908, were prerevolutionary politicians arrested, while many others escaped.[40] During the period before that collapse, an editorial in *Biwzandion* debated why Said Paşa had not dismissed the representatives of the ancien régime after the formation of his cabinet.[41] The editorial attempted to explain the situation by arguing that people should not forget that the empire existed in a revolutionary and chaotic period, during which freedom "is like a flowing flood, and the water of the floods cannot be entirely clean." The editorial asserted that this state could not be allowed to continue and that only liquidation of the ancien régime would allow a lawful, calm, and natural state of affairs to prevail.[42]

The main focus of the Armenian press was on Ahmed Izzet Paşa, one of the major figures of the ancien régime, who had played a crucial role in the Hamidian massacres of the Armenians.[43] One Armenian newspaper represented him as the person behind the massacres, saying that "there was a special policy in Yıldız [the palace] that stemmed from the monstrous brain of Izzet Paşa and spread all over the empire to annihilate the Armenians morally, financially, and physically."[44] His collapse, along with the collapse of Said Paşa's cabinet, in a sense, symbolized the demise of the ancien régime.[45] Despite developments such as the downfall of Izzet Paşa, many citizens still believed in the power of the ancien régime.[46] The sultan, however, was generally excluded from this discourse of blame.[47] Only after the Counterrevolution did the sultan became the target of all the ethnic groups' criticism, because he was seen, fairly or unfairly, as its main instigator.

In comparison to other newspapers, the Armenian press dealt most intensively with the concept of the ancien régime in its postrevolutionary rather than its prerevolutionary form. One such editorial in *Biwzandion* particularly sought to enlighten the public about the danger of the situation, arguing that Armenians especially needed wisdom at that pivotal time. The article is crucial in that it predicts the upcoming calamity of the Counterrevolution of 1909, advising Armenians not to create any pretext for the eruption of agitations. It argued that it was the duty of Armenians to "act with love toward their Turkish brothers and be careful with every act and every word that could make them bitter against Armenians and incite the people of the ancien régime." The editorial particularly warned against any appearance of Armenian separatism: "We repeat that we need to be careful about shouting 'Armenian' or talking about an independent Armenia. . . . The majority of the nation is in agreement that reforming the condition of the Armenians of Turkey is dependent on the reform of Turkey."[48]

This brings us to the issue of reform in general and the condition of the Armenians in the eastern provinces in particular, which became dominant issues in the political discourse on the ancien régime. The spread of freedom and constitutionalism in the eastern provinces took some time to be realized. This shows another dimension of the Young Turk Revolution: political changes taking place in the Balkans and Istanbul cannot reflect the situation in Anatolia or the Arab provinces, where many officers of the ancien régime were reluctant to declare freedom. Once freedom was declared in the center, thousands of letters poured into the Armenian Patriarchate, the offices of the ARF, the CUP, and the most important Armenian newspapers in Istanbul, expressing grief, sorrow, and anxiety about the unbearable situation in the eastern provinces where the ancien régime still prevailed. These letters were published by the Armenian press under the title "The Condition of the Provinces."[49] Upon hearing about the conditions in the eastern provinces, the locum tenens of the Armenian Patriarchate of Istanbul immediately sent a telegram to Minister of the Interior Hakkı Bey, asking him to send an urgent telegram to address the crisis in the provinces. Hakkı Bey chose to approach this critical issue in a different way, by sending a telegram to the governors of Muş, Erzurum, Van, Diyarbekir, Harput,

Bitlis, Sivas, Adana, and Aleppo, in which he made calls for harmony and unity among the different elements of society, advised people to live in harmony with each other, and instructed that measures be taken to achieve these goals.[50]

Hakkı Bey's telegram agitated the Armenian press, and editorials began to be written on the subject. One such editorial argued that although two months had passed since the declaration of the constitution and freedom, letters and telegrams were still pouring into the capital every day, indicating that "in many parts of Armenia the ancien régime is still ruling . . . [with] their oppression and exploitation of the population [and] by cooperating with the Kurds . . . whose acts and deeds are left unpunished."[51] Another article sympathized with the position of the government and argued that due to limited time and resources, the government did not have the means to destroy the anticonstitutionalists. It suggested that if the government could not send ardent constitutionalist officials to the provinces, it should at least distribute weapons to the people for self-defense and consider them civil guard soldiers.[52] Other authors believed autonomy was the only solution to the situation. For example, one argued that the remedy for the situation lay not in sending out investigation committees but rather in appointing Armenian and Greek governors to the regions in which those groups were the majority.[53]

A week later, the Ministry of the Interior issued a declaration indicating that complete tranquility prevailed in the Armenian provinces and that the telegrams and letters pouring into Istanbul from the provinces were forgeries published by the ARF to promote hidden agendas. In fact, this position was taken up by people in positions outside the government as well.[54] An article on October 26 in İkdam, the semiofficial newspaper of the Liberals, echoed the same concern upon receiving a telegram from the Cilician Catholicos about the potential for massacres in the provinces.[55] İkdam shed doubt on the telegram, saying that it did not want to believe in the existence of such dangers and that those who disseminated this type of news "have a special aim and that aim is naturally directed against the constitutional administration."[56] In addition, İkdam accused the ARF of sending letters related to the 1895 massacres from the provinces in order to push the Ministerial Council into implementing Article 61 of the Treaty of Berlin (1878).[57] In response, the ARF issued a statement rebuffing the allegations of İkdam, arguing that they were baseless and that the telegrams from the provinces reflected the real situation.[58]

Although the theme of the ancien régime's afterlife was more endemic to the Armenian than the Arabic or Hebrew/Ladino presses, some articles in those newspapers did tackle the issue. For example, the Egyptian newspaper *Al-Muqaṭṭam* argued that people needed to pay attention to the lingering spirit of division and despotism, contending that people should not be deceived by the festivities and celebrations of the Revolution. In this particular case, the loyalties of religious leaders were called into question when the article recommended that people should monitor the movements of community religious leaders, since they had the greatest effect on achieving the general good. In fact, the author specifically argued that the majority of these leaders were inclined toward the divisions of the previous period of ignorance while pretending to be the friends of the victorious people.[59]

In a phenomenon that brought together anxieties about the continued influence of the ancien régime and preexisting cultural divisions, similar trends appeared in the Hebrew and Ladino presses concerning the plight of the Jews of Baghdad. After the proclamation of the constitution, tensions were high in Baghdad against the Jews. *Habazeleth*, a Hebrew newspaper in Palestine, reported that during this time many reactionaries had gathered under the rule of local notables belonging to the ancien régime to threaten the governor. *Habazeleth* alleged that these reactionaries had threatened to kill Christians and Jews in the city if the constitution was reinstated. The newspaper also reported that the reactionaries had attacked Jews in the marketplace, injuring four of them before thousands of people gathered in the government building to demonstrate against the constitution.[60]

The Future of Ethnic Groups in the Empire

The public sphere during the Young Turk Revolution provided a venue through which ethnic groups could discuss the fate of their communities in the empire. What kinds of political systems did they envision? What did they expect from the government? How did they see intra- and interethnic relationships? It would be a bit presumptuous to argue that there was a specifically Armenian, Jewish, or Arab policy. Such representation would be superficial and problematic, since a wide variety of contending, ambiguous, and contradictory policies existed within each ethnic group.

While revolutionary festivities and euphoric feelings were reaching their apex after the July Revolution, the ethnic press began formulating policies for their own groups. For example, *Biwzandion* ran a series of editorials under the title "Our Political Platform." The subjects covered were Armenian-Turkish and Armenian-Kurdish fraternity, the position of Armenians in the forthcoming elections, Armenians in the Ottoman army, Armenians in the public service, and national education. Like the other Armenian newspapers, *Biwzandion* emphasized the necessity of establishing good relations with the Turkish element in the empire, because both groups "have sacrificed for the cause of the reform of all the empire."[61] Likewise, regarding the Kurds, "the policy of the Armenians in the constitutional system is to live like brothers with the Kurds."[62] As to the enlistment of Armenians in the army, the editorial noted that Armenians had wholeheartedly accepted the principle of furnishing soldiers to the Ottoman army, earning them the right to enter military academies.[63]

Most articles and editorials about the Armenian position indicated that whatever the Armenian people's political platform might ultimately be, such a policy could be realized only within the context of a unified, reformed Turkey. To underscore this point, an article in *Biwzandion* on August 27 highlighted the advantages that Armenians of the Ottoman Empire had over their counterparts in Russia and Iran, noting that "Armenians are doing much better in Turkey." Thus, the author argued, Armenians of the Ottoman Empire should put all their efforts into preserving the integrity and inviolability of Turkey.[64]

The Revolution of 1908 paved the way for the reemergence of traditional ethnic political parties, which projected their influence from exile into the political arena in the Ottoman Empire. In addition, new political parties representing different ethnic and interest groups were formed. The platforms and declarations of these political parties, which were printed in the ethnic press, provided another dimension to the discourse concerning political policy in the aftermath of the Young Turk Revolution. Although these points of confluence and conflict can be confusing, it is important to understand the orientations and aims of these political parties, since a good number of them played important roles in the political arena of the Ottoman Empire.

The immediate task of the political parties was to publish articles and give lectures to enlighten their communities about the policies they should embrace. For example, the Executive Committee of ARF made a declaration after the Revolution demanding that the constitutional government apply the following measures: free circulation (traffic) in the Armenian provinces; return of properties belonging to the Armenian community seized during the Hamidian period; abolition of the measures of persecution against Armenians created from 1895 to 1908; and return of the Armenian émigrés, who numbered over ninety thousand. The declaration argued that ARF, in agreement with the other nationalist parties, would deploy all its power to obtain full liberty in

the elections and to revise the constitution in ways that adhered to the principle of decentralization.[65] In addition, the party initiated a series of public lectures in Armenian neighborhoods, both in the capital and in the provinces,
to enlighten the public on the political and economic dimensions of their envisioned system. These lectures dealt with subjects ranging from the socialist
agenda of the party to the dynamics of the federal system and called upon the
different Armenian denominations to unite.[66]

The position of the other important Armenian party, the Hunchak, was
conveyed through several public lectures.[67] The first of these was a speech delivered by Sabah Gulian, editor of *Hunch'ak*, on September 6, 1908, in Gedikpaşa.[68]
Gulian argued that, although the constitution should be hailed, it did not suf-
ficiently deal with "the real demands of the people." These demands, according to him, were the implementation of a democratic constitution and local
autonomy for the people of the empire. He concluded his speech by warning
that if any group attempted to endanger the rights achieved by the people, "we
will be the first ones, arms in our hands, to go to the public in order to protect
these rights."[69]

Armenians were not alone in these efforts to establish political platforms.
In Istanbul, about twenty-six hundred Arabs gathered in a theater to discuss
the establishment of a society representing all Arabs in the provinces, as well
as the publication of a newspaper that would explain the principles of constitution, freedom, and fraternity to Ottoman Arabs. The Ottoman-Arab Brotherhood Society was established by the dismissed Arab functionaries of the ancien
régime.[70] This new society decided to publish a newspaper in both Arabic and
Ottoman Turkish—an act meant to simultaneously signal national solidarity
and ethnic autonomy. There were, nonetheless, concerns that this new organization harbored separatist agendas. For example, coverage in *Al-Muqaṭṭam*
indicated that Ottoman Turkish newspapers in the capital were critical of
the name of the society, fearing that it might suggest something like an Arab
union.[71] In practice, the program of the Ottoman-Arab Brotherhood Society
staunchly preached unity among all elements of the empire.[72]

Similarly, the Jews of Palestine formed the Association of the Ottoman Jews
(Agudat ha-Yehudim ha-'Ot'manim) to protect the rights of Jews and increase
their participation in the political sphere.[73] To attain these goals, the association
published newspapers, held lectures, and taught the Ottoman Turkish language
to Jews in evening classes. Within the Jewish sector, however, the body politic
was divided between the Zionists and Sephardic Jews. *El Tiempo*, whose politi-

cal discourse was inclined toward Young Turk Ottomanism, was the dominant mouthpiece of the Sephardic Jews in Istanbul.[74] Zionist publications were more likely to express strong ambitions toward political autonomy. For example, after the Revolution, *Ha-Po'el ha-Tza'ir* dealt with the future of the Jews in the post-revolutionary empire. The newspaper argued that in order to create political power for the Jews in Palestine, Zionists needed to unite all the Ottoman Jews in Palestine and train them for political autonomy. The author demanded that administrative decentralization be given to areas in Palestine in which Jews formed the majority (Jerusalem, Safed, and Tiberias) and that the official language in these areas be Hebrew. He concluded the article by advocating for a political position more openly aimed at Jewish autonomy, declaring that "the time of negotiation for Zionism has gone. Now our national desires and aims should be open, in regard to our demands."[75]

But there was disagreement even within Zionism. In the periodical *Ha-Shiloach*, another Zionist author expressed more caution regarding demands for autonomy because, according to him, "forces of darkness have not yet died; they only descended for a while from the stage." He argued that to the extent that caution and moderation were engraved on the Young Turks' flag, they should be engraved even more deeply on the Jewish flag. He argued that Jews should not add to a sense of division that, he predicted, would already be deep, explaining that most Christians in the empire would desire decentralization in the new government, while the Muslims, including the Arabs, would promote a centralized vision. He lamented the condition of Jews in "Asiatic Turkey," asserting that they were in decline and losing their cultural values, blaming AIU for this state of affairs. Contrary to other idealist Zionists at the time, this author seems to be more pragmatic regarding the political ambitions of Zionism, arguing that "it was only an empty dream that brought us to Uganda and did not let us move immediately to the Land of Israel [*Erets Yiśra'el*]." Ultimately, though, he did believe that the goal of practical Zionism was going to be realized through Jewish population of Palestine and Jewish land purchases in the region. Hence, he called for the establishment of a land fund that would give land in Palestine to Jews in exchange for long-term payments and give credit to those Jews who wanted to build factories and businesses there. Despite this optimism, he continued in a pragmatic vein, noting that there are also others— the Arabs—living in Palestine and that they would not want to be separated from Turkey. "We cannot exist as a weak sheep among hungry wolves," claimed the author.[76] He expressed his concern that it would be extremely difficult to establish a Jewish state in an area that was vastly populated by Arabs and had great significance to the Christians and Muslims alike.

As these examples indicate, the Young Turk Revolution caused serious changes in the dynamics of power inside the ethnic groups. In fact, most of these ethnic groups, which were represented by religious leaders, saw the Revolution as the beginning of a new era, during which their own ancien régimes had to be changed along with the old order of the nation as a whole. This was very much evident, for instance, in *El Tiempo*, which after 1908 immediately began a campaign against the acting chief rabbi of the Grand Rabbinate, calling him "the tyrant Moshe Halevi."[77] This brings us to the role of ecclesiastical leaders in the postrevolutionary period and their vision regarding the political system of their communities in this historic juncture.

In an interview that Archbishop Izmirlian gave to the Armenian daily *Zhamanak* prior to his election as the patriarch, he was asked whether he could reconcile the principle of equality with national privileges.[78] In response, he argued that these values were actually inseparable: "Of course. National privileges are given to the non-Muslim public by tending to the principle of equality. . . . The privileges given us in the past by the state constitute our national essentiality, so we cannot give them up in exchange for anything."[79] Religious leaders of other ethnic groups also used the press to explain and propagate their agendas. For example, in an interview given to the Jerusalem-based Hebrew newspaper *Hashkafa* before his election as the chief rabbi of the empire, Rabbi Nahum Paşa outlined his vision of the new era for the Jewish community in the Ottoman Empire. One of his first goals was to see that young people in schools were fluent in Hebrew. Furthermore, he advocated the establishment of societies in every city that would strengthen and develop morality and spread the wisdom of Israel among the Jewish nation.[80] The opinions of the religious leaders in the postrevolutionary period are extremely important because they demonstrate their involvement in the political sphere of Ottoman society in general and their respective communities in particular, something that contradicted the vision that the Revolution strove to achieve in which ethnic groups were going to be stripped of their ethno-religious privileges and become equal Ottoman citizens.

The Future Political System

One of the major points of contention among the ethnic groups during this period was the future political system of the empire. Most ethnic groups had high expectations regarding the political system, as most of them adhered to the idea of a decentralized administrative system because it was going to provide them more autonomy. The main champion of decentralization was Prince Sabahaddin, representing the Liberal faction of the empire, who was criticized by the CUP for his political views. For example, Hüssein Cahid argued that Sabahaddin's private initiative (*teşebüs-i şahsi*) approach was beneficial to the country and such an initiative should be part of the program of every constitutional party.[81] However, he was fervently against decentralization, arguing that Prince Sabahaddin had gone to extremes in his approach, which could not at all be beneficial to the country.[82]

The pro-decentralization position was widely discussed in the Armenian press and at public lectures by Armenian leaders. A little more than two months after the July Revolution, Nihad Bey, a representative of the Sabahaddin party, gave a talk at the Holy Trinity Church in Istanbul that emphasized Armenian-Turkish harmony and the principles of decentralization.[83] During the lecture, Nihad Bey praised decentralization as the most beneficial administrative system. After the lecture, one of the founders of ARF, Simon Zavarian, seconded Nihad's lecture by rising to the podium to explain decentralization more fully, praising both the system itself and his theory of it. Zavarian argued that, particularly in a place like Turkey where there were differences of race and language, local autonomy was most desirable.[84]

In another lecture, the editor of *Hunch'ak*, Sabah Gulian, argued that the Hunchak Party had one condition that needed to be acceptable to "every enlightened Ottoman": extension of responsibility (*tevsi-i mezuniyet*).[85] "Why should an Istanbulite individual who is not aware of all the conditions of the provinces run the affairs of these places?" he asked. Gulian argued that provincial authorities urgently needed to open canals, establish schools, and drain swamps, but because they did not have permission to implement such projects, they were obliged to wait for orders from the central government. To make matters worse, Gulian asserted, the central government often was unaware of local conditions and therefore refused to implement essential projects.[86]

As in other matters of policy, even when ethnic groups agreed in general, they tended to disagree about particulars. While Armenians like Zavarian and Gulian argued for the implementation of Sabahaddin's program nationally on the macro level, others argued that it should be implemented on the micro level within the Armenian community.[87] "From now on," editor Puzant Kechian argued in *Biwzandion*, "we do not have to await every order and decision from the [Armenian] Patriarchate, and we do not have to attribute every default to the political condition of the empire." On the issue of national privileges he argued that the Patriarchate should keep its church privileges and that it was the duty of all future Armenian deputies and senators to defend the ancient rights and privileges of the Armenians in the Ottoman Empire. In fact, Kechian warned that these privileges were "essential to our national and ethnic existence, because in Istanbul, as well as in Izmir, a chauvinist section of the Young Turks thinks of rescinding the privileges enjoyed by the Patriarchates and eliminating the national schools."[88]

The Ashkenazi Jewish press was more inclined toward decentralization than the Sephardic press. In this context, the Ashkenazi aim seems to have been to gain some kind of autonomy in Palestine. For example, the Zionist newspaper *Ha-'Olam* (The world) argued that the Revolution would result in the development of the "big national enterprise," which is the "Yishuv enterprise in the land of the ancestors [*be-Eretz ha-Avot*]."[89] Another Zionist newspaper in Palestine argued that the demands of the Jews should be similar to the demands of the country's other ethnic groups regarding local government and issues pertaining to language.[90]

Some Zionists were cautious not to raise the issue of political decentralization in this period, but they still believed that such a goal could be realized only through populating Palestine with Jews. Moshe Kleinman, an important Zionist intellectual who later became the editor of *Ha-'Olam*, for example, urged the Jews to move fast and work hard for the realization of the Zionist goal, arguing that the question of the Jews of Turkey was not only a cultural but a territorial one. Kleinman pressed Jews to hurry and buy lands in Palestine because "every negligence on this side will be a historical distortion that cannot be fixed."[91] Nevertheless, he made it clear that what Zionists wanted was not complete autonomy. "There is not a sound Zionist," he claimed, "that would think that we are now seeking a Jewish state in the Land of Israel [*Erets Yiśra'el*]. Nor are we seeking autonomy, which the Arabs, who are the majority of the inhabitants, could make use of." Rather, he asserted, the aim of the Zionists was to move to Palestine and enjoy "political and national rights in the country of our ancestors." Kleinman thought that in Palestine, the national culture of the Jews would be developed and strengthened as a "LIVING NATION IN ITS HOMELAND."[92] As a result, he believed the Jews would fulfill their duties as citizens. As to the current condition of Palestine, he represented it as "a country without a nation," waiting for the return of its sons. Kleinman concluded his article by reciting a line from a poem: "Bring a land without a people to a people without a land."[93]

Other Zionists also argued that if the Jews wanted a charter in Palestine, they would have to become the majority population in the country. "Zionists need to clarify to themselves," said David Tritch of Berlin, "that a Jewish Charter that is not based on Jewish majority in the Land of Israel is an impossibility." He urged Jews to start thinking seriously about autonomy, as well as to consolidate their strength by obtaining Ottoman citizenship for all the Jews in Palestine and initiating negotiations to that end with the Ottoman government.[94] This was the tone of the decision taken during the Zionist congress in Cologne in August 1908, which seemed excited about the Revolution. "In the foggy future of the development of Turkey," the congress declared, "a clear line of light pierces: Our historical and cultural role in the homeland of our ancestors. . . . The recognition that our East has risen to new life encourages us."[95]

The question of whether to adopt a centralized or decentralized political system was also high on the agenda of the Arabs in the provinces. Some of these commentators indicated that the administrative councils in the provinces would complement administrative decentralization if they adhered to the principles of the constitution.[96] Others, such as Edwar Murqus, explained that Prince Sabahaddin was right, if he was not an extremist, as some of the capital's newspapers had claimed. Murqus said that if Sabahaddin wanted administrative decentralization for the provinces along the lines of Germany and America, in which "every province will take care of its budget inside and outside, remove and appoint high and low officials, and make the provincial council as a miniature of the Parliament, I think he is going too far."[97]

The issue of what kind of political system should be adopted was very much evident in the case of Mount Lebanon, where the Ottoman parliamentary elections were seen as a threat to the privileges that Mount Lebanon enjoyed under the Règlement Organique of the *mutasarrifiyyah* of Lebanon, which had been promulgated in 1861 after the bloody civil war of 1860. Members of the Lebanese administrative council were not excited about electing deputies to represent the administrative division, since that meant an abatement of their privileges.[98] As a result, the people of Lebanon were divided into two groups: one believed that it was necessary to send deputies to the Ottoman Parliament to ensure political enfranchisement, whereas the other thought that Lebanon should defend its privileges by declining to send any delegates.[99]

Those who supported Lebanese inclusion in the Ottoman Parliament were called the Liberals. They maintained that the *mutasarrifiyyah* of Mount Lebanon was an integral part of the Ottoman Empire and should have deputies, as

Beirut and Syria did, in order to avoid being considered aliens within the empire.[100] Furthermore, the Liberals asserted that the Règlement Organique did not encompass all the needs of Mount Lebanon because things had changed and reforms needed to be made according to the spirit of the time. On the other hand, those who opposed sending delegates argued that Lebanon was a privileged province like Egypt, Bulgaria, Samos, and Crete and that these provinces did not fall under the jurisdiction of the constitution. Furthermore, they explained, there was no need to abide by any regulation superseding the Règlement Organique, because such an action would minimize the territory's freedom and threaten the basis of its privileges.

Shakib Arslan, a Druze prince who was an influential politician and writer in Lebanon, dealt with both approaches in a lengthy article. He concluded that both groups agreed on the importance of preserving Mount Lebanon's privileges. Arslan, who himself supported the inclusion of Mount Lebanon in the Ottoman Parliament, maintained that the territory was an integral part of the Ottoman Empire and could not survive without it. Thus, he argued, the inclusion of Mount Lebanon in the Parliament guaranteed, rather than nullified, its privileges. In other words, Arslan believed that the Lebanese would benefit from the constitution while keeping their special privileges. According to him, participation in the Ottoman Parliament was the best way of getting rid of the one-man dictatorship in Mount Lebanon.[101]

The editors of Al-Ittiḥād al-'Uthmānī, a strong supporter of the CUP, seemed to hold similar points of view regarding the political future of Mount Lebanon. For instance, in a lengthy article, Dawud Maja'es discussed the rumors circulating in Lebanon's newspapers about the Liberals. In particular, these newspapers claimed that public opinion in Lebanon was against the views of the Liberals. He vehemently criticized these claims, arguing that the Liberals did not seek to abolish Mount Lebanon's privileges but instead, in accordance with public opinion, wanted to ensure the participation of all the protected domains in the Ottoman Parliament.[102] According to Maja'es, such universal participation would guarantee the privileges of Lebanon.[103]

Another important subject in the political discourse of the nondominant ethnic groups was education. What kind of educational system should exist during the postrevolutionary period? If everyone was an equal citizen, did this mean that people were going to lose their privileges in the ethnic/private schools? While many members of the ethnic groups perceived state education as a threat to native languages, they also understood the need for children to learn the Ottoman Turkish language and history. As a result, some commentators argued that in order to protect the ethnic schools, Ottoman Turkish language and history should be equally weighed with other subjects. However, they vehemently refused to accept the fact that the Ministry of Education was going to inspect the private elementary schools of the Christian populations and that its duty should be only to support these institutions.[104]

This discourse concerning education was echoed in the Arab provinces. For instance, one writer in the Arab press attributed all the troubles of the empire to the lack of education. He made it clear that Arabic should be given priority over all the other languages in the public schools in the provinces, followed by Ottoman Turkish, French, and English.[105] Another provincial writer agreed, criticizing the teaching of Ottoman Turkish in the elementary schools:

> We the inhabitants of Syria and our brothers, the people of Iraq and the Arabian Peninsula and Egypt and the West, speak the Arabic language, and it is the language of our fathers and grandfathers from the time of the emergence of Islam. Every child of ours is born with it and practices Arabic in the lap of his mother and in the hands of his father and near his neighbors. And when he is seven years old, we send him to school, so in which language should we teach him? How should the child know the meaning of these morals that have been put in the Turkish books? . . . How should he learn the Qur'an and the Arabic dictation when the teacher is not an Arab? . . . And how should he know the history of his nation without his mother tongue? . . . I say that if the child masters his own language, he will learn Turkish in a shorter period of time. How could he not, when half of it or one-third of it is taken from Arabic?[106]

The quotation is important, as it indicates the way in which certain segments of the Arab population in the provinces reacted to the policy of the Young Turks to emphasize Ottoman Turkish as the first language of the empire. They did insist on Arabic as the principal language of the Arab provinces and expressed their willingness and the necessity to learn Ottoman Turkish as a secondary language.

On the other hand, some of the Jewish press strongly advocated for all Jewish citizens to learn Ottoman Turkish. For example, writers such as Moise Cohen called for the establishment of organizations and associations for promoting the Ottoman Turkish language.[107] This trend was most evident in Palestine, where evening language classes were held in Jerusalem for learners at all levels.[108] The Zionist newspapers criticized the education systems in Palestine, which taught French rather than Ottoman Turkish. In addition, the Zionist papers criticized the Sephardic community for not learning Ottoman Turkish, since that left them unable "to develop a personal culture and demand national rights." They compared the Jews in the empire to the Armenians and the Arabs, arguing that earlier in many parts of the provinces, Armenians also spoke Ottoman Turkish. However, the situation was changing because the Armenian language was increasingly being spread through the schools. The Arabs were also teaching the Arabic language in the schools run by Russians. He lamented the situation of the Sephardic Jews, who seemed not "concerned at all about reviving Israel."[109]

Conclusion

Examining the political discourse in the ethnic newspapers during the immediate aftermath of the Young Turk Revolution reveals that several conflicting discourses existed, competing against one another to define the important themes of the period discussed in this chapter. In addition to serving as a sounding board for these ideas, the ethnic press played the role of an educator attempting to discipline the masses during the fragile postrevolutionary period. This educational role is particularly manifest in the newspapers' struggles to define and elaborate on the concept of freedom in its different dimensions.

As the nation sought to construct an identity in opposition to the ancien régime, French revolutionary ideas became an important part of the discussion. In particular, the concepts of fraternity and equality became important components in the struggle over identity. It certainly was not clear exactly how these ideals would play out: whereas Ottomanism entailed that all ethnic groups be brothers and equal citizens, it also required that all the groups abandon their previously established privileges. This caused much anxiety among the ethnic groups whose communities enjoyed privileges bestowed on them by previous regimes. At the same time, some members of the dominant group were also skeptical about the implementation of Ottomanism, as they hoped to reaffirm their position as the ruling nation (*millet-i hâkime*) in the empire. Members of the nondominant groups, of course, saw this tendency among the dominant as a breach of the principles of constitutionalism to which the new nation was dedicated.

The struggle over space in the political discourse of the empire demonstrated how the different groups perceived the new political system in which they participated. For example, while some Armenian political parties argued for administrative decentralization as the ultimate panacea to the problems facing the empire, others vehemently disagreed with this proposition. And while Arabs in Mount Lebanon faced a dilemma about the political future of the *mutasarrifiyyah*, the Zionists began seriously debating the future of the Jews in the empire in general and Palestine in particular.

The Revolution not only shaped the discourses of the different ethnic groups with regard to the future path of the empire but also opened the door for intraethnic discourse concerning the status of their respective communities in the new era. That discourse became more vivacious and tense after the emergence of new interest groups posed an imminent threat to the legitimacy of the traditional forces that ruled these communities for the *longue durée*. The tension between tradition and modernity among the ruling elite(s) that peaked in the postrevolutionary period also manifested itself among the nondominant groups. This was especially true in debates concerning representation and citizenship, on the one hand, and religion and secularism, on the other. The Revolution not only created a new space in which ambiguous and contending ideas floated but also led to serious changes in the dynamics of power among these groups in the different geographic areas of the empire. Thus, as the next chapter demonstrates, the 1908 Revolution inspired the empire's different ethnic groups to initiate their own microrevolutions, claim their own victories, and hail the new era in tandem with major transformations taking place in the empire.

3 THE "HISTORICAL PERIOD" AND ITS IMPACT ON ETHNIC GROUPS

SIX DAYS AFTER THE REVOLUTION, Puzant Kechian, editor of *Biwzandion*, wrote a lengthy article about the downfall of the Armenian patriarch Maghakia Ormanian (1896–1908). "The strong current of freedom took away Ormanian," Kechian crowed. "A day does not pass when we do not see the collapse of a major representative of the ancien régime. It is true that we are living in a historical period, as it was for France in 1789 and in 1848 for all Europe."[1] Kechian's words reverberated positively among some ethnic groups. For others, though, the period became a critical historical juncture that threatened their power, prestige, and status. Regardless of their outcome, revolutions profoundly change the dynamics of power within their respective states and societies, and the 1908 Revolution was no exception. For those disenfranchised people who were dreaming of freedom, equality, and justice, the Revolution became their savior—the means by which a new and better future would be achieved and by which they themselves would be freed from the shackles of tyranny. For those traditional elites who were wary of the Revolution, however, it became their worst nightmare, shaking the pillars of their authority, endangering not only their power but also their survival.

In recent years, excellent macrohistorical analyses have traced the impact of the Revolution on the Ottoman state in terms of the transition of power from the sultan to the Ottoman Parliament and the CUP, the interplay between the constitution and the *şeriat*, the tension between the executive and legislative authorities, and contention among the major political parties.[2] In contrast,

comparative examinations of the Revolution's impact on the multiethnic composition of Ottoman society have been scarce.[3] Such studies are particularly
challenging because the differences among the societal structures, religions,
ethnicities, languages, and cultures of these groups outnumber their similari-
ties. A comparative cross-cultural examination of these groups would provide a
better picture with regard to the impact of and the reaction to the Revolution. It
would demonstrate how these different groups negotiated and redefined their
positions by adapting themselves to and navigating through the new, unstable
period attained by the Revolution.

On the eve of the Revolution, these divergent groups were living in societal
structures that were centuries old. This does not, however, mean that those societies were stagnant. Despite the prevailing status quo, these diverse groups
were influenced by global and regional currents of change that affected the
gradual transformations of their societies. Nonetheless, the Revolution acceler-
ated these transformations and attempted to create a rupture with the previous
era. This sudden, radical transformation became a major threat to those entities
with a keen interest in preserving the status quo. For those seeking change, the
Revolution provided a major boost and the ultimate opportunity for change.
A third group would jump onto the revolutionary bandwagon not because of
its members' sincere commitment to revolutionary ideals but because of their
desire to preserve their own interests. Examining the impact of the Revolution
on different social groups reveals the deep-rooted antagonisms that existed not
only within the different stratums of the society in general but also within the
different institutions of society: religious, military, and political alike. These
antagonisms would manifest themselves in the postrevolutionary period and
demonstrate why revolutions are a more complex phenomenon than just an
attempt by many people within the society to topple a government and create
a new one.

The Impact on the Armenians of the Empire

One of the major changes occurring among Armenians of the Ottoman Empire
after the 1908 Revolution was the change in leadership and the transfer of the
center of power from the Armenian Patriarchate to the Armenian National Assembly (ANA). The downfall of Patriarch Maghakia Ormanian represented the
downfall of the Armenian ancien régime and the beginning of a new era. Thus,
the Young Turk Revolution became a milestone in defining intraethnic relationships in the empire's Armenian *millet*. It resulted in a microrevolution, culminat-

ing in the reinstatement of the Armenian National Constitution, the (re)opening of the ANA, and the election of Madteos II Izmirlian as patriarch of Istanbul.

Whereas the ancien régime of the Ottoman Empire during the postrevolutionary period was embodied in the Yıldız Palace clique,[4] the Armenian ancien régime was embodied in one person: Patriarch Ormanian. Puzant Kechian described Ormanian's dominance in the community this way: "He was everything, and as Louis XIV said, 'L'État c'est moi.'" Certainly, Ormanian could truly have declared, "I am the patriarch, Patriarchate, religious council, political council, economic committee, financial trustee, judicial committee, and educational committee." Thus, the Armenian microrevolution eliminated competing centers of power more successfully than the larger Young Turk Revolution because Armenians were able to get rid of Patriarch Ormanian, whose "regime was nothing but a miniature of the Ottoman ancien régime in the national arena."[5]

In addition to garnering resentment for his stranglehold on power, Ormanian was criticized by Armenian revolutionary groups for his policies in general and his "collaboration" with the Yıldız Palace in particular. The Dashnak official organ, Droshak, hailed Ormanian's collapse and ferociously attacked him, calling him the "Tatar Patriarch," who was mourning the Revolution like his superior, the sultan.[6] These criticisms intensified as a result of rumors about his candidacy for the post of catholicos in Echmiadzin.[7] As a result of these attacks, Patriarch Ormanian resigned immediately after the Revolution.[8]

While his opponents protested outside ANA headquarters in Galata, Ormanian appeared before the mixed council of the ANA, chaired by Kapriel Efendi Noradoungian, to submit his resignation.[9] After long deliberations, Ormanian's resignation was accepted and Archbishop Yeghishe Tourian was chosen as the locum tenens of the Armenian patriarch by the "will of the people."[10] Things did not, however, end there. Immediately after his resignation, rumors spread in the capital that ex-Patriarch Ormanian had appropriated thirty thousand gold pieces from the Patriarchate's treasury and was planning to run away. The rumor caused much agitation among the capital's Armenian population. On August 7, 1908, people gathered near Ormanian's residence and demanded that he go to the Patriarchate to account for his actions. The demonstrators threatened that if he refused to do so, they would take him by force.

As the demonstrations intensified, Taksim's chief of police attempted to disperse the masses, but without success. That night, he entered Ormanian's residence and convinced him that for safety's sake, he should be taken to the Ministry of Police under their protection. Ormanian left his residence in a carriage surrounded by policemen, but the crowd followed him, shouting, cursing, and demanding that he be taken to the Patriarchate instead. Consequently, the masses succeeded in seizing his carriage and taking him to the Patriarchate. In the process, Ormanian became the ultimate spectacle of humiliation.[11] Moreover, this procession of public degradation represented the humiliation of the ancien régime, which had to be dragged into the streets and scolded in order to fulfill the aims of the Revolution. After CUP's intervention on his behalf, Ormanian was returned safely to his house.[12] The downfall of Ormanian's regime was finalized by the (re)election of Archbishop Madteos Izmirlian on November 4 as patriarch of Istanbul.[13]

As in the capital, local prelates were dismissed by the Armenian population in many parts of the provinces. For example, in Harput, the Armenians succeeded in dismissing their bishop.[14] In Diyarbekir, the local prelate escaped, along with his mother, uncle, servants, and four soldiers, leaving behind "the anger and dismay of the community."[15]

The reinstatement of the Armenian National Constitution and the ANA, which became the center of Armenian policy making in the empire, were important political processes in the postrevolutionary period. The ANA contained most of the prominent Armenian clerical and lay figures in the empire, including members of the Armenian political parties, Armenian members of the Ottoman Parliament, and representatives of different Armenian societies.

An examination of debates in the assembly sheds new light on the Armenian leadership's position during the postrevolutionary period up until the Counterrevolution. In fact, an examination of the twenty-five sessions of the ANA reveals that utmost importance was given to the Armenian constitution. Constitutionalism became a key factor upon which the community's affairs were administered. The authority of the Armenian National Constitution was even placed above that of the highest Armenian cleric, the patriarch. Partially as a result of this reorientation, the ANA became a mini-parliament that (at least in its earlier stages) discouraged partisanship and advocated loyalty to the empire. When he was chosen to be president of the ANA, Minas Cheraz made the following statement:[16]

> Delegate Reverends and Gentlemen, thanks to the reinstatement of the Ottoman constitution, the Armenian constitution, which has been paralyzed by despotism for years, was also reinstated. The rebirth of both constitutions is an equally happy occasion for us because, if it is the call of the Ottoman constitution to administer the affairs of the country according to the principles of justice, it is also

the call of the Armenian constitution to administer its national affairs according to the principles of justice: principles whose anchor is the popular right or, according to an old expression, "the voice of many, the voice of God."[17]

In general, three issues dominated the debates in the ANA during this period: the formation of a commission to investigate ex-Patriarch Ormanian,[18] the question of the eastern provinces, and the "Question of Jerusalem."[19] Of these, the situation in the provinces proved to be the most urgent issue.

The Question of the Eastern Provinces

One of the major questions facing the ANA during the postrevolutionary period was the situation of Armenians in the eastern provinces. In some parts of these provinces, the constitution prevailed within two to three months of its proclamation, but in other areas the ancien régime continued to rule. For example, the declaration of the constitution did not bring about any reform in Muş, and the Hamidiye Regiments and Kurdish tribes (aşirets) affiliated with the ancien régime oppressed the Armenian population there.[20] The case of Muş attracted much attention in the Armenian press, and assembly members were pressured to respond meaningfully.[21] Likewise, in Bitlis, the announcement of the constitution was followed by a violent reaction. The Kurdish tithe farmers there continued to oppress the population, and the government stated that the matter would be resolved with the arrival of the new governor.[22] Both the reaction of local groups—such as the Kurdish aşirets or the Hamidiye Regiments after the Revolution—and the counterreaction should be seen in the context of changes in power dynamics in the eastern provinces brought about by the Young Turk Revolution that led to an erosion of social and political stability. By disturbing precariously balanced power equilibrium, the Revolution produced a great deal of dissatisfaction within some segments of the population.

The ANA discussed the situation of the provinces in depth. Krikor Zohrab proposed that a government investigative commission be sent to the provinces. It was decided that the task of preparing a petition for the investigative commission and presenting it to the ANA would be given to the assembly's Political Council. On October 17, the petition was submitted to the assembly, recommending that the government send an investigative commission to the provinces and, toward this aim, an official delegation headed by the locum tenens should pay an official visit to Grand Vizier Kâmil Paşa.[23] It also recommended that the commission consist of honorable, honest, and liberal men of different nationalities under the authority of a minister or marshal who had not participated in the previous regime and who enjoyed public trust. The commission would be charged with dismissing corrupt provincial officers, removing Hamidiye Regiments, arresting criminals who had been set free, returning confiscated property that belonged to Armenians, providing the level of aid given to Muslim refugees (*muhacirs*) to all Ottomans returning to the empire, punishing the *ağas* (chieftains) who were oppressing the Armenians, providing wheat and seeds to Armenians suffering from impoverishment and famine, and issuing a special order that the military authorities should assist with implementation of the investigative commission's work.[24]

On November 4 a delegation from the ANA headed by the locum tenens Archbishop Yeghishe Tourian met with Grand Vizier Kâmil Paşa and delivered the petition.[25] Kâmil Paşa promised that the necessary steps would be taken on the question of the provinces but also emphasized the government's preoccupation with other urgent issues in the empire. A couple of months later, the issue of the provinces appeared again, this time on the agenda of the ANA, when some deputies inquired about the fate of the petition submitted to the government. Some members argued that a new memorandum should be sent to the government. While Zohrab and Bedros Haladjian Efendis (MPs) argued that the Armenian deputies in the Ottoman Parliament were already working on the issue and that there was no need for a new petition, others insisted that it was extremely important to formulate a new one. While the debates about the provinces were taking place, the Counterrevolution and the Adana massacres of 1909 took place, events that elevated the level of the concern and occupied a central position in the assembly's debates.

Armenian Political Parties in the Postrevolutionary Period

The Revolution also paved the way for Armenian political parties that were active in exile to return to the empire. It is important to mention that some of these political parties were already active in the provinces, but all of them were underground groups, outlawed by the government for allegedly trying to destabilize the serenity of the empire. After the Revolution, they became legitimate groups whose focus was politics rather than armed struggle. Most of the political prisoners connected to these parties were released from prison, and the revolutionary groups handed in their weapons.[26] Thus, the Revolution transformed these groups from revolutionary groups to legally sanctioned political parties. However, the public sphere in which these groups acted would also contribute to a fierce and sometimes bloody competition between the parties over controlling intracommunal public opinion and the right to represent the Armenian nation. Their center of activity was Istanbul, from which they issued orders to the provinces.[27]

Immediately after the Revolution, the Dashnak members in exile arrived in Istanbul and began to organize a series of lectures to enlighten the public about their party's political and economic platform.[28] The party's major policies were to cooperate with the CUP for the preservation and protection of the constitutional regime, reestablish all branches of the party in the provinces, create a powerful bloc in the Parliament, return confiscated land, and gradually implement a basic administrative-cultural decentralization.[29] In the ARF's first public address in Galata on August 23, 1908, Khachadour Maloumian (Agnuni) explained the party line to a capacity crowd:

> Compatriots, you are not Ottoman subjects anymore. Rather, you are free Ottoman citizens. You can be sure of the eternity of your freedom: there is not any fear of the reinstatement of the previous regime. The aim of Dashnaktsʻutʻiwn became to create this freedom in despotic Turkey. From now on, its effort will be to preserve and spread this freedom at any cost: with cannon, swords, arms, and powder. The different elements that cooperated with the Dashnaktsʻutʻiwn at the Paris Congress agree to this idea. Dashnaktsʻutʻiwn will seek to create for Turkey a free federated state on the basis of the principle of coexistential equality, whose different parts, being autonomous, will be supporters of the Ottoman fatherland.[30]

As part of its activity in the provinces, the party decided to establish new newspapers in Van, Erzurum, and Harput that would be their semiofficial organs. It even suggested the creation of a French newspaper in Istanbul under the editorship of Pierre Quillard, editor of *Pro Armenia*.[31] However, the party postponed establishing its official organ in the empire until June 1909, when it established *Azatamart* (Fight for freedom) under the editorship of Rupen Zartarian.

The ARF also spread widely in the provinces. In Muş and Van, the party was in control of the local church diocese.[32] Nevertheless, the Young Turk Revolution presented a major challenge to the Armenian revolutionary groups in the provinces. It created a revolutionary class whose existence became an "unnecessary thing, a rusted rifle left in a dark corner,"[33] because the Revolution had already been achieved. A glimpse of this situation was provided by Rupen Der Minassian,[34] who observed the crisis happening among these revolutionaries. The CUP argued that because the constitution had now been reinstated and freedom proclaimed, there was no need for revolutionary groups. Therefore, it maintained that members of these groups should either be disarmed or enter the ranks of the Ottoman army.[35] This crisis was also reflected in the relationship between the political center of the Dashnaks residing in Istanbul and the revolutionary fringe in the provinces. While the leadership in Istanbul, most of which came from abroad, was optimistic about the postrevolutionary government, the leadership in the provinces was highly pessimistic about the situation, and some were reluctant to hand in their weapons.

The Revolution also paved the way for other Armenian political groups to act in the empire. After the Revolution, the Hunchak Party's leadership returned to Istanbul and began organizing its branches in the provinces.[36] The Hunchaks had a clear-cut policy: political autonomy for Armenia within the framework of a constitutional empire.[37] They were reluctant to enter into any form of cooperation with the CUP. Upon their arrival in Istanbul, they conducted several meetings with CUP representatives to discuss issues pertaining to both parties, but these meetings yielded no results.[38] The Hunchaks' two main aims became establishing branches in the empire and arming the people. Despite their differences, the Hunchaks and the Dashnaks met before the parliamentary elections of 1908 to campaign on the same platform. But these meetings also did not yield any results, as the Hunchaks were very skeptical about the Dashnaks' intentions because of their close relationship with the CUP. The Hunchaks were ready to cooperate and sign agreements with the Dashnaks if the latter openly declared that they had cut all their ties to the CUP.[39]

Two other parties became active in the empire: the Armenian Constitutional Democratic Party (Sahmanadir Ṛamkavar Kusakts'ut'iwn, also known as the Ramkavar Party), founded in Alexandria on October 31, 1908; and the Reformed Hunchakian Party.[40] In its platform, the Ramkavar Party argued in favor of the people's sovereignty, advocated for all the nations constituting the Ottoman Empire to preserve their national uniqueness, and promoted the extension of responsibility in the provinces based on administrative decentralization. In addition, it demanded the abolition of the Hamidiye Regiments, an end to the *aşiret* system, and the subjugation of the beys and the *ağa*s to the law.[41]

A fierce and sometimes bloody competition began between these political parties, a state of affairs reflected in the partisan press, the ANA, and the provinces, especially in Van. The Hunchaks and Ramkavars were extremely critical of the Dashnaks' policy and of their relationship with the CUP. After the Adana

massacres in 1909, the ARF continued its close relationship with the CUP, leading to a great deal of tension among the empire's Armenian political parties.

Struggles within the Jewish Millet

On January 25, 1909, Jacques Bigart, secretary-general of the Alliance Israélite
Universelle (AIU),[42] wrote to the chief rabbi of the Ottoman Empire, Haim
Nahum,[43] expressing his contentment with the Revolution: "Thus it may well
be said that the whole Turkish revolution is like the triumph of our ideas,
ideas that are so moderate yet so liberal and solely inspired by love of the
common good."[44] The Young Turk Revolution's impact on Jews in the empire
should be analyzed from two perspectives, one pertaining to the microrevolution that occurred inside the Jewish *millet* and the other to the increased
Zionist activities in the empire after the Revolution.[45] The Revolution paved
the way for the Jewish progressive movement in the empire to start not only
reforming their own communities but also taking an active part in the political and economic life of the empire. However, unlike the relatively smooth
transition of power in the Armenian community, change in the Jewish community met with some resistance from people loyal to the previous administration of Rabbi Moshe Halevi.

The Jewish progressive movement's first task, then, was to take control out
of the hands of Rabbi Halevi, who had occupied the position of locum tenens
without any formal appointment for more than thirty-five years and was under
the influence of the black camarilla (Ladino, *banda preta*), a group of Jewish
notables.[46] On August 17, the progressives succeeded when Haim Nahum was
chosen as locum tenens.[47] The *Jewish Chronicle* of London hailed the election, reporting that Nahum was receiving many congratulatory telegrams.[48]
The newspaper's depiction of the mood in the empire was, however, rather
misleading. It is true that many telegrams arrived from the provinces congratulating Haim Nahum, but his appointment also caused much anxiety in
Jewish circles.[49]

This anxiety was especially evident in the conflict between *El Telegrafo* and
El Tiempo,[50] which "produced a painful impression among our coreligionists of
the capital and those of the provinces."[51] *El Telegrafo* claimed that Nahum's election was illegal and that *El Tiempo* should be held responsible for it.[52] Nahum
himself described the resolution of this dispute in one of his letters to J. Bigart:
"I must tell you in passing that the paper *El-Telegrafo*, my predecessor's organ,
after having tried to create problems for me by proclaiming the illegality of the

council that appointed me, has finally come over to my side, on pain of seeing its paper put on the index by its own readers and subscribers."[53] In the same letter, Nahum expressed much optimism about his election as chief rabbi.

On Sunday, October 18, 1908, a meeting organized by the Seekers of Truth (Rodfey Emet) and attended by about fifteen thousand participants, took place in Hasköy, a "manifestation that does not have an equal in the annals of the Jewish community of Constantinople."[54] This meeting seems to have given a boost to Rabbi Nahum Paşa, as he indicated in one of his letters to J. Bigart.[55] The government seems to have fully supported Nahum's candidacy for the position. In his first visit to the Sublime Porte, Nahum was received by Grand Vizier Kâmil Paşa, who promised his support: "All the efforts which you will make to improve the condition of the Jewish communities in the Empire will have my entire approbation, and you may rely on my support."[56] In order to strengthen his position, Nahum paid official visits to important figures: for example, on September 8 he visited Prince Sabahaddin;[57] and on September 10 he visited Archbishop Madteos Izmirlian, who, according to El Tiempo, was "a very liberal person [and] suffered a lot during the ancien régime."[58]

The tensions emanating from Nahum's appointment as the locum tenens were the outcome of tension between the Zionists and the AIU that escalated after the Revolution. In order to oppose the movement of the AIU in Istanbul, the Zionist founded the Maccabi gymnastic club branch, which became an important society that gained momentum in the postrevolutionary period.[59] This tension was caused by competition between Germany and France, aligned with the Zionists and the AIU, respectively, for influence over the empire's Jews. German Jewry was against Nahum's appointment because that would mean greater French influence over the Middle East.

Like the election of the locum tenens, the election of the chief rabbi of Turkey occupied a central position in the Jewish press in Istanbul. According to the Jewish millet's organic laws, five candidates were chosen by the temporal council to fulfill this task.[60] The candidates were Haim Nahum, Avraham Danon (Nahum's father-in-law), R. A. Shimon (chief rabbi of Cairo), Moshe Haviv (chief rabbi of Bursa), and Yosef Halevi (member of the general and religious council [meclis-i umumi-ruhani] of the Grand Rabbinate of Istanbul).[61] In this case, however, controversy focused more on the terms of the appointment than on the candidates. The Salonica community asked that the appointment of the chief rabbi be limited to three to five years, a suggestion supported by the community of Edirne. In an attempt to force the question, both provinces refused to send their representative to the General Assembly for the election. The Salonica community also demanded the elections be postponed on the pretext that modifications to the Jewish organic law were necessary.[62] The assembly unanimously rejected the motion, but the debate lived on in the press.

On January 24, 1909, Haim Nahum was elected chief rabbi with seventy-four votes.[63] His opponents protested the election, arguing that only three-fourths of the delegates participated in the election. Nonetheless, the vast crowd that had assembled in the confines of the synagogue received the news of Nahum's success with great jubilation.[64] *El Tiempo* announced that the election results were received with joy and happiness from all the empire's provinces, as evidenced by the numerous telegrams, letters, and articles the newspaper had received.[65] Indeed, the grand rabbi of Salonica, Ya'kov Meir, sent a letter to the newly elected chief rabbi of Turkey, expressing his congratulations and happiness.[66] And, in the end, the government itself ratified the election on March 2, 1909.[67] Nahum was ushered into office with a policy focus that emphasized the reorganization of Istanbul's Jewish community in order to centralize power by attempting to bring the provinces under his grip.

Even before Nahum's election, letters had begun to pour into the office of the chief rabbi from the provinces, demanding that Nahum, as locum tenens, dismiss their spiritual leaders because they represented the ancien régime of their communities.[68] The Jewish communities of Jerusalem, Damascus, and Sayda held demonstrations against their rabbis.[69] In Jerusalem, letters were sent to the Grand Vizierate and the Ministry of the Interior demanding the removal of Rabbi Elyahu Panigel, who held a provisional appointment. In Damascus, the Jewish community demanded the removal of Rabbi Mirkado Alfandari, "who has a mentality and an education that is not at all compatible with the new order of things." In Sayda, the people demanded the removal of the chief rabbi, under "whose administrative tyranny the population suffered for many years."[70] The governors of these communities also telegraphed the Sublime Porte, arguing in support of the demonstrators. In addition, the minister of justice wrote to the locum tenens, demanding that he take action without delay. Finally, on September 3, the Secular Council convened under Nahum's presidency and decided to dismiss these three rabbis.[71] Of these three, dismissing the locum tenens of the Rabbinate of Jerusalem became the most important and complex issue that preoccupied the Jewish press in the empire. It came to be known in the local press as the "Question of Jerusalem," as did its Armenian and Greek counterparts.[72]

An Opportunity That Could Not Be Missed:
Zionist Activities after 1908

On February 2, 1909, Vladimir (Ze'ev) Jabotinsky, a Zionist leader, wrote an article in *Ha-'Olam* discussing postrevolutionary conditions: "The new situation in Turkey has opened in front of us new and wide horizons, but in order to make use of this situation, it is necessary that we have energy and tactics, and it is difficult to say what more: tactics or energy."[73] The 1908 Revolution did indeed provide important venues for Zionist activities in the empire and for the realization of Zionist aims.[74] Even prior to the Revolution, the Zionists felt that they needed a permanent representative in Istanbul in order to realize their goals. David Wolffsohn, president of the World Zionist Organization,[75] had expressed this view during the meeting of the Inner Action Committee (Engeres Aktions-Comité) in Cologne, where he reported on his visit to the Ottoman Empire. He argued that there was a serious inclination at the highest levels of the Ottoman government to deal with Zionism and the time was ripe for political activity.[76] At the same meeting, Dr. Avigodr Jacobson, a Russian Jew who was director of the Anglo-Palestine Bank branch in Beirut, was appointed to represent the organization in Istanbul and charged with promoting the interests of Zionism in the empire.[77] While these plans were being made, the Young Turk Revolution took place, opening up new possibilities for Wolffsohn and others who hoped that the Young Turks would not pursue the anti-Zionist policies of their predecessors.

Jacobson arrived in the empire on August 26, 1908. From Istanbul, he communicated with Wolffsohn two to three times a week, updating him about the situation. Their correspondence, housed in the Central Zionist Archives, indicates the importance that Wolffsohn gave to developments in Istanbul.[78] In one of his first letters to Jacobson, Wolffsohn described the role that Jacobson needed to play. According to him, Jacobson's immediate task was to gather information about the political conditions and conduct a series of important meetings with key figures in both the Jewish community and the Ottoman political milieu more generally without entering into negotiations.[79] This task involved meetings with the leaders of Jewish communities in Istanbul, Izmir, and Salonica, as well as with Emanuel Karasso, Rabbi Haim Nahum, Nissim Mazliah, Nissim Russo, Bekhor Efendi, and Vital Faradji.[80] In his first letter to Wolffsohn, Jacobson described the situation in Turkey, expressing his hopes for the promulgation of new laws regarding the purchase of lands that would be beneficial to the Zionist cause.[81]

Jacobson, however, wanted to do a more active job of promoting the Zionist approach to the empire's Jewish communities and enter into negotiations with the Ottoman authorities. He believed that such activity would be in accord with the AIU and the Ezra Society.[82] After meeting with Vital Faradji, Jacobson wrote to Wolffsohn that Faradji thought it was not the right time for Zionists to make demands for territorial concessions. Concerning the issue of Jewish immigration to the Ottoman Empire, Faradji told Jacobson that it would be possible to get support from a number of leaders, but it was also not the right time to start a campaign in the press toward that end.[83]

While Jacobson was building the basis for future Zionist activities in the empire, a competition was taking place over the empire's Chief Rabbinate (Hahambashlık). The Zionists attempted to gain points in this competition by backing Rabbi Ya'kov Meir of Salonica as their candidate. Nevertheless, when Rabbi Nahum, who was not fond of Zionists, was elected, Wolffsohn immediately sent him a letter of congratulation.[84] Although the Zionists had not openly opposed Nahum's candidacy, they had tried to create obstacles for him indirectly by mobilizing both Orthodox Jewry in Germany and the Ezra Society.

In early 1909, the Zionist leadership seemed optimistic about their activities. One of their main achievements in Istanbul during this period was the mobilization of two Jewish Parliament members, Nissim Mazliah and Nissim Russo, to represent their interests. Both were influential and expressed a keen interest in Zionism.[85] Wolffsohn sent them a letter in which he thanked them for meeting with Jacobson and maintained that the parliamentary way would be the best path to achieving the aims of Zionism. He also asked them to explain in the Parliament that Zionism did not have "a separatist aspiration [*une aspiration séparatiste*]" and concluded his letter by urging the Ottoman Jews to defend the Zionist cause.[86] A week later, Jacobson updated Wolffsohn about Russo's activities. Russo had met with one of the leaders of the Young Turks, who had expressed his readiness "to support the immigration of the Jews to Turkey."[87]

Meanwhile, however, there were disagreements between Jacobson and Wolffsohn about how to proceed. In the letter including the report on Russo's efforts, Jacobson argued once again for the necessity of influencing public opinion in Turkey, this time in an angry tone: "I proposed another idea, and I do not understand why it is not clear to you. We have to buy the public opinion of Turkey, to gain the support of the parties, the Parliament, and the Ottoman government."[88] Wolffsohn, in his reply, expressed concern about Jacobson's proposal, arguing that they needed to be cautious about their activities.

"Zionist Associations," stated Wolffsohn, "could be very useful but also could do a lot of harm."[89] Still, Wolffsohn seemed to keep the door open regarding other political currents. In early 1909, he sent Albert Fua to Istanbul to meet with the Liberal factions. Jacobson opposed this move. In his response to Jacobson, Wolffsohn said, "It is forbidden for us to identify with any party; rather, we need to be neutral and consider all the factors. If the Liberals do not have a chance now, the political situation could change once more."[90] Wolffsohn believed that the Liberal faction in the empire might be more sympathetic to the Zionist cause than the other mainstream faction.

As Zionist influence expanded, one of Jacobson's major tasks became the establishment of a newspaper in Istanbul that would promote Zionist ideas, a process that began as early as 1909. Jacobson had been interested in such a project at least as early as the end of 1908. In a letter dated October 21, 1908, he expressed his thoughts on this subject to Wolffsohn, insisting that such a paper was "the only way we will be able to instill the Zionist ideas in Turkish society." Furthermore, he argued that the newspaper would touch on issues pertaining to the Jewish minority, Jewish autonomy, and immigration problems and said it was better to print the newspaper in French than in Ottoman Turkish. Jacobson also proposed that a committee be formed in Istanbul to deal with publicity.[91]

Such a committee was not finally formed until after the Counterrevolution in March. The members of the committee were David Jacobson, Ze'ev Jabotinsky, and Sami Hochberg. Together, they decided to publish a French newspaper in Turkey that would deal with the general issues of the country, including Zionism.[92] They also formed a Hebrew periodical, *Ha-Mevasser* (Herald), and gave support to four other newspapers in which Zionism would be promoted.[93]

Zionists also made a special effort to propagate their ideas in Salonica.[94] Despite opposition from the local Jewish community, the political ground there was much better prepared than it was in Istanbul, a fact reflected in press coverage from this time.[95] In Salonica Chief Rabbi Ya'kov Meir; Dr. Itzhak Epstein; Joseph Naor, mayor; and Sa'adi Halevi, editor of *La Epoka*, the main Jewish newspaper, were all very sympathetic to Zionism. In fact, when Ze'ev Jabotinsky was sent to advocate Zionism in Salonica,[96] *La Epoka* covered his lectures on its front pages.[97] *La Epoka* also played the role of educating the people about Zionism.[98] These efforts bore fruit, including the support of Emanuel Karasso, the Jewish deputy of Salonica and a prominent figure of the Young Turk movement, who was regarded as the greatest political gain for the Zionist efforts in Salonica.[99]

The power dynamics that emerged in the empire's Jewish community as a result of the Revolution were complex. The rise of Haim Nahum to the Rabbinate was a tremendous victory for the progressive movement among the Jews. The Revolution also opened up new horizons for the Zionists, but it created a major obstacle for the realization of their goal: Haim Nahum, chief rabbi of the empire. Nahum and David Fresco, editor of *El Tiempo*, became the main opponents of Zionist activities in the empire.

In addition to these external threats, Zionists suffered from serious internal divisions. On the one hand, the leadership in Cologne, as Wolffsohn's letters to Jacobson attested, was very concerned not to raise the fears of the Young Turks regarding Jewish immigration to Palestine.[100] The Cologne leadership's position was reflected in a major article in *Die Welt* by Nahum Sokolow, general secretary of the World Zionist Organization, in which he declared the "charter is dead" and that Zionism did not aim to establish an autonomous Jewish state in Palestine. "Our plans will not be realized in a Jewish state [*Judenstaat*]," stated Sokolow, "but rather in a homestead [*Heimstätte*]."[101] On the other hand, in its General Assembly in 1909, the Odessa Committee (Ḥovavei Tzion) severely criticized the Cologne leadership in general and Wolffsohn in particular. As a result of these divisions, at the end of March, Wolffsohn decided to go to Istanbul to be closer to the issues and look into publishing a journal. However, just before his departure, the Counterrevolution took place. His plans were delayed, and his attempt to unify the party was put on hold.

CUP versus the Politics of the Notables

The impact of the Young Turk Revolution on the Arab provinces should be viewed not only from the perspective of the Arab provinces themselves but also from that of the imperial palace. After all, it is there that the close confidants of the sultan from the Arab provinces, who played the role of intermediaries keeping a fine-tuned balance between the local notables and the palace, lost their power.[102] On first glance, it appears that the Revolution did indeed cause serious changes in the dynamics of power in the Arab provinces, but making a generalization about the impact of the Revolution on these provinces would be misleading. The euphoric feelings and mass demonstrations in the cities of the Arab provinces after the Revolution should not be perceived as the beginning of a mass movement. Though every locality was influenced by the Young Turk Revolution, the impact varied from district to district, depending on local exigencies.

When news of the Revolution arrived in the Arab provinces, local authorities received it with reservation and were unwilling to declare the constitution valid.[103] Some were skeptical about the news, while others feared that such a step would lead to the erosion of social and political stability. In addition to the local officials, the notables and the *ulema* were stunned by the news, and some began to voice their opposition to the activities of the junior officers. They were afraid that the Revolution and the shift of the center of power from local authorities to the CUP would endanger their traditional source of legitimacy, power, status, and prestige. These fears certainly had a basis in fact: after the Revolution, CUP branches and clubs mushroomed in Syria, and although these organizations began as local initiatives, they eventually were taken over by the Central Committee of the CUP in Salonica. The CUP branches threatened the notables and the *ulema* by temporarily becoming the de facto force in local politics in the Syrian districts during the postrevolutionary political gap. In some cases, people associated with the ancien régime entered the ranks of the CUP without having any ideological affinity for the party and with the sole aim of preserving their status. In addition to bringing CUP branches to Syria, the Revolution resulted in the creation of Arab political movements, the first of which was the Ottoman-Arab Brotherhood Society, established in Istanbul by the dismissed Arab functionaries of the ancien régime.

Damascus

Among the Arab provinces, Damascus was an important center for the activities of the *ulema*, in part because the Ummayad Mosque made Damascus a traditional place of Islamic learning. Additionally, the notables in Damascus, numbering around fifty families, were a powerful force running the political mechanism.[104] As in other localities, the Revolution became the ultimate threat to the notables and the *ulema* class. With its slogans of constitutionalism, parliamentarianism, freedom, and equality, the Revolution meant the existing orders of the ancien régime would no longer be the centers of power. This transformation was, however, less successful in Damascus than in other areas of the empire. In Damascus, the traditional networks of the notables and the *ulema* were stronger than the newer ties of the Revolution. The old power structures were, nonetheless, affected by the Revolution, which resulted in the emergence of new actors on the political scene, a mixture of military personnel and civilians, mostly members of the newly emerging CUP branches. As in other areas, young military officers initiated the establishment of constitutional clubs under the name of the CUP.[105]

The temporary political gap created after the Revolution was filled by these CUP branches as they began running the affairs of the administration.[106] As the CUP assumed that role, its first task in Damascus was to remove the ancien régime's officials from positions of power. Hence, they pressured the governor to dismiss the head of the Administrative Council of the province, the mufti of Damascus, the chief clerk of the *şeriat* courts, the *kaymakam* of Zabadani, and Busra Eski-Sham, along with several other district officials.[107] These actions caused some discontent among the *ulema* class,[108] resulting in the establishment of an association meant to protect its interests.[109]

Tensions in Damascus were also reflected in reactions to Rashid Rida during his tour in Syria after the Revolution. Toward the end of October, Rida arrived in Damascus and began to give a series of lectures in the Ummayad Mosque. During one of these sermons, Salih Sharif al-Tunisi, one of the mosque's teachers, interrupted to accuse Rida of heretically preaching Wahhabism.[110] This caused a public uproar against Rida, forcing him to leave the mosque. In response to this disturbance, the deputy chief of police, who also happened to be a prominent member of the CUP, arrested al-Tunisi. Events reached a crisis when thousands of people carrying weapons began gathering on the streets and in the markets. Many of them went to the municipality, while others went to the government building, all of them demanding al-Tunisi's release. The mob attacked the government building and released al-Tunisi. They wanted to kill As'ad Bey, the CUP de facto ruler of Syria,[111] but he escaped to Beirut.[112] This was yet another success for the notables, who were able to silence one representative of the new regime and run his confederates out of town. This antagonism between the *ulema*/notables and the CUP also bore fruit during the parliamentary elections, which resulted in the defeat of the Damascene CUP candidates.[113] In fact, the *ulema*/notables were able to beat the CUP in the election by playing on religious sentiments and accusing the CUP of secularism.

Latakiyya

In Latakiyya, there were minimal celebrations for the proclamation of the constitution, but the transition of power was, nevertheless, uneventful.[114] As a result of orders from the CUP branch in Salonica, a committee was chosen to represent the party locally.[115] Additionally, a CUP delegation arrived in Latakiyya as part of the Central Committee's larger delegation to the Arab provinces.[116] This group established a central body whose task was to preserve the constitution and resist any reactionary moves by adherents of the ancien régime.

Along with this central body and the local committee, a CUP club was established where speeches were given. In his memoirs, Yusuf al-Hakim, an attorney in the Ottoman courts of Latakiyya, says that two additional aspects of the club's activity were particularly important: purging people associated with the ancien régime from the administration and dismissing officers whose conduct was poor.[117] The first target of these efforts was the local *mutasarrif*, despite his reputation as an honest and straightforward person.[118] In his memoirs, al-Hakim mentions that the CUP in Latakiyya did not distinguish between good and bad functionaries of the ancien régime, simply removing all of them from power. These easy successes did, however, have a price: there was a serious gap in the city's administration, and chaos prevailed until the arrival of the new *mutasarrif*.[119]

Nablus

News of the Revolution reached Nablus on July 24 from the governor of Beirut. Celebrations began right away, led by the Ottoman officers and their friends. This group also established a club and considered themselves part of the CUP, as attested by the telegram they immediately sent to CUP headquarters in Salonica that informed officials about their activities and formally requested the CUP's consent.[120]

As in most other areas, the CUP in Nablus quickly emerged as the center of authority, and people began sending them letters complaining about the functionaries of the ancien régime.[121] The CUP asked the *mutasarrif* of Nablus, who was honest but weak, to resign, appointing a replacement from the CUP. In response to such actions, some members of the ancien régime, fearing for their positions, began to show support for the CUP, such as Sheikh 'Abbas Haj Tawfiq, president of the National Society (al-Jam'iyyah al-Waṭaniyyah). He sent the CUP telegrams congratulating it on the constitution and arguing that the National Society had preached justice and order long before the Revolution. Despite these protestations of affinity, the CUP was wary of Tawfiq because of his affiliation with Sultan Abdülhamid's regime. This distrust, as it turned out, was justified. *Al-Muqaṭṭam* mentions that Tawfiq's society had five thousand members and opposed the CUP, and in the society's first publication, it accused the CUP of being heretical. Later, during the Counterrevolution, the society would turn against the CUP.[122]

Beirut

As in Nablus, celebrations in Beirut began immediately after the proclamation of the constitution, and many junior military officers positioned in the city took part.[123] In his memoirs, Salim 'Ali Salam, deputy of Beirut to the Ottoman Parliament, mentions that the CUP emerged with full force, becoming the sole authority in the city.[124] Indeed, a CUP branch, composed of one hundred officers and civilians, was established immediately. On August 8, the British consul, H. A. Cumberbatch, informed the British ambassador in a confidential letter that the CUP of Beirut was in free communication with the Central Committee at Salonica.[125]

As elsewhere, the CUP's first task was to move against associates of the ancien régime, particularly the governor, the chief of police, and the commandant of the gendarmerie, along with many other local officials.[126] Telegrams arrived ordering the removal of these functionaries while local newspapers began a campaign against Beirut's administrative council, calling for its reform.[127] The governor, Muhammad 'Ali Bey, escaped to Alay upon hearing about his dismissal, planning to flee to Cyprus and place himself under the protection of the British.[128] His plan failed, however. The next day, after being arrested, he and other dismissed officials became spectacles of public humiliation. They were forced to move in a procession toward the harbor while thousands lined the streets, cursing the governor and his colleagues.[129]

Mount Lebanon

As mentioned earlier, since 1861 Mount Lebanon had enjoyed local autonomy under the Règlement Organique, which was guaranteed by international powers and the Ottoman government. In Mount Lebanon, news of the reinstatement of the constitution was received with a certain amount of reservation, since society there was split over the question of whether Mount Lebanon should take part in the Ottoman Parliament. The centrality of the Maronite Patriarchate is a key factor in understanding the impact of the Revolution on Mount Lebanon, where clerical and anticlerical politics intertwined with the dynamics of regime change.[130] The Maronite clerical circles opposed sending representatives to Parliament, whereas Druze, Greek Orthodox, and other minority sects were in favor of it.[131] On August 20, however, the British consul reported that the movement in favor of sending representatives had grown stronger when a liberal Maronite party split off from the rest of its organization to join the pro-parliamentary group. The consul further reported that although this party belonged to clerical circles, it was showing an inclination to associate itself with the Liberals, many of whom were Freemasons.[132]

These dynamics indicate that the constitution not only created tension between the different sects in Mount Lebanon but also opened a new door for the anticlerical Maronite movement, or as Dennis Walker calls them, "the post-Christian lumpen-bourgeois element," to rid itself of its own ancien régime through the inclusion of Lebanon in the Ottoman Parliament.[133] In so doing, they would subvert the authority of the Maronite patriarch, Ilyas Butrus al-Huwayyik (1843–1931; patriarch from 1899). As a Conservative, the patriarch shared Sultan Abdülhamid's opposition to any social or political change. For both al-Huwayyik and Abdülhamid the Young Turks and the post-Christian bourgeoisie Maronites threatened the stability of the existing order. With the success of the Young Turk Revolution, the anticlerical movement in Mount Lebanon grew stronger, and they increased activities to "curtail the baneful influence of the Maronite clergy and to introduce greatly needed administrative reforms."[134]

Existing tensions in Lebanon came to a head in the celebration of the sultan's enthronement, which took place in Bayt al-Din, the Governor's Palace, on September 2, 1908. On the same day thousands of Druze and Maronites from Dayr al-Qamar gathered in Bayt al-Din, carrying arms with long pikes.[135] Skirmishes took place between the Druze and the Christians, leading to the death of one person from each side and the injury of many others.[136] On September 5, members of these factions held a meeting in Beirut and drafted a list of five demands for the governor of Lebanon: proclamation of the constitution in Mount Lebanon, dissolution of the administrative council of Mount Lebanon and election of new council members, dismissal of corrupt officials, abolition of new taxes, and formation of a provisional advisory committee.[137] Governor Yusuf Paşa refused to agree to any of these demands.

A week later, on September 12, an eighty-person deputation of the Liberal Party presented the governor with five additional demands in Bayt al-Din,[138] in what came to be known as the incident of Bayt al-Din.[139] When the governor refused to accept these demands, arguing that they did not represent the people's wishes,[140] the deputation went to the telegraph office to communicate with the CUP at Salonica.[141] Meanwhile, the Ottoman military reinforcement at Bayt al-Din sympathized with the demonstration and refused to comply with the governor's order to disperse the people who had gathered to support the deputation.[142] Finally, under pressure, the governor succumbed to one of the deputation's demands and took the oath of fidelity to the constitution. He was then forced to promise that he would proclaim the constitution immediately, procure the necessary sanction of the Ottoman government for dissolution of the administrative council and the election of new members on a reformed electoral basis, and reorganize Mount Lebanon's finances through the new administrative council.

The paşa was also forced to dismiss high officials who, according to the British consul, were "all personal rivals of one or other of the members of the deputation." The consul claimed that this deputation's action "evoked expressions of disapproval on all sides, even among leading Maronites and Druzes, and it will probably lead to counterdemonstration, instigated by the Maronite partisan of Mir. Keblan."[143] Indeed, counterdemonstrations, organized by the friends of the five dismissed officials, did take place a few days later. The organizers of these demonstrations sent deputations to the governor and drew up petitions protesting the Liberal deputation's actions. The British consul also reported that the governor was being secretly pressed by the CUP in Beirut to take steps for parliamentary elections.[144]

Although they are important sources of information, reports of the British and French consuls in Lebanon require a cautious approach. As Shakib Arslan, the leading Druze representative in Mount Lebanon, notes in his memoirs, the British and French had a strong interest in preserving the status quo in Lebanon and in preventing representation of Mount Lebanon in Parliament.[145] It is no surprise that H. A. Cumberbatch, who disliked Arslan,[146] referred to the Druze and Greek Orthodox as radicals.[147] That tone was echoed by the French consul, M. Fouques-Duparc, who reported to the French embassy that many Lebanese citizens feared that the Bayt al-Din movement was fictitious and had been founded on the spot under the pressure of "more or less ambitious individuals who did not understand the privileged status of their country." The consul argued that the Maronites, who constituted the majority of the population, wanted to preserve the international treaties concerning Lebanon and that Arslan was pressuring the governor to change his policies. Fouques-Duparc also contended that Cumberbatch, his English counterpart, thought the Druze had found a means, in their support of the constitution, "to efficiently fight the alleged predominance of the Maronite element in Lebanon."[148]

In the end, the status quo won out. On October 30, Cumberbatch sent a letter to the British ambassador, claiming that the inhabitants of Lebanon persisted in their refusal to send deputies and that petitions against parliamentary representation continued to pour into the consulates general.[149] After much debate in political circles, the administrative council of Mount Lebanon voted against representation in the Ottoman Parliament. In a lengthy book published in 1909, Bulus Mus'ad laid out the perspective of the winning side in this debate. He argued in depth, from both a legal and historical perspective, that Mount Lebanon should not participate in the Ottoman Parliament and should not give up its privileges. He heavily criticized the "radical Liberals" and their arguments. In his conclusion, Mus'ad argued that the people of Mount Lebanon were faced with two choices and there was no middle ground between them: either they gave up all their rights and joined the Ottoman Empire or they preserved their privileges.[150]

Conclusion

The changes in the dynamics of power within the three ethnic groups in the empire have been examined through the Young Turk Revolution's impact on them. Postrevolutionary ethnic politics in the Ottoman Empire should not be viewed only from the prism of political parties but also through ecclesiastical politics, a key factor in defining inter- and intraethnic politics. Interestingly, even though the Revolution attempted to create the modern secular Ottoman citizen whose loyalty was going to be to the state, it nevertheless strengthened the ethno-religious political centers of the ethnic groups. It did so by creating the space in which fierce competition began among the different actors within these communities for control over the power positions. In the Jewish case, the center of power remained in the Hahambashlık. The election of Haim Nahum as chief rabbi strengthened the hamambaşı's role as the ethno-religious representative of Sephardic Jewry, but this became increasingly difficult in a period when new actors entered the public sphere in the Ottoman Empire. The Zionists, who aimed at winning over the public opinion of the Sephardic Jewry of the empire for their activities, were considered an undesirable element by the Chief Rabbinate and many other prominent Sephardic figures. Some Sephardic Jews feared that the Zionist goal of creating a Jewish state in Palestine could arouse the Turkish and Arab elements of the empire. In the Armenian case, the center of power shifted smoothly from the Patriarchate to the Armenian National Assembly, which became the representative of the Armenian ethnic group in the empire. Unlike the Jewish case, the ANA included representatives of most of the Armenian religious and political currents. And after the Adana massacres of 1909 it became a battleground between the different Armenian political groups. The Revolution also paved the way for the strengthening of Armenian political groups, most prominently the Dashnaks, who, by propagating their "grandiose role" in the great Revolution, tried to strengthen their status in Armenian circles. They used their close ties to the CUP to claim to be the representative of the Armenian ethnic group in the empire.

In geographic areas where intricate political realities were characterized by ascendancy of the notables, the Revolution threatened to disrupt this fine-tuned balance and transfer power to emerging politicians, who were primarily representatives of the CUP. It is, however, evident that the new politicians lacked a crucial tool that the notables enjoyed in the provinces: their traditional role in their own indigenous societies and religious organizations. To break the bonds forged by tradition and religion proved to be a difficult task.

Removing the ancien régime from power in the Arab provinces also proved particularly difficult because power in the Arab provinces was not embodied in a single person or an institution as it was in Armenian and Jewish communities. It was embodied in a multiplicity of notables, so it was more difficult to remove many traditional leaders from power than to oust a single functionary.

For these reasons, despite the emergence of CUP branches in the Arab provinces and despite their temporary control over the government, they lacked the support of the majority. As indicated by the cases in this chapter, the CUP was unable to mobilize anywhere close to the number of people that the notables or the *ulema* could. In other words, the basis of their legitimacy was much stronger than that of the new politicians.

In the case of the *mutasarrifiyyah* of Lebanon, however, the situation was more complex than in Damascus, Latakiyya, Nablus, or Beirut. For more than half a decade, the Règlement Organique had created what Akarlı called "the long peace."[151] Despite this equilibrium after the events of 1861, some elements of Lebanese society remained discontented. The Young Turk Revolution provided these elements with the opportunity to change the balance of power on Mount Lebanon. The Administrative Council of the *mutasarrifiyyah*, which was more important than the administrative councils of other regions, became a battle zone, contested by the notable families of Mount Lebanon, the Maronite church, and the laity. Nevertheless, although local notables retained their positions in society, even in Lebanon, most Arab functionaries of the ancien régime in the other provinces lost their grip on power.

4 FROM THE STREETS
TO THE BALLOTS

IN ONE OF THE FIRST EDITORIALS to appear prior to the elections, Puzant Kechian argued that from then on, the fate of the Ottoman Empire would stem from the Ottoman Parliament:

> The king reigns, but he does not rule. From now on, the ruling authority of the empire will be the Ottoman Parliament. It is true that the Ottoman Parliament is not as democratic as the British or the French constitution. . . . Now the biggest need is to satisfy the people and not to flatter the caprice of the sovereign.[1]

Kechian's expectations from the elections were very high. He confidently argued that Armenians were familiar with the electoral process, noting that provincial delegates to the Armenian National Assembly were elected through two-stage balloting.[2] In the weeks that followed, Kechian contended that Armenians had the right to elect ten deputies from the provinces, but he also cautioned his readers that Armenians needed to work in harmony with the Turks during the elections to achieve this aim.[3]

The 1908 elections fell short of fully democratic standards, yet they were competitive elections that reveal much about the social, political, and ideological evolution of ethnic groups in the empire. Although the main competition was between the CUP and the Liberal Party, other groups also played an important role. The elections required two-stage balloting: primary and secondary. Every tax-paying male citizen above the age of twenty-five was entitled to vote in the primary elections in order to elect the secondary voters. Afterward, the secondary voters, numbering between five hundred and seven hundred, would vote to determine the members of the Ottoman Parliament. The elections were not based on proportional representation but on the numbers specified for a particular electoral district.[4] In some cases, deputies were chosen prior to the balloting process, a circumstance demonstrative of the preelection deals endemic to the elections of 1908. Nonetheless, these elections represented one of the first electoral endeavors in the Middle East. Through political participation, mobilization, and lobbying, ethnic groups struggled both internally and with one another in legitimizing the Parliament. This was an important development in the history of the Middle East's "process of democratization," which is still unfolding in the twenty-first century.

What is most interesting about this process, then, is not the election's balloting procedure but rather the phase prior to the balloting, during which intensive negotiations took place among and between the different ethnic groups. These negotiations, after all, whether successful or not, would decide the course of the elections. In addition, these procedures indicate that some groups were not wholeheartedly committed to exercising their "civic duties" as "Ottoman citizens" for the sake of the Ottoman fatherland or in the service of a pan-Ottoman platform. The elections were overshadowed by complex ethnic politics and lobbying efforts among and between the different ethnic groups—a fact that highlights the multifaceted tensions manifest in the campaigns, negotiations, alliances, policies, and deals surrounding the critical phase of the elections. Although the ethnic groups' electoral campaigns and policies were influenced by one another, their main position during the elections was charted in relation to the platform of the dominant group—the CUP. Thus, the electoral campaign phase was extremely important in defining the different ethnic groups' political *Weltanschauung* and foreshadowed the major political divisions that would appear in Parliament, which were not monolithic. The political disagreements among all ethnic groups, as discussed in the preceding chapters, were a testament to the complexity of electoral behavior and elections in the postrevolutionary period.

Expectations for the Elections

The euphoria that followed the Revolution of 1908 raised the ethnic groups' expectations of proportional representation, increased fairness, democracy, and equality in the electoral process. The gap between these expectations and the actual results of the elections created contradictory feelings among some ethnic groups. While some were extremely frustrated by the results, others were content, despite the shortcomings of the process.

It is noteworthy that the parliamentary contests were not the only electoral processes that the Armenians and Jews were preoccupied with in the post-revolutionary period. These groups were also busy electing their national assemblies and spiritual heads. The Armenians were involved in elections for the ANA, the municipality of Istanbul, local councils, and the Armenian catholicos of Echmiadzin. The Jews were engaged in electing the chief rabbi of the empire and local rabbis in the provinces.

The attitudes of Armenian leaders toward the parliamentary elections differed greatly. An optimistic viewpoint appeared in a lengthy article by an Armenian lawyer in *Biwzandion*, who enthusiastically urged all Armenians to work hard to ensure good results in the parliamentary elections, especially since seats would not be distributed along ethnic lines. This meant that the demographic representation per deputy would be uneven. In some cases, one deputy would be chosen for fifteen thousand Armenians; in others, a single deputy would represent seventy-five thousand. The author argued that in areas where Armenians and Turks constituted the majority of the population, one Turkish and one Armenian deputy should be chosen. He confessed, however, that "all these plans are very easy on paper, but in practice it will be very difficult . . . because there are places in which people have not yet perceived the meaning of the constitution." The author predicted that three or four Armenian deputies would be elected from Istanbul and thirty to forty would be elected from the provinces.[5] On the other hand, one of ARF's leading intellectuals, Rupen Zartarian, expressed a more pessimistic view. Over the course of the elections, Zartarian expressed great dissatisfaction with the electoral system, saying that the Turks, "relying on their numerical advantage through a series of dirty activities, are taking their unjust victory." He argued that the two-stage balloting system prevented the peasants and the professionals from ensuring their candidates' success.[6] Yet another, anonymous Armenian intellectual believed that the election could satisfy everyone only if it was done through proportional representation (*hamematakan nerkayatschut'iwn*). He argued that this was the only way to solve the electoral issue because "the people constituting the Ottoman Empire are extremely different in race, language, religions, glories, and ideas, and they cannot elect independently with the same spirit and feelings."[7]

Since they were a majority population in the Arab provinces, Arabs' expectations for the elections were not the same as those of the Armenians or

Jews. As a result, Arab representatives made no demands for proportional representation. Although most of the Arab deputies in the provinces were CUP candidates, there was still competition between the CUP candidates and their rivals, the Arab notables (*ayan*) and the *ulema*, who ran as independent candidates. The Arabs' primary concern regarding the elections was choosing good candidates, a focus reflected in the press. For example, an article in *Lisān al-Ḥāl* cautioned all candidates that simply stating their names was insufficient and advised them to explain their political platforms.[8] Another article appealed to the people of Beirut, advising them to elect qualified candidates: good, honest, educated people who were well aware of the rules and regulations of legislative authority.[9]

The Jewish press expressed much satisfaction about the prospect of the elections and even called the electoral process a sacred act and duty that all the empire's Jewish citizens should fulfill.[10] Furthermore, they called for the election of qualified candidates, arguing that unqualified deputies "who do not possess the necessary qualities for representing the members of the nation in a legislative assembly commit a crime of lèse-majesté."[11] The concern about electing qualified Jewish candidates for the elections was echoed in Ya'kov Friman's article in *Ha-Zvi* (Gazelle) in Palestine.[12] Friman argued that during this time, it was difficult to find qualified people for Parliament and that the government was "looking with a torch for qualified people":

> This lack of [qualified] people is especially felt among the Jews. We do not have a number of Jews who deserve to serve in the government. The disadvantage of not knowing [Ottoman] Turkish, the language of the country, is strongly felt among our brothers [of] the new generation, since most of them were educated in the AIU, which dealt only with [the] French language. Should the association mentioned above know its duty? Will it change its program to make it more suitable to the spirit of the time? Or it will say, like its honored headmaster: "Chez nous pas da [de] progrés."[13]

Friman argued that only through educational reform would it be possible to produce people who were more qualified. He urged that reformed schools be both Jewish and Ottoman and warned that if the empire could not succeed in creating such schools, "we will feel sorry."[14]

Jews were more confident that they would be able to elect Jewish deputies in Istanbul, Salonica, and Izmir than in Palestine. In particular, the Zionists' main concern was whether the Jews would be able to elect a candidate representing

Jerusalem.[15] The candidate they proposed as offering the best chance of election there was Yitzhak Levi, manager of the Zionist Anglo-Palestine Bank, whose knowledge of Ottoman Turkish would "help him in his work in Istanbul as a representative of the Jerusalemite Jew." The Zionist paper Ha-'Olam criticized the rival Jewish candidate, Albert Antebi, who was the principal of the AIU school. "Though the person is talented," the paper's editorial explained, "I think he is not the right person, because his first act will be to obey the commands of the French association, which will care less about the national condition of the Jews of Eretz Israel and Turkey."[16]

Although the Ottoman Turkish press also expressed its desire to see qualified deputies elected to Parliament, they still expressed much concern about elections. Hüssein Cahid, editor of Tanin, expressed his concern that the electoral laws were written in a rush and needed to be "written taking into consideration the psychological condition of the people, [their] applicability, and then [their] benefits."[17] The major concern of the Young Turks, however, was the political aspirations of the non-Muslims in general and the Greeks in particular.[18] The Young Turks who supported universal representation criticized the idea of proportional representation among non-Muslim elements of the population.[19] In a lengthy article on the issue, Hüssein Cahid openly opposed proportional representation, arguing that the empire would become like the Tower of Babel if that policy were implemented. Cahid did, however, suggest that the election of non-Muslim deputies to Parliament should be facilitated. He believed the electoral laws made it unlikely that non-Muslims would win many seats, since the sancaks were assigned as electoral districts and few sancaks had Christian majorities.[20] In another article with an even stronger tone, Cahid criticized what he saw as non-Muslims' sectarian approach to the elections, arguing that the electoral law did not differentiate among groups. He asserted that, on the contrary, election law stipulated that the different elements of the empire should jointly elect deputies for Parliament. Finally, he argued that Ottoman subjects should not vote along religious or ethnic lines but based on the candidates' virtues and honor.[21]

Proportional representation, then, was the key concept in the electoral battle among the empire's ethnic groups. While many of the ethnic groups were in favor of proportional representation, the Young Turks who had led the Revolution feared that applying proportional representation to the elections would cause an imminent political threat to them from the non-Muslim population. This was especially true of the Greeks, who had a long tradition of holding elections and were even backed by the Greek government in their electoral efforts.

The electoral platforms of the empire's ethnic groups provided an important medium through which they demonstrated their political worldview and the agenda they would pursue in Parliament. Furthermore, these political platforms influenced the ethnic groups' stances toward each other. For analytical purposes, the platforms can be divided into two types: partisan and individual.

Partisan Platforms

One of the first parties to issue its platform was the ARF.[22] The platform's introduction stated that for a multilingual empire like the Ottoman Empire, the best political system was a federal, decentralized one. The reasoning behind this ideal was that the different regions, with their separate geographic, economic, and ethnographic characteristics, would harmoniously strengthen the empire when they enjoyed internal administrative autonomy. Along these lines, the platform argued that all the provinces should enjoy a large degree of autonomy in conducting their internal affairs. This would entail constitutional revisions based on the idea of decentralization. Within this system, Turkish Armenia would constitute an integral part of the Ottoman Empire and conduct its local affairs in a way that would equally benefit all the other nations of the empire. In keeping with these ideals, the platform urged that the teaching language of national schools would be the mother tongue of the respective populations, with Ottoman Turkish taught in schools beginning in the fourth grade. In addition to Ottoman Turkish, local languages would be used in administrative institutions, including the courts. Other points in the platform included equal conscription, the reduction of compulsory military service to two years, the return of all lands seized during the Hamidian period, and fundamental change in the tax system.

In a lengthy article on the front page of *Tanin*, Hüssein Cahid criticized the Dashnaks' political platform, accepting some of its points but refuting others.[23] Its editorials determined that the party appeared to be socialist and was convinced that it would achieve its aim gradually by working with all the other political parties. Cahid claimed that this was opportunistic and that the Dashnaks' socialism existed only in their minds. Cahid saw no need to change the constitution according to the Dashnaks' decentralization scheme, arguing that extension of responsibility was already part of the constitution. Cahid also stated that if the aim of ARF was to establish autonomy in the name of decentralization, then he was against it.[24]

On October 6, 1908, a month after the ARF electoral program was published, the Young Turks' CUP published its own platform in *Şura-yı Ümmet*.[25] The platform included a statement of the cabinet's responsibility to the House of Deputies, a proposal for the election of one-third of the senators by the sultan and two-thirds by the people, a call to lower the voting age to twenty, an assertion that Article 108 of the constitution be implemented, and an endorsement of extension of responsibility in the provinces.[26] It also included an affirmation of Ottoman Turkish as the official language of the empire for all government correspondence, and a declaration that Ottoman Turkish should be the language of instruction in elementary school classes. In military matters, the CUP platform also advocated the conscription of non-Muslims into the army and a decrease in the term of obligatory military service.[27]

Predictably, Cahid praised the CUP's program, saying that it dealt mainly with how to move the constitution forward.[28] In another article, Cahid claimed that many Ottoman compatriots and foreigners considered the CUP program a Turkish program because "all the Turks today have united around the CUP; they have established this party as a center of gathering because power results from unity and, since the majority of the people in the CUP are Turks, the program has been a Turkish one."[29] Cahid then discussed the CUP's reaction to the other ethnic groups' electoral programs. He argued that the CUP followed a sincere and just aim and that there was no need to talk about (non-Muslim) privileges, since the Ottomans had not assaulted anyone's religion or confession and the issue of privileges would be solved by Parliament. Finally, in praising the CUP platform's statements concerning Ottoman Turkish as the official language, Cahid criticized the non-Muslims' multilingual educational systems, which, he said, were far "from pursuing Ottoman Unity."[30]

In reaction to the CUP platform, ARF's official organ, *Droshak*, was highly critical of the CUP program: "It is undeniable that the platform of the Young Turks is a nationalist one, and that, as expected, it is their endeavor that in the upcoming Parliament the Turkish or the Muslim element should have as much voice as possible, and in an inseparable way, to forge the 'basic' law of the country."[31]

The Advisory Committee of the Ottoman Parliamentary Elections (Ōsm. Eresp̔. Endrut̔iants Khorherdaktsakan Hantsanzhoghov), which was formed by the Armenian Patriarchate, published its platform under the title "The Platform of the Armenian Members of the Ottoman Parliament."[32] The twenty-four articles of this platform stressed that the committee rejected any separatist ideas and that Turkish Armenia formed an integral part of the fatherland. Some of the more important points in the platform included the preservation of privileges enjoyed by different nations and communities, including control over educational affairs; complete administrative extension of responsibility in the provinces; the necessity of employing local languages in the courts and in police matters; the return of confiscated properties from the Hamidian period; the abolishment of nepotism; and Ottoman Turkish instruction in all of the empire's schools, beginning with the third grade.

The ethnic groups' electoral platforms did not operate in a vacuum; they influenced one another. For example, the Jewish newspaper *La Epoka* lamented what it saw as the Jews' lack of political presence in Salonica, noting that the CUP, the Bulgarian Constitutional Club, and the Greeks had already published their electoral programs. "And we Jews," argued the newspaper, "have not yet adopted a program. We have not made it look like we exist."[33] Sa'adi Halevi, editor of *La Epoka*,[34] rhetorically asked of the Salonica Jews: "Should they follow the lawyer who said, 'We are so few that we do not count'?" In order to avoid such a situation, Halevi proposed the formation of a committee of fifteen to twenty individuals from Salonica's Jewish community whose task would be to draft a platform. Halevi also suggested that the Bulgarian platform could serve as the basis for the Jewish committee, arguing that the Bulgarians' demands for their schools, children, and local administration should be emulated by the Jews.[35]

Individual Platforms

The press also provided a medium for individual and independent candidates to publish their political programs. Regardless of whether these candidates succeeded in winning seats in Parliament, their platforms provide insight into another dimension of the electoral campaigns that is devoid of any partisan dimensions. The electoral platforms of Arisdages Kasbarian, Jurji Efendi Ghammashi, Maystro Izzak Efendi Taranto, and Bedros Haladjian, among many others, are particularly illuminating and provide us a glimpse of the major issues that preoccupied such candidates.

In his electoral platform's introduction, Arisdages Kasbarian, a lawyer from Adana, stated that reform must start with the country's laws, which must be based on justice, equality, and freedom.[36] To achieve this aim, he argued, reform must start with the constitution. The first article of Kasbarian's platform indicated the need to add a section to Article 5 of the constitution: "It is obligatory that the sultan, in front of the Parliament, take an oath to preserve the constitution and to implement it point by point." Other articles dealt with the freedom of the press within the limits of the law "on condition that it [a newspaper] not be subjected to censorship before being published." In his platform, Kasbarian dealt with the extension of responsibility, arguing that governors, *mutasarrifs*, and *defterdar*s should be appointed by the center (Istanbul), whereas the other offices, such as the *nahiye müdür*s (township administrator), *kaymakam*s, and officers from the sancak, should be appointed by the center of the province. He also promoted administrative decentralization but was against political decentralization, "which simply means autonomy, something that the main defenders of the decentralization system do not accept."[37]

Jurji Efendi Ghammashi of Beirut published his electoral platform in *Lisān al-Ḥāl*. Ghammashi divided his platform into three sections: a political plan, a reform plan, and a prosperity plan. In the political section, Ghammashi indicated that he would "protect the constitution until the last minute of my life by amending some of its articles so that it is more applicable to the principles of freedom, constitution, and changing what is necessary with the rest of the regulations." In the reform section, Ghammashi indicated that he would support the "sacred CUP." Furthermore, he argued that he would work to preserve the special status of Bulgaria, Bosnia, and Herzegovina and would remove traditional political privileges slowly, as conditions allowed. In his plan for prosperity, Ghammashi called for the establishment of agricultural, commercial, and industrial schools in the center of the provinces, as well as for the establishment of Ottoman companies.[38]

Maystro Izzak Efendi Taranto of Izmir, a lawyer for the Ministry of Foreign Affairs, presented his candidacy and published his electoral platform.[39] Taranto called for absolute political equality among all the races and religions of the empire and opposed any act that would lead to dissolution of the empire. He also advocated for free access to public posts for members of all ethnic groups, establishment and consolidation of budgetary equilibrium, facilitation of land transactions for all Ottoman subjects without distinction and for foreign subjects under the restrictions of Protocol Number 7, obligatory military service for all Ottoman subjects, and integral maintenance of the privileges and religious jurisdictions of non-Muslim communities.

Of these independent electoral platforms under study, the lengthiest and most detailed was that of Bedros Haladjian, a member of the CUP from Istanbul.[40] Haladjian's case is interesting because of his attempt to reconcile his

ethnic affiliation with his partisan inclinations. His platform was first delivered as a speech on September 27, 1908, in Hasköy and was later published as
a booklet.[41] In the introduction, Haladjian argued that through the organization of freedom, the existence of unity, and civilizational advancement, the
Ottoman nation would become one of the most prosperous nations on earth.
The first article of his platform stated that Armenian parliamentary deputies
would "protect completely and totally the equality of rights of all the elements
and the individuals, and on that basis, [they would protect] also the unity
and integrity of the Ottoman Empire totally and completely."[42] Other articles
dealt with the sultan's accountability toward the Parliament and protection of
the special legal position of the Armenian nation. In keeping with his ethnic
views, Haladjian refused to use the word "privileges" in describing the Armenians' status:

> In order to express these special positions, the word "privilege" is being used.
> It is said that the Armenian nation is enjoying privileges. That is completely
> wrong. The Armenian nation does not have any kind of privileges. The Arme-
> nians are simply found in special conditions in the different religious, education,
> and legal issues, as are other elements, which are the result of their ethnic and
> religious differences in a country where an official religion exists, in which many
> legal issues have religious particularity, and in which ethnicities and languages
> are extremely different.[43]

Like the other candidates, Haladjian supported administrative decentralization. However, he rejected political decentralization and advocated a limited
extension of responsibility. In addition to these issues, Haladjian argued in
favor of mandatory Ottoman Turkish instruction in the Armenian schools,
military service for both Muslims and non-Muslims, and search for a remedy
for the Armenian confiscated property during the prior thirty years.[44]

In general, the partisan/national and individual platforms agreed on many
points. The major points of disagreement between the CUP and the nondominant ethnic groups were centered on the political system, the status of religious
institutions, and education. The Armenians, Albanians, Greeks, and Bulgarians—and to a certain extent the Jews—promoted the extension of discretion.
Furthermore, they all supported administrative decentralization, the preservation of religious and national privileges, and mandatory teaching of mother
tongues in the national schools. The CUP, on the other hand, was vehemently
against administrative decentralization and argued that extension of responsi-

bility already existed in the constitution. They promoted centralization as the means by which the empire ultimately would be governed. In addition, they promoted the removal of all ethno-national privileges enjoyed by non-Muslim ethnic groups, and wanted to make teaching of the Ottoman Turkish language mandatory for all the ethnic schools on both the elementary and the secondary levels. The Armenians, in particular, considered the CUP's electoral platform to be a radical statement of Turkish nationalism.

Electoral Campaigning Committees

More systematic electoral campaigns aimed at mobilizing their members in the elections and negotiating their place in Parliament were initiated by special bodies created by the empire's ethnic groups. It is noteworthy that most of these electoral committees were established by ecclesiastical entities (e.g., Patriarchates and the Chief Rabbinate) in a way that demonstrates once again the active role that these bodies played during the elections. Ecclesiastical involvement in the elections generally reinforced the *millet* system and totally contradicted the CUP's vision of a new political order based on the concept of a secular Ottoman citizenry. Uniting the different political currents in a specific body was, however, not an easy task. Although these electoral campaign committees managed to strike deals among the ethnic groups prior to and during the elections in some provinces, electoral battles among Armenian, Jewish, and Arab candidates still took place in many others.[45]

One of the more prominent electoral campaign committees was the Advisory Committee of the Ottoman Parliamentary Elections (ACOPE). This committee, established by the Armenian Patriarchate, included major Armenian figures.[46] All the elected members of the ANA, the editors and managers of the Armenian newspapers, and representatives of both Armenian Catholics and Protestants were invited to participate. It held regular meetings in the ANA in Galata. In addition to examining Ottoman parliamentary members' political paths, the Patriarchate gave the committee the task of examining the qualifications of the deputies and the elections.

Cautious of making radical demands, the committee members decided to put aside party platforms and embrace a minimal, consensus-building platform.[47] In its preliminary meetings, chaired by the Patriarchate's locum tenens, the committee considered twenty-two potential candidates for the post of deputy. From these, the two most qualified would be chosen as candidates for Istanbul. After lengthy deliberations, the committee decided to hand the issue of nomination over to the representatives of the two Armenian political groups, the Dashnaks and the Hunchaks.[48] On November 5, Krikor Zohrab was elected to candidacy by the committee's newly formed Ottoman Constitutional Armenian Body, and on November 7, Bedros Haladjian was elected as well.[49] On November 18, the Constitutional Body held a meeting during which the members initiated substantial arguments about the committee's policy. Zohrab argued that the Armenians should wholeheartedly unite with the Turkish constitutionalists and shun unity with the Greeks, which he said would be detrimental to Armenian interests. He nonetheless asserted that Armenians should maintain religious fraternity and friendly relations with the Greeks. Zohrab also argued that the Constitutional Body should immediately seek consensus from the Young Turks regarding their candidates.[50]

The CUP, unhappy with Zohrab Efendi's candidacy, sent a letter to the Armenian Patriarchate's locum tenens, claiming that it had received complaints about Zohrab from certain individuals in the provinces. The letter also noted the party's concern that unless necessary steps were taken, the two Armenian candidates would fail to win seats.[51] Nevertheless, the CUP leadership declared that it would honor its protocol to elect two Armenian deputies.

On December 8, ACOPE convened to discuss the CUP's letter.[52] Zohrab himself prepared a bill that asserted the obligation of the CUP and the Election Facilitation Committee to respect the protocol they had signed. The bill also demanded that the Ottoman Turkish press call on their Turkish compatriots to vote for the Armenians in the name of harmony. The committee decided that its two candidates for Istanbul would be Krikor Zohrab and Bedros Haladjian.[53]

Within the Constitutional Body was a subcommittee chaired by Harutyun Boyadjian, the Committee of Electoral Campaign (Ēntrakan Paykari Hantsnakhump). On December 11, this group met to discuss its policy regarding the Greek deputies.[54] Boyadjian argued that the Armenian votes should be given to the two Greek candidates whose names had been forwarded by the Greek Patriarchate. The assembly decided that if no Greek candidate was nominated, votes should not instead be given to an Armenian or a Turk, since that might deprive the Greeks of their two seats in Istanbul. Boyadjian assured those in attendance that by evening they would receive an answer from the Greek Patriarchate and accordingly notify the second-degree electors.

When the committee meeting was over, the Constitutional Body convened. During this meeting, Zohrab asserted that the Constitutional Body's real work would start after the elections, when the Armenian deputies would not only have to face their consciences but also be responsible to the Constitutional Body. He suggested that the Constitutional Body should be made a permanent organization, internal regulations drawn up, and a list of Armenian senators compiled. CUP member Haladjian Efendi opposed Zohrab's suggestion, saying that since Armenian deputies were elected based on the trust of the body, they should be given full authority to act in Parliament. "I take it on myself to protect your platform with all my power," argued Haladjian, "but I do not promise that I am going to abide by your decisions."[55] Zohrab and Harutyun Shahrigian Efendi both opposed Haladjian's statement. This represented the tension that also existed among the other groups. Would the members of Parliament of certain ethnic groups be directed by their ethno-religious institutions, or would they perform their duties as independent Ottoman citizens?

The Jews also formed a committee to oversee the electoral process in Istanbul. *El Tiempo* indicated that this was a necessity while also asserting that Jews in the Ottoman Empire did not need a distinct political program, since their only program was "the defense of the Ottoman constitutional laws." At the request of Haim Nahum, the Chief Rabbinate's locum tenens, thirty Jewish notables from different Istanbul communities gathered to determine the Jews' policy in the first-stage elections. Before those deliberations, however, the Jewish Committee for Parliamentary Elections, composed of ten people and headed by Colonel Moise Bey Dalmedico,[56] met to determine how the Jews should proceed in the elections.[57] As one of its first acts, this committee entrusted *El Tiempo* to urge those who ran the Jewish community's affairs in Istanbul to encourage other Jews to show up to participate in the elections in their assigned municipal circles.[58] This body later negotiated electoral deals with the other ethnic groups. For example, Moise Bey Dalmedico and David Fresco, editor of *El Tiempo*, met with CUP leaders to tell them, "in the name of the Hebrew nation," that they wanted Vital Faradji elected to represent Istanbul's Jews.[59]

Elections in the Provinces
The elections and electoral deals in the provinces were more difficult to administer than those in Istanbul and led to the rise of inter- and intraethnic tensions. In some places, like Kayseri and Adana, Greeks united with the Turks against the Armenians. In other places, Armenians sided with the Turks against the Greeks. Amid this confusion, one thing seems obvious: ethnic electoral

campaign committees established in Istanbul did not have full authority over the electoral campaign bodies in all of the provinces. For example, the Dashnaks had far more influence than ACOPE in the provinces.

Electoral campaigning in the provinces took place through lectures and pamphlets aimed at enlightening the electors about the different candidates and their political agendas, but not everyone clearly understood the election's aims. Mardiros Toumanian, a second-degree elector from Pazar district (Tokat), addressed this situation when he argued that the people did not understand the meaning of the constitution and therefore were ambivalent about the elections.[60] A letter from Adana indicated that many people eligible to vote did not register because a rumor spread that the registration was actually for conscription purposes.[61]

Alliances in the provinces also created surprises and disappointments that led to tensions. In the sancak of Adana, there were two electoral districts: in one the Armenians nominated a candidate and the Turks nominated their own candidate. The Armenians were sure that their candidate, Arisdages Kasbarian, whose electoral platform we dealt with earlier, would win, but Greek electors voted for the Turkish candidate "despite the fact that they had declared that they were going to unite with the Armenians in order to elect Arisdages Kasbarian."[62]

Furthermore, agreed-upon alliances sometimes broke down when individual voters failed to toe the party line. In Tokat, the Armenians and Turks had agreed on three candidates, the editor of the weekly *Beyen ul-Haq* (Statement of truth), Hoca Mustafa Sabri Efendi (who lived in Istanbul); the lawyer Hattatzâde Ismail Paşa (who also lived in Istanbul); and Bunjukian Hagop Efendi (who was from Tokat but lived in Bulgaria). The Armenian second-degree electors, who were a minority, kept their word and voted for these three candidates. However, according to a reporter for *Biwzandion*, only some of the Turkish voters in the periphery voted for the Armenian candidate, and none of those in the district centers did.[63]

In other cases, alliances held fast despite intraethnic conflicts that had lasting effects. For example, the majority of Armenians in the provinces were located in Van, where Armenian leaders expected to elect four deputies, since they estimated the Armenian population at around two hundred thousand. But prior to the election, the Responsible Body of the ARF had agreed with the CUP that one Turk and one Armenian deputy would be elected in Van. The candidates were Dr. Vahan Papazian and Tevfik Efendi Demiroğlu. This agreement was not mentioned in the daily newspapers of the period.[64]

But Van was the center of Armenian intraethnic tensions during the elections. Dr. Papazian, one of the candidates agreed upon in the official Armenian-Turkish alliance in Van, was also backed by the Dashnaks, since he was one of their revolutionary leaders. In opposition, the Ramkavars nominated Avedis Efendi Terzibashian, a rich Armenian fluent in Armenian and Ottoman Turkish.[65] This caused a fierce electoral battle among the Armenians that was manifested in extensive meetings and lectures. The Dashnaks also intensified their electoral campaign in Van's cities and villages. Dashnak activists, including candidates Papazian and Tevfik Efendi, gave lectures in Armenian and Ottoman Turkish.[66] The Hunchak minority, seeing that the Dashnaks would win the elections, had no choice but to unite with them, forming the Dashnak-Hunchak bloc. And, finally, both the Dashnak-Hunchak bloc and the Ramkavars were opposed by the Armenakan Party, which nominated its own candidate, Dr. Kalust Aslanian of Salonica.

As the campaign advanced, the three parties praised their own candidates and attacked one another's. Terzibashian's opponents described him as bourgeois. Aslanian's adherents portrayed him as a student of Mguerdich Portukalian (founder of the Armenakan Party) who was fluent in Ottoman Turkish and French and had played an active role in the CUP Salonica Committee. His opponents, however, argued that he had been outside the empire for a long time and did not understand the pitiful condition of the country. Papazian's opponents attacked his candidacy on the basis of his not knowing Ottoman Turkish, while his supporters claimed that he could learn the language in a couple of months and that he had a keen understanding of the political situation in the empire.[67] Since neither the Armenakans nor the Ramkavars could successfully oppose the Dashnaks alone, they united around Aslanian's candidacy.[68]

When the first-stage elections were over, the Dashnaks had won the majority of the Armenians' votes as well as those of the Kurdish farmers and Assyrian villagers. As campaigning in Van intensified prior to the second-stage elections, the Dashnaks gained the support of Armenian, Turkish, Kurdish, and Assyrian villagers on the premise that they would return property confiscated during the Hamidian period.[69] In the end, both candidates (Papazian and Demiroğlu) supported by the Dashnaks and the CUP were elected deputies for Van.

In Palestine, both intraethnic and intraparty conflicts played a complex role in the development of alliances. There, many Zionists were optimistic that with the help of the Muslims, they would be able to elect at least one Jewish candidate in the sancak of Jerusalem.[70] But correspondence between Arthur Ruppin, director of the Palestine Bureau (also known as Eretz Yisrael Office), and David Wolffsohn, president of the World Zionist Organization, reveals pessimism regarding the prospect of electing a Jewish deputy in Jerusalem.[71] Ruppin argued that only eight thousand of the fifty thousand Jews living in Jerusalem were registered Ottoman subjects, whereas more than four thousand Muslims and more than four thousand Christians were registered.[72] Furthermore, Jews made up a minority of the electorate because only a small number of them owned property, which was one of the preconditions for suffrage. Ruppin further argued that the electoral districts were defined in a way that was disadvantageous to the Jews.[73] As a result, he suggested that it would be best to support Muslim candidates who were sympathetic to the Jews. Meanwhile, the Zionist office in Palestine took upon itself to campaign for the Jewish candidate.[74]

As these developments unfolded, an Ottoman-Jewish Association was established to prepare for the elections in Jerusalem, headed by Dr. David Levi, Dr. David Yellin, and A. Ben-Yehuda. However, a rift between Albert Antebi and Dr. Levi, who was the Zionists' favorite candidate, divided the Jewish community soon after the association's formation.

In the meantime, Ruppin informed Wolffsohn of two potentially friendly Arab candidates: Hafez Bey al-Sa'id and Ruhi al-Khalidi. Taking into consideration both his previous arguments and the newly developed division within the Jewish public, Ruppin suggested that they support the Muslim candidates. For this reason, Levi and one of the Arab candidates, Husseyn Efendi Hashemi, campaigned together.[75]

On October 24, the elections took place for the sancak of Jerusalem. Three deputies were elected: Ruhi Efendi al-Khalidi (consul general of the Ottoman Empire in Bordeaux), Sa'id Efendi al-Husseyni (from the notables of Jerusalem), and Hafez Bey al-Sa'id (from the notables of Jaffa).[76] Ruppin's predictions had proven accurate: the Jews were unable to elect one of their own as a deputy in Jerusalem. The election did, however, result in the victory of the two Arab candidates Ruppin and Wolffsohn had endorsed. *Al-Ittiḥād al-'Uthmānī* praised the three candidates, saying that al-Khalidi "left his six thousand grush salary and consented to being paid little because of his love of serving his dear fatherland."[77] As both deputies left Jerusalem to Istanbul, a large crowd of Muslims, Jews, Armenians, and Greeks gathered in the train station to bid them farewell.[78] Speeches were delivered by 'Abd al-Salam Efendi, editor of *al-Quds al-Sharīf*; Sheikh 'Ali Rimawi; and David Efendi Yellin.[79]

Beirut was an important center of CUP activities in the Arab provinces. Eighteen candidates were running for two deputy positions, and *Lisān al-Ḥāl* detailed descriptions of all the candidates.[80] From descriptions, it appears that two important qualifications were prerequisite to their candidacy: knowledge of Ottoman Turkish and expertise in laws and regulations. *Lisān al-Ḥāl* argued that the newspaper would not favor any candidate over another and that it was the people's duty to decide on qualified parliamentary members.[81] On November 7, elections took place in Beirut in the presence of political leaders, spiritual leaders, and the inspection committee, resulting in the election of two deputies: Rida al-Sulh and Sulayman Efendi al-Bustani.[82]

In Syria, alliances played almost no role, since the CUP was one of the only organized political parties to campaign for the elections. Indeed, the CUP had a strong presence there, since it had active branches in Syria and the party had sent delegates from Salonica as early as October. The CUP did not make any electoral deals with the local populations of Syria, as they had in other places. Harran argues that the reasons for this were, first, that the Syrians were predominantly Muslim and therefore had an interest in the survival of the ancien régime, and, second, that they did not yet show any signs of an organized national movement.[83] At any rate, the CUP nominated most of the deputies in Syria. The candidates in Syria were from different social backgrounds, but, as in the case of the vilayet of Beirut, most of them served the state in some capacity and came from prominent families.[84] In short, the deputies in the Arab provinces came from three backgrounds: *ulema*, landowners, or professional men from the towns.[85]

Most of the Arab deputies from the urban and rural notables in Syria were supported by the CUP, but in Damascus, the CUP faced a fierce challenge from a strong group of influential *ulema* and notables, who rallied thousands of people behind them, forming an alliance based on religious ties. The elections in Damascus, therefore, resulted in the CUP candidates' defeat and the election of five deputies representing the notable class.[86]

In Salonica, a heated electoral campaign took place between Jewish and non-Jewish candidates.[87] On August 24, *El Tiempo* reported that two Jews from Salonica had nominated themselves: Emanuel Karasso, a lawyer originally from Salonica, and Nissim Efendi Mazliah, originally from Manisa and a member of the Commercial Tribunal of Salonica.[88] The newspaper also stated that two of the community's notables had nominated themselves: Vitalis Efendi Strumza, former inspector of agriculture for the vilayet of Salonica and Hilmi Paşa's last secretary, and Binko Efendi Shaltiyal, a Jewish notable from the community.[89] *El Tiempo* reported that Strumza's candidacy was received favorably by the Salonica Jews because of his intellectualism and his reputation as an "excellent deputy for the Jewish confession."[90] Emanuel Karasso, the CUP's candidate, was supported by the Jews in Salonica. The general opinion among the Jews was that Karasso would be a good deputy and "an honor to the Jewish element who would elect him."[91] The elections in the sancak of Salonica resulted in the selection of six deputies, including Karasso.

Elections in Istanbul

Because of Istanbul's strategic position, the major newspapers in the capital focused on elections there. The Armenian, Jewish, and Greek electoral committees, along with the religious authorities (e.g., the patriarchs and hahambaşı), entered into negotiations with the CUP about their candidates. Cooperation among the ethnic groups was evident during this period. For example, an Armenian delegation that included Krikor Zohrab and Bedros Haladjian visited the Greek Patriarchate to request the patriarch's support in the electoral campaigns. Although the patriarch recognized the advantage of such an alliance and believed it to be in his community's best interests, he could not declare support for the Armenian candidates without consulting the patriarch's two councils (Temporal Council and Religious Council) so called a meeting of the two councils to discuss the matter.

On October 29, 1908, delegates from the CUP, along with the Greek and Armenian Patriarchates, held a meeting to discuss the elections. After long deliberations, the delegates reached an agreement regarding the Istanbul elections and drew up a protocol. The Greeks were ready to sign the protocol, but the Armenian delegation declared that it was not authorized to do so. According to the understanding, Istanbul would be represented by ten deputies in Parliament: four Turks, three Greeks, two Armenians, and one Jew.[92]

On election day, Istanbul was very animated. Large processions carried ballot boxes to the various mosques, churches, synagogues, police stations, and other public buildings where voting would take place.[93] Three Jews had declared their candidacy for the Istanbul elections: Vital Efendi Faradji, a lawyer and legal adviser to the Régie Tobacco company; David Efendi Rusi, also a lawyer; and Ferer (Albert) Efendi Aseyo, a functionary of the Imperial Bank in Salonica.[94] Vital Efendi Faradji was almost unanimously supported by members of Istanbul's Jewish community, who campaigned vigorously for him.

In accordance with their agreement with the CUP, the Jews of Istanbul were poised to elect all the candidates nominated by the CUP. On December 9, prior to the elections, a functionary of the Armenian Patriarchate delivered a letter from ACOPE to the locum tenens, Rabbi Haim Nahum, asking him to designate a candidate from the Jewish community of Istanbul so it could recommend that the Armenian second-stage voters vote for him. Rabbi Nahum responded that Faradji was the Jewish candidate and asked for the Armenian candidates' names so he could inform the Jewish second-degree electors. Two hours later, the officer of the Armenian Patriarchate presented the rabbi with an official document stating that the Armenian candidates were Haladjian Efendi and Zohrab Efendi. Rabbi Nahum immediately communicated these names to the Jewish electoral delegates.[95]

The Ottoman Constitutional Armenian Body cooperated with the CUP to elect Istanbul's two Armenian deputies.[96] Prior to the elections, the Armenian Electoral Campaign Committee invited the Armenian second-degree electors to the Armenian National Assembly at Galata.[97] Chairman Hampartsum Efendi Boyadjian officially informed the Ottoman committee about the five Turkish candidates and one Jewish candidate, M. Faradji, who were backed by the CUP. Boyadjian also asked the committee to vote for that slate of candidates so the Turks would vote for the two Armenian candidates. The chairman officially stated that the Armenians needed to vote for the two names that were sent by the Greek Patriarchate, and there was some question during the meeting as to whom the Greeks would nominate.

The Turks also began encouraging their compatriots to vote for the CUP candidates. Hüssein Cahid called upon the Muslims in Istanbul to take an active part in the elections, saying that "the non-Muslim compatriots are very much used to the norms of election; they know every detail and every aspect of the elections. As for the Muslims, they are not used to elections. . . . Hence, we should encourage the Muslims to vote and awaken them."[98]

Elections for the ten deputies of Istanbul took place on Friday, December 11, in the Postal and Telegraphic Office. In total, 507 electoral delegates participated. The voting procedure was filled with ceremony and rejoicing.[99] The ballots were proctored by the Inspection Committee, which included two Armenians and one Jew. After the elections, a Muslim religious man prayed and the Inspection Committee signed the ballot box. Then the box was put on a carriage and delivered to the Municipality Building. On Saturday, the ballot boxes were opened in the city's prefecture in the presence of many

functionaries, dignitaries, and religious representatives and the votes were
counted:

Candidate	Votes
Refik Bey Maniasizâde	503
Mustafa Asim Bey	475
Ahmed Rıza Bey	472
Vital Faradji Efendi	461
Bedros Haladjian Efendi	455
Ahmed Nessimi Bey	425
Krikor Zohrab	392
Kostantin Kostantinidis Efendi	369
Hüssein Cahid (Yalçın)	354
Pandelaki Kozmidi Efendi	340

In the aftermath of the elections, Rabbi Nahum, along with an official delegation from the Jewish General Council, paid a visit to Armenian patriarch
Madteos Izmirlian in Kum Kapu to congratulate him on the Armenians' success in the elections. Patriarch Izmirlian, surrounded by many members of the
religious and political council, received Rabbi Nahum warmly. The two religious leaders expressed reciprocal, cordial sentiments and vowed to work to
strengthen communal relations "in the name of a single fatherland." Nahum
Efendi thanked the Armenian patriarch for the benevolence of the Armenian
second-degree electors, which was manifested in their voting for Vital Efendi
Faradji, the Jewish community's candidate.[100]

Facing the Election Results

Many of the empire's nondominant ethnic groups, especially the Greeks and
Armenians, had high expectations of the elections. Some groups were, however, very disappointed by the election results, as was attested in the Armenian
press. Overall, ten Armenian deputies were elected to Parliament out of the
thirty they had hoped for. The Armenians' greatest success in the provinces was
in Erzerum, where they were able to elect two deputies.[101] Results elsewhere
were generally poor.

The Armenian leadership's postelection disappointment and frustration
were reflected in a lengthy editorial written by Puzant Kechian and published
in *Biwzandion*. He argued that CUP delegations were sent from Salonica to the
provinces to stifle the voices of the Armenians. Although the Armenians had

praised these delegations and treated them well, Kechian argued that they had persistently worked against the Armenians by inciting the Turkish masses not to vote for Armenians. Kechian also criticized the activities of fellow Armenians in the provinces, who "did all their best in order to see the Armenian revolutionary element represented in the Ottoman Parliament, rather than strengthening the Ottoman legislative team with experienced elements."[102] Kechian was very critical of the Dashnaks, in particular, for this. He argued that there were only two or three Armenians who could orate eloquently and that these were from Rumelia, not Anatolia. Regarding the Armenian deputies of Istanbul, Kechian contended:

> The first deputy elected from Istanbul, Bedros Haladjian Efendi, was having a good time in Paris as a student during the revolutionary years, and he has always lived away from revolutionary and national affairs. He has also stayed away from Turkish life for a decade . . . and his [Ottoman] Turkish language is not that good. . . . The second candidate is Krikor Zohrab, also not a revolutionary, who has touched on national affairs only through literature.[103]

Kechian argued that Armenians should not be thankful to the CUP for electing two deputies for Istanbul, since the ardent stance of the Armenians with the CUP in Istanbul cost the Armenians one seat in Kasyeri, "by which we can assume that in Istanbul we have only gained one seat . . . like the Jews." The editorial ferociously criticized the election of *Tanin*'s editor as deputy to the Parliament and argued that the CUP elected him because his chauvinistic policy was in line with its own attitude and political direction. The editorial then ended by lamenting the results of the election.[104]

Another article by Hovhannes Asbeduni heavily criticized the election of Hüssein Cahid as a deputy for Istanbul. Asbeduni defined Cahid as an ignorant (*chahil*) who had been a promising literary figure and could have been an important Liberal but who, when freedom came, "immediately changed [literature] to a sword and took the appearance of a lion; fire and thunder began to fall; [he] shouted, roared, and threatened and gave destructive blows to the collapsed bases of despotism." Asbeduni argued that Cahid, "drunken from his easily attained popularity," found new victims for his "new, inexperienced swordsmanship." He became a defender of the nationalist current and of old-fashioned ideas like that of the Islamic state "that has been used tediously and worn out by the ancien régime, and that cannot be implemented after July 11 [24]." Asbeduni also argued that many Christians and Muslims had already distanced themselves from him. This claim was, indeed, corroborated by the low number of votes that Cahid received in the elections. However, those who defended him argued that Cahid had used the ideas of a ruling nation (*millet-i hâkime*) and an Islamic state for tactical reasons, to gain votes. These advocates predicted that the future would show how liberal Cahid was and that he would "stand as the champion for fraternity in the Parliament once more."[105] Asbeduni responded:

> Wrong! wrong! To incite the fanaticism of the people and use the tendencies of the ruling element in order to become a deputy. . . . But he is neither far sighted nor a politician. . . . And now it is not a secret to anyone that the Efendi, editor of *Tanin*, is a big-shot nationalist, even ultranationalist. And what are nationalism, jingoism, and chauvinism? But first let us define what is loving of the nation. . . . Now that our beloved Hüssein has become a deputy, he should turn his tongue in his mouth twenty times and not endanger the brotherhood, harmony, and future of the country, which has been arranged with great sacrifices and letters of blood.[106]

In contrast to these reactions, there was not much disappointment in the election results in the Sephardic community. In fact, Jewish newspapers hailed the election of four Jews to Parliament.[107] One newspaper editorial argued that the Jews gave "remarkable proof of their altruism by placing, in many instances, the interests of the country above their narrower interests." The newspaper reported that in recognition of this stance, the CUP supported the candidacy of a few Jews in the larger towns.[108] A huge, celebratory banquet, held in the hall of the National Hospital, Or ha-Khaim, was organized by the Temporal Council in Istanbul to honor the elected Jewish deputies.[109]

Some Zionists did, however, express greater discontent with the elections, particularly concerning the results from Jerusalem.[110] For example, A. Ben Yehuda argued that the Jews had been negligent in failing to elect a single Jewish deputy from the population of Jerusalem, the "majority of which are Jews."[111] This discontent even caused some skepticism concerning the Jewish candidates who had been elected. Ben Yehuda argued that the duty of Nissim Mazliah, deputy of Izmir, would be not only to protect the private rights of Jews in the empire but also to protect the "rights of the nation of Israel ['Am Yiśra'el] as a whole, as will the Greek and the Armenian deputies protect the rights of their nations." He concluded his article by advising Mazliah:

> We do not know if Mr. Nissim Mazliah is familiar with the affairs of Eretz Israel or if he was interested at all in issues pertaining to the Jews here; but I hope that

Mr. Mazliah understands that when he is a private person, he can be interested or not interested in this issue, but now that he is the delegate of a public, he should know these issues in depth, and with this hope we want to accompany our first deputy with blessing on his way to the capital.[112]

Unlike the Armenian and Jewish reaction to the elections, some Arab provinces felt a sense of consensus and satisfaction regarding the election results, as demonstrated by the Arabic press of the period.[113] *Lisān al-Ḥāl*, for example, hailed the victory of the two deputies from Beirut and argued that they were gifts from the city to the Ottoman Parliament.[114] In other areas of the Arab provinces, however, the opposite was true. The population of Haifa was not content with Sheikh Asʿad Efendi Shuqayr's election—supported by the CUP—as deputy of Acre. They sent complaints to the Central Committee of the CUP in Salonica denouncing his election and accusing him of corruption.[115]

Conclusion

To a certain extent, the real election took place before the balloting, but the 1908 Ottoman elections still represented one of the first organized, mass political performances in the Middle East. For that reason, the electoral behavior of the ethnic groups prior to and during the elections is of particular interest. The phase before the balloting was characterized by a heated battle over ideas in which every ethnic group declared its political platform, which became the blueprint for the political system that the ethnic group envisioned.

Many of these partisan/national and individual electoral platforms had much in common, including disagreement with the policies envisioned by the Young Turks' CUP. Therefore, administrative decentralization, ethno-religious privileges, national education, and proportional representation became key factors in the negotiation processes among the CUP, Armenians, Greeks, Albanians, and to a certain extent, Jews and Arabs. The CUP vehemently opposed the major points of the ethnic groups' political platforms because they contradicted its ideals of centralization and its version of Ottomanism.

The 1908 elections also witnessed the establishment of the ethnic groups' electoral campaigning committees, which attempted to unite different political currents and control the course of the elections. It is, however, evident that the CUP, with its branch offices and extensive networks throughout the empire, was the most active and effective political party, since it assured the election of its candidates wherever possible. The CUP had the strongest card in the electoral campaigns: it was the author of the Revolution and, hence, was able to exert its power and influence to secure its candidates' elections.

While some ethnic groups, including the Arabs and Jews, were generally satisfied with the election results, others, like the Greeks and Armenians, were extremely dissatisfied. Many members of these groups accused the CUP of both electoral irregularities in the provinces and gerrymandering. Others claimed that electoral districts were divided in a way that prevented non-Muslims from gaining large numbers of votes.[116] Within the Armenian community, dissatisfaction regarding the election was less apparent in the Dashnak camp and more apparent in non-Dashnak camps, perhaps because the Dashnaks acted independently in the provinces, relying on the wide networks they had created prior to the Revolution. In some areas, they even received the CUP's support.

An overview of the election reveals that most of the successful Armenian candidates came from professional backgrounds, such as law or medicine. In the Arab provinces, most of the deputies were notables and landowners who influenced the election results by using their sociopolitical status. The CUP had realized the importance of these notable families in the Arab provinces and owed some of its electoral success to backing them. Partially as a result of this policy, the only place where the CUP met with fierce electoral resistance was Damascus. The Sephardic Jews, meanwhile, were more successful in such cities as Salonica, Izmir, and Istanbul than in Palestine for two main reasons: their greater numbers and the CUP's support. The Zionists' greatest disappointment, however, was the sancak of Jerusalem, where they were unable to elect a single Jewish deputy to be their mouthpiece in Parliament.

The 1908 elections resulted in a landslide victory for the CUP.[117] Through its untouchable position as the author of the Revolution, that party was able to dominate the Chamber of Deputies. Despite the inequities caused by the CUP's preeminence, however, the elections did result in parliamentary representation of most of the nondominant ethnic groups. Of 281 deputies from the first round of elections, there were 151 Turks, 56 Arabs, 25 Albanians, 22 Greeks, 10 Armenians, 5 Kurds, 4 Bulgarians, 4 Jews, 3 Serbs, and 1 Vlach. If we add to this list the 42 deputies elected through the by-elections, the figures for the first period of elections would be 323 deputies, of whom there were 170 Turks, 67 Arabs, 31 Albanians, 25 Greeks, 12 Armenians, 6 Kurds, 4 Bulgarians, 4 Jews, 3 Serbs, and 1 Vlach.[118] The dominance of the CUP in Parliament would not, however, go unchallenged. As the next chapter demonstrates, a weak opposition made up of the Liberal Union in cooperation with other nondominant ethnic groups tried tirelessly to undermine the CUP's parliamentary power. This opposition was formed by a diverse group of Liberals, bureaucrats, nationalist and proto-nationalist parties, Islamists, and socialists, among others.[119]

5 FROM THE BALLOTS
TO THE PARLIAMENT

THE POLITICAL PHASE after the first parliamentary elections in the empire represented a shift from the politics of the street to the politics of the Parliament. This shift did not, however, break the bond between the street and Parliament, nor did it mean that parliamentary politics were conducted behind closed doors. On the contrary, parliamentary politics became an important dimension in the public spheres created after the Revolution. As a result of newly gained freedoms, reporters and editors, as well as guests, were allowed to observe parliamentary debates. Most of the empire's major newspapers sent correspondents to Parliament and published transcripts of these debates on a daily basis in their respective languages. In addition, official parliamentary transcripts were published in *Takvim-i Vekayi*, the government's official gazette.[1] By publishing such accounts, newspapers became the medium through which the masses became acquainted with and connected to parliamentary politics. Moreover, some newspapers used large-font titles and subtitles to highlight or criticize the issues discussed in Parliament, which often reflected the newspapers' political orientations. In the theater of this modern political system, Parliament became the stage and the masses became the spectators, enthusiastically viewing modulating developments by identifying with their favorite political actors.

One cannot understand ethnic politics in the Ottoman Parliament without understanding the context of the ongoing struggle between the CUP and the

Liberals, between the dominant and subdominant groups, and between the legislative and executive branches of the government. Within this turmoil, some ethnic deputies were very vocal in representing issues pertaining to their respective communities and to the general Ottoman interests. The issues raised in Parliament demonstrate the interethnic bones of contention that prevailed in the postrevolutionary period.

These issues did not spontaneously appear on the parliamentary debate agendas but were manifestations of the many unresolved issues that haunted the empire for decades. As the architects of the Revolution, the CUP knew well that in the era of constitutionalism and legislative assembly they had no choice but to deal with those challenges through the modern political system they themselves had initiated. Nonetheless, after the landslide electoral victory that led to their dominance in Parliament, they were confident they would be able to abort or block any attempts by the executive power and opposition groups to endanger their political program.

As noted in previous chapters, constitutional assembly was a means for the CUP to implement its massive project of centralization to preserve the territorial integrity of the empire. Some of the nondominant groups had sincerely believed that Parliament ultimately would allow them to find a remedy for the maladies that inflicted the empire in general and their communities in particular. They would soon realize that their weak position in Parliament and the dominance of the CUP made such attempts futile. Thus, the dream of a constitutional assembly as the ultimate democratic institution of justice gradually degenerated into the reality of a one-party dictatorship.

At first, four main issues preoccupied the ethnic groups in Parliament: the Macedonian Question, concessions to foreign countries, reform in the Anatolian provinces, and restrictions on the right to assembly. During the first year Parliament was in session, no serious issues pertaining to the empire's Jews were discussed. Only in 1911 did Zionism become a major issue in Ottoman parliamentary debates.[2] An analysis of the four issues is crucial to understanding how representatives of the ethnic groups viewed themselves within the ongoing struggle to define their position in the Ottoman Empire. While these ethnic deputies tried to demonstrate their loyalty to the Ottoman Empire in Parliament, they also tried to protect the rights and interests of their ethnic groups. This created an obvious dilemma, since such political wrangling contradicted the ideal of united Ottomanism.

An Overview of the Political Situation

On August 5, 1908, Said Paşa resigned as grand vizier and was replaced by Kâmil Paşa.[3] Though the Greek, Armenian, Albanian, and Syrian deputies fully supported the government of Kâmil Paşa, the CUP only nominally supported the new cabinet. In order to appease the CUP, Kâmil Paşa made some ministerial changes, such as appointing Hüssein Hilmi Paşa, a Young Turk sympathizer, as minister of the interior. However, things changed in November and December, when Kâmil Paşa became more inclined toward the Liberal Union, a situation that made the CUP unhappy. The tensions between the new cabinet and the CUP became more strained when Austria-Hungary announced the annexation of Bosnia and Herzegovina on October 6, 1908, leading to the eruption of the First Balkan Crisis. That crisis provided the CUP with a good excuse to criticize Kâmil Paşa's government. Party members accused him of failing to come to an agreement with Bulgaria and Austria regarding the annexation of Bosnia-Herzegovina and the Bulgarian declaration of independence. On December 30, Hüssein Cahid, editor of *Tanin*, kept up the pressure when he gave an interpellation in Parliament asking for clarification from Grand Vizier Kâmil Paşa regarding the internal and external policies of his cabinet.[4] In response, Kâmil Paşa appeared before the chamber on January 13, 1909, and defended his cabinet's program.[5] He explained his cabinet's policies, praised the moderation and discipline of the empire's people, and declared that everyone should thank the sultan for the absence of bloodshed following the Revolution. His speech was followed by an informal vote of confidence, which carried unanimously. The interpellation and vote of confidence were considered a victory for the sympathizers of Kâmil Paşa and a defeat for the CUP.[6]

Less than a month later, however, the détente between the CUP and Kâmil Paşa ended when the latter dismissed the ministers of war and the navy on February 10. The new grand vizier tried to strengthen his position by appointing his own men. As a sign of protest, Hüssein Hilmi Paşa resigned. On February 11, parliamentary deputies submitted a series of motions asking for clarifications from the grand vizier regarding the latest ministerial changes.[7] On February 13, the chamber assembled to interpellate Kâmil Paşa. He, however, failed to appear for the interpellation, arguing that it was his right to postpone it. As a consequence, he was given a no-confidence vote of 196 to 8.[8] This was regarded as a victory for the CUP. Hüssein Hilmi Paşa was given the task of forming a new cabinet. On February 25, in order to prevent any protests from the Liberal Union or Kâmil

Paşa's sympathizers, the government issued a communiqué restricting public gatherings. The tension between the Liberal Union and the CUP continued until the Counterrevolution of March 31, 1909, which became a defining moment in the history of the Second Constitutional Period. Until the Counterrevolution, this conflict was an essential element of the ethnic politics in Parliament.

Vilayat-ı Thulth or Macedonia?

The most obvious ethnic tension in Parliament was evident during the debate over the Macedonian Question. This debate provided a venue in which Parliament discussed an ethnic issue pertaining to Ottomans, Bulgarians, Greeks, Vlachs, Serbs, Catholic and Orthodox, Albanians, Bosnians, Muslims, and Turks.[9] In particular, the debate over Macedonia focused on its three provinces (vilayat-ı thulth): Salonica, Manastir, and Kosovo. As in other geographic areas, the region of Macedonia acquired a political significance in the nineteenth century as a result of the revival of Christian nationalities and the contestation among Greeks, Bulgarians, and Serbs over the region, giving rise to the Macedonian Question.[10] It first began with the Greeks who wanted to secure the allegiance of the Christians in Macedonia. The Greeks and Serbs believed that they could achieve this allegiance by a policy of cultural and linguistic dissimilation of the Macedonian Slavs through educational and church propaganda. However, they were immediately challenged by the Bulgarians, who won ecclesiastical independence with the establishment of the Bulgarian Exarchate in 1870.[11] In the Treaty of San Stefano (1878) the region had been largely incorporated into the new Bulgaria, but after the Congress of Berlin (1878) it returned to Ottoman control. The contestation in the region increased and led to the formation of revolutionary organizations. In 1893, Slavs formed the Internal Macedonian Revolutionary Organization (IMRO) in Salonica to fight for the establishment of an autonomous Macedonia. In 1895, the External Macedonian Revolutionary Organization (EMRO), which favored union with Bulgaria, was established there. Thus, prior to the 1908 Revolution Macedonia had become highly contested terrain and a volatile region for violent acts by revolutionary committees and bands representing different ethnic groups (for example, Serbs, Bulgarians, Greeks, Vlachs, and Albanians).

The debate officially began on January 27, when a group of deputies interpellated Parliament regarding the situation in the three provinces.[12] On January 30, Hüssein Hilmi Paşa, who was still minister of the interior, came to Parliament to answer these inquiries. As the former inspector of Macedonia, he was able to give an overview of the situation in the troubled provinces, focusing on the struggle between the patriarchists, who were supporters of the Greek Orthodox patriarch of Istanbul, and the exarchists, supporters of the Bulgarian Excarchate, which he believed was the main reason for the violence in the region. The churches in the region, as he explained, were under the influence of the Bulgarian and Greek communities. In closing, Hilmi Paşa asked Parliament to form a special commission to compose a bill to resolve the issue.

For the next three days, fierce debates took place among the deputies in Parliament. When Hristo Dalchef (Siroz) used the term "Macedonia" to refer to the region, many members of Parliament, including Greek deputies, accused him of promoting nationalist propaganda.[13] The Armenian deputy, Krikor Zohrab (Istanbul), defended Dalchef, saying that if use of the term "Macedonia" was off limits, then the place-names of Albania, Arabistan, and Kurdistan should not be used either. Dalchef himself immediately clarified that he did not intend to give the term "Macedonia" a political meaning but simply to define an area formed of the *kazas* (districts) of Salonica, Manastir, Üsküp, and Edirne. In the same speech, however, Dalchef accused the ancien régime of backing the formation of Greek bands that wanted to destroy the Bulgarian bands (*çete*) in Edirne.[14] Dalchef argued that there were many documents backing his claims. In addition, he argued that all the churches were still running according to the status quo, although the constitution now fulfilled that role.[15]

In response, the minister of the interior rejected Dalchef's claims that the government was protecting the Greek bands and presented a long list of illegal acts perpetrated by the Bulgarian bands. Others, such as Riza Efendi (Karahisar-ı Şarki), argued that one should not view the church problem as a religious problem only, since what was hiding beneath it was a political problem, and it was impossible to solve the Macedonian Question without solving the Church Question.[16] Other deputies, including Karolidi Efendi (Izmir) and Riza Tevfik Bey (Edirne), insisted that the situation in Macedonia was the result of foreign intervention and that external factors—by which they meant the interference of European powers in Balkan affairs—were imminent.[17] As the debate continued on March 13, a State Council (Şura-yı Devlet) subcommittee took on the task of drafting a bill. The first-round discussion concerning the bill did not conclude until March 14. The first bill was submitted to Parliament on July 7, and Parliament ultimately voted in favor.

The debate over the Macedonian Question revealed the complexity of ethnic politics in Parliament, which were not necessarily divided along Muslim/

Christian lines. Rather, Parliament was divided along intrareligious and inter-ethnic lines in general and along Greek/Bulgarian lines regarding the Church Question. The dynamics of the debate also underscore the point that ethnic politics in the postrevolutionary period cannot be viewed solely from the per-spective of political parties but must also be understood from the perspective of ecclesiastical politics. In fact, ecclesiastical politics was one of the key factors in defining inter- and intraethnic relationships in the empire.

Arab Deputies in Parliament

The great majority of the Arab deputies in Parliament were elected either with the approval or support of the CUP. In the Parliament's first year, therefore, most of these deputies remained ardent supporters of the CUP bloc, so there was not an Arab bloc in Parliament for the first parliamentary year.[18] However, at the end of 1909, some Arab deputies were able to create a bloc that would play an important role in power politics from 1909 to 1912.[19] Shafiq al-Mu'ayyad and Rushdi al-Sham'a of Damascus, the leaders behind the creation of this bloc, were the same men whose election as parliamentary deputies had caused some anxiety among CUP circles in the Arab provinces. Other deputies who had been CUP supporters, including 'Abd al-Hamid al-Zahrawi (Hama), shifted to-ward al-Mu'ayyad's camp when they became disillusioned with the CUP party.

Shafiq al-Mu'ayyad had also raised hackles as a founder of the Ottoman-Arab Brotherhood Society in Istanbul, which welcomed the Arab deputies with a large reception. The society was criticized by both Arabs and Turks for hav-ing separatist tendencies.[20] Others defended the society's platform as one that aimed to preserve the constitution while spreading both education and trade among Arabs by cooperating with the government.[21] Despite the controversy it created, the society did not have any influence on parliamentary politics and cannot be regarded as the beginning of a parliamentary bloc.

The plan to form an Arab bloc went back to April 1909, when many Arab deputies had gathered at the house of the deputy of Beirut, Rida al-Sulh, to form the political party Al-I'tidāl (Moderation) and develop a political pro-gram. A reporter for *Al-Ittiḥād al-'Uthmānī* later explained that the party was neither a national nor a doctrinal one but rather an Ottoman party that opened its doors to members from different ethnic backgrounds.[22] Not until November 1909 did some forty deputies, a majority of whom were Arabs, convene at the Pera Palace Hotel, where they officially agreed on the necessity of forming a party and devised a political strategy. The party, which came to be known as the

Liberal Moderate Party (Al-ḥizb al-ḥurr al-Mu'tadil), also had some Armenian, Turkish, Greek, and Albanian deputies as members.²³

It was also at the end of 1909 that a heated debate took place over the Lynch affair, which related to the government's plan to provide commercial conces- sion in Iraq to a foreign enterprise: the British Lynch Company. The affair trig- gered a crisis between a number of Arab deputies and the government, leading to the resignation of Grand Vizier Hüssein Hilmi Paşa. This parliamentary op- position to foreign intervention in the economic and political interests of the empire through concessions did not, however, start with the Lynch affair. Its roots can be traced back to the Baghdad Railway discussions in Parliament during its first year of convention.

Four major issues were especially pertinent to the Arab deputies in the par- liamentary debates: ratification of the electoral results for four Arab deputies, including al-Mu'ayyad; the Mutran affair; the Hidjaz Railway; and the Baghdad Railway.

Arab Deputies under Suspicion
The tension that arose between the CUP and the Arab candidates during the elections was also reflected in Parliament, specifically concerning ratification of four Arab deputies' official electoral results. The first focus of controversy was the candidacy of Yusuf Shitwan, deputy of Bingazi, who was accused of being a spy for Sultan Abdülhamid II. He was also accused of having a bad character and us- ing political influence to guarantee his own election.²⁴ The second was Shafiq al- Mu'ayyad of Damascus, one of the founders of the Ottoman-Arab Brotherhood Society, who had been elected without the support of the CUP. Like Shitwan, he was accused of having ties to the sultan. The other Arab deputies were 'Umar Mansur (Bingazi) and Sayyid Talib (Basra). Despite some parliamentary depu- ties' objections to these members' candidacy, all but Shitwan were admitted to Parliament. Parliament ordered Shitwan to run for election again, claiming that he influenced some officers during the first round. Shitwan was successful in this second round of elections and was, therefore, admitted to Parliament.

One thing especially noticeable about these cases is that none of the Arab deputies from Syria, Palestine, Lebanon, Iraq, or Yemen defended these candi- dates. It is highly probable that since most of the Arab deputies were backed by the CUP, they did not want to risk their standing with the party by taking the side of deputies like al-Mu'ayyad or Shitwan. Riza Tevfik (Edirne), defended al- Mu'ayyad and refuted the charges that were brought against him.

Another deputy whose candidacy was questioned in the early phases of Parliament was Serdarzâde Mustafa (Karahisar-ı Şarki), who was accused of being an oppressor by the Armenian prelate of Sivas. Serdarzâde defended himself in Parliament, saying that there were about 10,000 Armenians and 160,000 Muslims in Karahisar-ı Şarki and that the Armenian minority was complaining about his candidacy since it was not able to elect its own deputy. Zohrab Efendi (Istanbul) criticized Mustafa's candidacy, saying that "atrocious people and criminals" should not sit in Parliament.[25] In response, Riza Tevfik (Edirne) requested that Zohrab not use words like "criminal," since there was no substantial evidence against Mustafa.

The Mutran Affair

Another issue touching on Arab loyalty to the empire was a declaration written by the Syrian Central Committee, founded in Paris,[26] and signed by Rashid Mutran, a Syrian Greek Catholic, that demanded self-government in Syria.[27] In December 1908, the declaration began to circulate within the empire, asserting that a Western-style constitution was an impossibility and that catering to the desires of minorities would lead to the disintegration of the empire (désagrégation de l'empire). In addition, Mutran suggested the establishment of an autonomous Syria backed by the Western powers.[28]

Reactions to this declaration from the Arab community were swift and primarily negative. Telegrams began to pour into Parliament from Damascus, Beirut, and Paris, denouncing the declaration and saying that there was no inclination for separatism (ayrılık) among the Arab people.[29] Ruhi al-Khalidi (Jerusalem) suggested that these telegrams be published, most probably in order to assert Arab loyalty to the empire. The deputy of Aleppo denounced Rashid Mutran's declaration, saying that "the action of such a cursed person was illegal and that he had fallen in the eyes of all the Arab and Ottoman people." The governor of Syria also sent a telegram to the Ministry of Internal Affairs, indicating that Mutran's declaration had greatly agitated the people of Syria.[30] On January 18, Muhammad Arslan (Latakiyya) indicated that some of the letters sent to Parliament were published in İkdam. One of the letters, which he read to the assembly, was written by Shamilzâde Ahmet, a Syrian notable. In addition to opposing Rashid Mutran's political views, the letter denounced his family. Arslan, on the other hand, argued that Mutran's family should not be held accountable for his actions and stated that they were among the first to condemn his actions. He asked that this condemnation be included in the parliamentary records.[31]

Apart from the controversy concerning several of the Arab deputies and the Mutran affair, no major issues pertaining to Arab loyalty were discussed in Parliament. Furthermore, it seems that historians have exaggerated the significance of the Mutran affair. Compared to other ethnic issues that arose in Parliament, such as the Macedonian Question and the situation of the Anatolian provinces, the Mutran affair appears to have had minimal impact.

This does not mean, however, that the Arab deputies did not take part in parliamentary debates. On the contrary, they frequently raised issues pertaining to their localities, especially concerning taxes. When discrepancies in the kinds of taxes being administered and in the methods of their collection in the Arab provinces were discussed, the Baghdadi and Yemenite Arab deputies participated energetically.[32]

The Hidjaz Railway

Two major issues pertaining to the Arab provinces did cause heated debate in Parliament. Both pertained to transportation, the Hidjaz and Baghdad Railways. The intensive intervention of the Arab deputies in the latter affair demonstrates their anxiety and opposition to concessions given to foreign companies that would threaten not only the sovereignty of the Ottoman Empire but also their regional and provincial interests.[33]

The Hidjaz Railway construction began in 1900, during Abdülhamid's administration, and was built mainly by the Ottomans with German advice and support.[34] The railway was built to strengthen the empire's grip over the Arab provinces; to establish a connection between Istanbul and Mecca, the most important holy center of Islam, to facilitate the pilgrimage; and to ease the transportation of military troops. The railway that ran from Damascus to Medina through the Hidjaz aimed at extending the preexisting line from Istanbul to Damascus. On September 1, 1908, the anniversary of the sultan's accession, the railway reached Medina, but the project's initial aim of reaching Mecca was never achieved.

On January 13, Syrian deputies Muhammad al-'Ajlani and Sulayman al-Barun demanded an interpellation from the minister of public works regarding the measures being taken to finish the Hidjaz Railway project. The interpellation described the abuse that plagued the railway's administration.[35] The interpellation was accepted by Parliament, but the minister of public works did not show up to respond to it. In his place, the director of the Hidjaz Railway, Zihni Paşa, came to Parliament on January 21. In his reply, Zihni gave a long description of the project's status and admitted that the line from El-'Ula to Medina, which was three hundred kilometers long, had not been constructed. He accused the operating manager of negligence. As a result of this testimony, a special commission was formed to complete the project. The commission's first task was to terminate the manager named by Zihni and appoint in his place Muhtar Paşa, a graduate of the Engineering School and head of the technical branch, who had proved his ability and skill in building the railway's Haifa section.

Zihni gave a brief account of the reasons for the project's delay and stated that a more detailed account of what had been done and what was going to be done had been prepared. Tahir Receb Efendi (Hudayda) commented on Zihni's report, saying that a more detailed account was needed concerning how much money had been allocated for the project and how much had been sent by Muslims living abroad. He demanded that the other registrars of the railway project be brought in for examination and argued that a committee needed to be formed to investigate the matter.[36] Others, like Hakki Bey (Baghdad), argued that there was no need to form an investigation committee, but Krikor Zohrab (Istanbul) disagreed and criticized Zihni's report. Zohrab remarked that it was strange that Zihni put the blame on the prime minister, which meant the company's agent was accusing the client of wrongdoing. Zohrab argued that there were two ways to tackle the issue: either an investigative committee composed of a wide range of authorities could begin investigating as soon as possible, or the directorate's report could be distributed prior to an investigation. Zohrab himself concluded that there was no benefit in delaying the investigative commission until after the distribution of the report and urged immediate formation of the committee.[37] Nonetheless, the two motions were put to a vote, which went in favor of those who wanted the commission to form after the report was circulated.

The Baghdad Railway
It is interesting that despite the importance of the Hidjaz Railway to the hajj pilgrimage, a good number of those involved in the debates were not Arab deputies. The Baghdad Railway project attracted more attention than the Hidjaz project in Parliament, both from Arab and non-Arab deputies. This mainly stems from the project's strategic dimension and the involvement of international powers.

The Baghdad Railway, including an already-constructed Orient Express line, was initiated under German control during the Hamidian period.[38] In

1888, a company sponsored by Deutsche Bank was given concessions by the Ottoman government to build railways from Haydar Paşa to Ankara and from Istanbul to Izmir. The company began operating in March 1889 under the name Société du Chemin de Fer d'Anatolie, and after thirteen years of negotiations with the government was awarded the concession for the Berlin-Baghdad Railway in 1902. For this purpose a special subsidiary was formed in 1903, Société Impériale Ottomane du Chemin de Fer de Baghdad. Through this railway, the Germans were planning to insinuate themselves into the Persian Gulf, establishing a port there. For its part, the Ottoman Empire aimed at maintaining its control over Arabia and expanding its influence to the Red Sea, which was by then controlled by the British.

The Arab deputies vehemently criticized the concession for the Baghdad Railway, which can be understood as part of the Arab deputies' overall struggle against foreign intervention that eventually would be reflected in their reactions to the Lynch affair. The government's plan to give the Lynch Company a long-term monopoly over transportation on the Tigris River led to a vehement attack on the government by "Iraqi" and other deputies, which, in turn, led to the resignation of Grand Vizier Hüssein Hilmi Paşa.[39] The "Iraqi" deputies were wary of British penetration and acted as a lobby to prevent granting a concession to the British. Thus, the roots of the Lynch affair can be traced back to late February 1909, when the case of the Baghdad Railway resulted in lengthy and detailed discussions in Parliament, raising such issues as whether giving concessions to foreign companies threatened the Ottoman Empire's sovereignty.

The issue was raised mainly by Ismail Hakki Bey (Baghdad), who demanded information about the Baghdad Railway from the ministers of public works and foreign affairs.[40] In his interpellation, Hakki Bey argued that the various contracts concluded by the government with the railway scheme's promoters had been concealed (mektûm) from the Ottoman people. He argued that the only source of information the Ottoman people had about the subject was the biased European press, and the people were asking for explanations. Attached to Hakki Bey's interpellation was a motion from Sulayman al-Bustani (Beirut) calling for an examination of the status of the Baghdad Railway.[41]

On February 27, 1909, Minister of Public Works Zihni Paşa came to Parliament to answer Hakki Bey's interpellation. In response to the question about concealment of the Baghdad Railway contract, Zihni argued that when the project had begun thirty years earlier under the ancien régime, it was not customary for the kinds of concessions included in the contract to be advertised.

He explained that he could find nothing in the contract agreement that violated Ottoman sovereignty and declared that the government would tolerate no interference with Ottoman sovereignty.[42] He also urged the project's continuance under the old contract, arguing that its completion would put the empire in a strong political and economic position.[43]

In response, Hakki Bey repeated his question as to why the government kept the contract concealed. He declared Zihni's claim that fifty copies of the contract had been published to be inadequate, since the project involved the lives of millions. While hundreds of articles about the subject were being published in Europe, he noted, nothing had appeared in Istanbul's newspapers. Hakki Bey agreed with Zihni that the contract agreement did not violate national sovereignty but said that, nonetheless, he saw no national benefit in it. He strongly criticized the whole project, contending that the privileges that came with the concessions were totally unfair. One of these privileges, for example, pertained to the right to build tax-exempt factories along the railway line.[44]

Other parliamentary deputies also spoke out against the contract. Sulayman Efendi al-Bustani (Beirut), who had prepared a lengthy report, indicated that most of the issues he wanted to raise had already been mentioned by Hakki Bey, so he submitted a written version of his report to the parliamentary president. The Armenian deputy, Zohrab Efendi, also strongly criticized the whole project, saying that the damage that would result from the contract had not been discussed. He suggested the formation of an independent committee whose task would be to modify the contract agreement. In contrast to Zihni, who had described the railway as the life and nerves of the empire, Zohrab Efendi characterized it as "nothing but a killing venom." In reply, Zihni reiterated his claim that the project would improve the empire economically and politically and that, "if in the coming ten years we will suffer for it . . . our children will see the [positive] benefits in the future."[45]

Several days later, on March 3, al-Bustani again asked for the formation of a committee to consider necessary changes to the Baghdad Railway contract. Hakki Bey continued arguing that the clarifications that Parliament had found satisfactory pertained only to the explanations made by the minister of public works and did not ratify the contents of the contract. He also suggested that the abuses within the contract should be examined by a council, a committee, or the Public Works Council.[46]

The discussion concerning the Baghdad Railway project represented one of the earliest instances of opposition by some Arab deputies to foreign con-

cessions in the Ottoman Parliament, a trend that culminated in the Lynch affair seven months later. It also demonstrated the concern of other, non-Arab
deputies that concessions to foreign powers would harm the empire's economic interests.

Language Issues

One of the main factors that hampered Arab deputies' from being more active
participants in Parliament was their poor knowledge of Ottoman Turkish, as
pointed out in an editorial in *Al-Muqtabas* in March 1909. The article encouraged its readers to hope that more qualified deputies would be elected to the
second or third term of Parliament.[47]

On the other hand, newspapers such as *Al-Muqaṭṭam* and *Al-Ittiḥād al-
'Uthmānī* defended the Arab deputies and stated that the people of the Arab
provinces should be content with the deputies' performance. Lacking strong
oratory skills was, they claimed, common among all the deputies of the chamber, not just among the Arab deputies.[48] *Lisān al-Ḥāl* alleged that it had received
many inquiries from Arabs regarding the Arab deputies' silence in Parliament.
Therefore, the newspaper interviewed 'Abd al-Hamid Efendi Al-Zahrawi and
Sulayman Efendi al-Bustani, who shifted the discussion away from language
fluency by explaining that Parliament had recently convened, the deputies did
not know each other, and they did not yet have the self-confidence to make
arguments. Like the editors of *Al-Muqaṭṭam* and *Al-Ittiḥād al-'Uthmānī*, they
argued that these disadvantages were not confined to the Arab deputies. The
newspaper praised the deputy of Aleppo, Nafi' Paşa, as the best Arab orator in
Parliament and a sign of hope for fuller Arab participation.[49]

Armenian Deputies in Parliament

From the opening of Parliament until the Counterrevolution, there were three
significant issues pertaining directly to Armenians: the inspection committee
assigned by the government to examine conditions in the Anatolian provinces;
the discussion about status of the public order in the empire; and the right
to assemble. Though Armenian deputies participated extensively in parliamentary debates, their intervention intensified when these three issues were
discussed and was particularly pronounced when discussions concerned the
eastern provinces. Furthermore, in these three instances, most of the Armenian
deputies acted as a bloc, supporting each other in the debates. This should be
viewed as the application of policies drafted by the Ottoman Constitutional

Armenian Body, the two most important and vocal deputies of which were Krikor Zohrab and Bedros Haladjian.

Reform Committee to the Eastern Provinces

The roots of the grand vizier's bill—sending an inspection commission to the eastern provinces—which was read in Parliament on February 8, 1909, can be seen in the Armenian National Assembly's lobbying efforts after the Young Turk Revolution.[50] The ANA decided that an official delegation headed by the Armenian Patriarchate's locum tenens should pay an official visit to Grand Vizier Kâmil Paşa to demand that the government send an investigation committee to the provinces. The delegation did meet with the grand vizier, who promised that necessary steps would be taken on the issue of the provinces but also emphasized the government's preoccupation with the western provinces.

The bill submitted to Parliament on February 8 dealt specifically with this issue, arguing that order and public security had been violated in the provinces of Trabzon, Erzurum, Van, Sivas, Mamuretülaziz, Diyarbekir, and Bitlis, and that to prevent conflict and strife and reestablish order, a reform committee should be sent to the provinces. The bill explained that the committee would be headed by Galib Bey, a member from the Senate, and composed of Mustafa Zihni Paşa, Sheikh Nazir Efendi, and Cemal Binbaşı Zeki. The bill also requested that salaries be allocated to these committee members.[51]

In fact, the bill was sent to Parliament for purely financial reasons. The grand vizier had not submitted the bill to Parliament for its approval but rather to ask that it fund the committee's expenses. Many deputies, however, insisted that a committee be formed to further discuss the bill. Still others thought it should be debated in Parliament. The president of Parliament, Ahmed Rıza Bey, on the other hand, suggested that it be sent to the Financial Committee.

Other deputies attacked the bill more directly. For example, Arif Ismet Bey (Biga) demanded that other deputies reject the bill because the constitution had already given every governor the responsibility to reform his province, and governors who proved unqualified to administer their provinces' affairs could simply be replaced. In conclusion, he said that sending inspectors was absurd (*saçma*). His speech was followed by enthusiastic applause from some deputies. However, not everyone agreed with this assessment. The Armenian deputy, Vartkes Serengülian (Erzurum), opposed Arif Bey, saying that more direct intervention was called for. "It is true," argued Vartkes, "that we have *valis*, *mutasarrifs*, and *kaymakams*, but we know better than everyone that these *valis* and *mutasarrifs*, being old people, attached to the ancien régime, were thickened with old blood and veins." He argued that these officers had strictly followed orders for the past twenty to twenty-four years and were unable to rule in accordance with the constitution after only five or six months. He continued:

> I am going to ask from this body that a committee be formed by the Parliament [Interruptions: "It cannot be!"] and now should be sent to Anatolia and Rumelia. I ask you to listen . . . let us think of something else. Any conscience will not accept the situation in Anatolia, the injustice in Anatolia. You also know that the injustice suffered by the people [*ahali*] of Anatolia, the assaults on the people of Anatolia, the exertion, and the blood in Anatolia have not taken place anywhere else. Our first [Interruptions from many places: "Explain!"] . . . Yes I am explaining; I am giving an explanation. The things that have happened to the people of Anatolia until now, even the famine that is taking place in Anatolia now, is the work of ancient injustice.[52]

Despite the interruptions, Varktes continued his speech, saying that a committee should be sent to the provinces to examine the situation in depth and find remedies that would provide for the happiness and prosperity of the people. Haladjian Efendi (Istanbul) immediately came to Vartkes's aid, saying that the executive authority had deemed it necessary to send a committee and that Parliament, as the legislative authority, could not interfere in measures taken by the executive branch. He also explained that the executive authority had not asked Parliament to decide on the measure's validity but rather to approve the financing of the committee. Hence, he agreed with the president's suggestion that the bill be sent to the Financial Committee for examination. Haladjian noted that if Parliament wanted to interfere in the work of the executive authority, it also would become participants in its responsibility. According to him, this violated the constitution.[53]

The Armenian deputy Hampartsum (Murad) Boyadjian (Kozan) supported the arguments made by his fellow Armenian deputies, commenting that although the governors, *mutasarrifs*, and officers in the provinces had administrative authority, the cabinet's decision to send a committee to the provinces was based on a massive number of complaints arriving from the provinces. Boyadjian said he supported dispatching a committee to the provinces, since that would allow the government to investigate who was responsible for the injustices and to remove those people from their positions. He argued that according to reports arriving from Diyarbekir, Bitlis, Muş, and Adana, there was a great deal of deception in those areas, where the old political system was continuing:

> It seems that it is necessary to send such a committee. I beg you pay attention to this point. I also do not want us to spend more money, but if there is a solution, if you have another measure, you should start now and give the necessary orders to the *valis*, *mutasarrifs*, and *kaymakams* to prevent this impertinence. If preventive measures are going to be taken for these impertinent situations, then I would say that there is no need for the committee; however, since the present situation is continuing, to that aim I want to draw your attention, I beg you, examine these things very well.[54]

Boyadjian asserted that since past committees had been ineffective, Parliament should determine the members of the committee and the government should then officially appoint them.

The Armenians encountered resistance from other deputies. Haci Ilyas Efendi (Muş) opposed their approach, saying that dispatching a committee to the provinces contradicted the constitution and would set a precedent for committees to be sent annually. Kozmidi Efendi, the Greek deputy of Istanbul, took another approach, arguing that the procedure behind the bill was illegal and procedural errors could not lead to true constitutional administration. He suggested that Parliament should have investigated the committee's legality before proposing a law that would have to go through the Senate to the central government for consideration. Kozmidi also asserted that the cabinet sent the bill to Parliament to avoid responsibility, resolving, "We are going to tell the cabinet, 'If you see the necessity to take extraordinary measures, the responsibility is yours.'"[55]

Other deputies argued that there was no legal basis for dispatching such a committee. Ömar Lütfi Efendi (Budur) supported Kozmidi's arguments. Emphasizing the existence of internal laws and regulations for each province, he asked on which regulatory code the inspection committee would base its findings. Ömer Lütfi Bey (Dersim), in turn, shed doubt on the possibility that the commission would achieve any success in the provinces, and his speech was followed by raucous applause from the deputies. Izzet Bek (Trabzon) suggested that his province be removed from the list, since there was no need, according to him, for an inspection committee there.

The Armenian deputies were not alone in supporting the bill. Arif Efendi (Bitlis) argued that people in Anatolia were suffering and everyone there was anticipating the dispatch of the committee. "In the name of the poor and oppressed people," said Arif, "I am demanding that a committee be sent to Anatolia."[56]

Parliament's mood worsened when the discussion became more personal and particular. Ismail Bey (Tokat) started criticizing Galib Bey, head of the reform committee to be sent to Anatolia. Riza Paşa (Karahisar-ı Şarki) suggested that the deputies from Anatolia should conduct preliminary investigations to determine whether committees were necessary, since they knew their respective provinces better than anyone else.[57] Others argued that certain areas in Anatolia, such as Dersim, were in particularly bad shape. Ismail Mahir Efendi (Kastamonu) urged that Dersim be given utmost priority by the inspection committee, but Ömer Lütfi opposed dispatching a committee to his province precisely because the situation there was urgent and he was convinced that the committee would be ineffective.

This, in turn, led to more discussions of procedure and legality. The deputy of Kastamonu argued that inspection bodies must be sent out in accordance with the law. Hence, he suggested the formation of a draft law for the bill. Seyfullah Efendi (Erzurum) agreed that a law must be passed to identify the committee's tasks and fix committee member's salaries. Anything done prior to this, he argued, would be against the law.[58]

Other deputies agreed that an inspection committee should be sent to Anatolia but demanded clarification of its duties. Müftüzâde Selim Efendi (Konya) asked how the committee would be formed and how it would coordinate with local authorities: "I just have one important question that also reflects the thoughts of many members, and that is, 'What is the duty of this inspection body?' Will they be respecting the constitution, or are they going to establish martial law? [If so], they have to demonstrate the necessity for a military administration."[59]

After many deputies expressed their support for or opposition to the bill, the president, Ahmed Rıza, closed the debate. Afterward, fourteen motions were presented by groups of deputies. These generally can be divided into three categories: some accepted the bill, some denounced it, and others wanted to modify it.

The first motion was prepared by Talat Paşa (Edirne), Arif Bey (Diyarbekir), Ahmet Müfit (Izmit), and Ruhi al-Khalidi (Jerusalem). Their motion described the necessity of drafting a law that would describe the duties and authorities of the committee and be sent to Parliament for ratification. Another motion, prepared by deputies Mehmet Ubeydullah (Aydın), Mustafa Nail (Canik),

Mehmed Rifat (Aleppo), Bedros Haladjian (Istanbul), Sulayman al-Bustani (Beirut), Mahir Sait (Ankara), Hafez Bey al-Sa'id (Jerusalem), and Vartkes Serengülian (Erzurum), argued that if Parliament took no action, it would be entrusting an urgent issue to the Financial Committee by default. Other motions opposed the whole project, arguing that it would be unproductive. The first motion was accepted, but this vote did not end the matter, which was raised again in the next session.[60]

It is interesting that the Armenian deputies, who staunchly supported dispatching an inspection committee to the provinces, were able to gain support from a wide range of deputies from the Arab provinces for their motion. Of course, when Armenian deputies, such as Serengülian or Haladjian, used the phrase "people of Anatolia," they surely meant the Armenians of Anatolia. However, it seems that Armenian deputies were cautious to avoid the phrase "Armenians of Anatolia" lest this be viewed as a strictly ethnic issue. In addition, by speaking of the "people of Anatolia," the Armenian deputies hoped to strengthen their case, since it would appear that they were advocating on behalf of all the inhabitants of Anatolia.

Was Public Order Violated?

The issue of the Anatolian provinces raised another major question at the beginning of the 25th session: Had public order in the empire been violated? This question was brought up when an interpellation motion was signed by almost sixty deputies, asking the Ministry of the Interior to delineate what measures the government had taken against the lack of public order in Istanbul and the provinces, intervention in government affairs, and transgression against the provisions of the constitution. All these factors, according to the motion, had a negative effect on both Ottoman public opinion and external politics.[61]

The motion caused heated debate in Parliament between those deputies who believed that public order had been violated and those who did not, although deputies from both sides of the debate sometimes agreed in their attacks on the motion itself. Ismail Hakkı Bey (Gümülcine), who believed that public order had been violated, criticized the motion, saying that one must differentiate between a lack of public order and the crimes that were committed during such a period. From his point of view, crime was the result, not the cause, of a lack of public order.[62] Although Yorgo Bosho Efendi (Serfiçe) did not believe public order had been violated, he supported Ismail Bey's position, arguing that the motion must specify where public order had been violated and why the government had not taken necessary steps to resolve these problems. Furthermore, Bosho criticized the excessive deployment of troops wherever a problem existed: "Like old doctors, sulfate cannot be prescribed for every illness."[63] Parliament, according to Bosho, should instead demand basic reforms from the cabinet. The solution to problems of public order, he believed, was to strengthen the police and the gendarmerie in the provinces and give them wider authority.[64]

In opposition to both Ismail Bey and Bosho, Zohrab argued that from a legal perspective, there is little difference between a lack of public order and an abundance of crime. He argued that implementing new laws in the provinces would not suffice and asked the deputies to consider a regulation dealing with the extension of responsibility, one of the major principles outlined in the political platforms of parliamentary deputies. According to Zohrab, the Ministry of Interior Affairs had already asked why Parliament had not passed a law concerning extension of responsibility. For Zohrab, the extension of responsibility was both an important aspect of implementing the constitution and one of the key factors to establishing order in the empire.[65]

Yusuf Kemal Bey (Kastamonu) criticized Zohrab's focus on extension of responsibility. He argued that it would be more effective to implement regulations pertaining to the general administration and to form general councils in the provinces. He also argued that there was no need to ask for clarification from the minister of interior affairs regarding the extension of responsibility.

Bedros Haladjian, on the other hand, criticized Ismail Bey, arguing that public order could not last in a country experiencing a sudden change of government. "It is our duty," stated Haladjian, "to ask the government what kinds of measures it is following, what kinds of measures it is taking, in the situation under which this public order is violated."[66] Haladjian was confronted by some deputies who asked him to specify where public order had been violated, and he responded that many deputies from Anatolia agreed with him on the issue. He also explained that he did not want to bring the minister of the interior to Parliament for a vote of no confidence. Rather, he simply wanted further clarification on this issue. Haladjian asked Parliament not to reject the motion that was submitted by the sixty deputies, since he believed that rejecting the interpellation meant Parliament would surrender the right to request clarification from the executive authority on important issues.

Hüssein Cahid responded to Haladjian sarcastically, saying that at first he thought the motion was a translation from a well-known newspaper.[67] He then rejected Zohrab's conception of extension of responsibility, saying that it would already have been implemented if it existed in the constitution. Cahid explained that even if such a provision did exist in the constitution, one must first prove that public order had been violated in order to implement it. He added that the grand vizier had already clarified the internal political issues and concluded his remarks by rejecting the interpellation.[68] At this point, Zohrab intervened in the debate, saying that regulations relating to the extension of responsibility should be implemented according to the necessary laws. He argued that the existence of such laws did not mean that deputies would abrogate the extension of responsibility.

In the end, the interpellation was put to a vote, but it received the support of only a minority. Since the Armenian bloc in Parliament had failed to get Kâmil Paşa's inspection committee's bill passed, it turned its attention to the interpellation motion asking the minister of the interior to account for the absence of public order in the empire. CUP members, led by Hüssein Cahid, vehemently attacked the motion, arguing that there was no need for an interpellation, and they succeeded in obstructing it.

The Armenian deputies' attempt to bring the situation of the Anatolian provinces to the floor of Parliament did not end with these two motions. On March 10, the Armenian deputy of Izmir, Stepan Efendi Ispartaliyan (Spartalian), submitted a third motion dealing with measures needed to reform the situation of the people of Anatolia. This motion did not get a majority vote, so it was not put to a discussion. The three attempts by Armenian deputies to bring debate about the situation in the Anatolian provinces to the agenda in Parliament is an extremely significant matter that would haunt Armeno-Turkish relations until World War I. The inability and reluctance of both the executive and legislative power in the Ottoman Empire to reform the deteriorating condition of the eastern provinces (that is, Armenian provinces) prior to and after the Counterrevolution and the Adana massacres of 1909 would lead to a dramatic acceleration of the intervention of European powers in the internal affairs of the Ottoman Empire. This intervention would culminate in the Armenian Reform Project of 1914, which became an intolerable burden for the CUP and one of the factors for its decision to enter World War I.[69]

The Restriction of Public Gatherings

The last issue pertaining to the Armenians in Parliament in the period under study was restriction of public assembly in the empire. Debates concerning this issue took place against the backdrop of the collapse of Kâmil Paşa's government and the establishment of a new government headed by Hüssein Hilmi Paşa and supported by the CUP.

On the night of February 25, 1909, the government issued an official communiqué, declaring that it had received reports of imminent public meetings that were intended to compromise the harmony of the empire.[70] The government, therefore, had decided to monitor such assemblies to ensure public security. The communiqué stated that the police should be notified of any assembly twenty-four hours in advance and that meetings without prior authorization from the police would be prohibited. It seems likely that the communiqué was issued in response to an article published in the opposition newspaper *Serbesti* (Liberty), which demanded the restoration of Kâmil and Nazim Paşa to power.[71]

The issue was raised in Parliament on March 3, 1909, through two interpellations, one of which was submitted by Bosho Efendi and the other by Mehmed Rifat Bey and his friends. Bosho Efendi's interpellation asked two questions: Why had the government revoked the right to assemble, which was guaranteed by the constitution, and was there any reliable intelligence that the empire's harmony and security been threatened?[72] Taking a more direct approach, the interpellation submitted by Rifat Bey, Kozmidi Efendi, Ismail Kemal (Berat), and Mahir Sait stated that the government had restricted the right to assemble without sufficient reason. Their interpellation argued that the official communiqué violated the spirit of the constitution in two ways, by implying that the government had the authority to completely ban public gatherings and by insisting that assemblies obtain official permission twenty-four hours prior to gatherings. The interpellation asked how the cabinet, which had just stated that it was committed to preserving the constitution and freedom, could take such steps.[73]

Hüssein Cahid immediately supported the government's position, noting that the communiqué said there was no clarity in the law regarding the right to assemble. Cahid agreed with this assessment, arguing that the right to assemble was not guaranteed in the constitution. Nevertheless, although it was not clearly stated in the constitution, the government accepted it in principle. "But the right to assemble is not a right that is given randomly," argued Cahid. "We all know that freedom does not mean we can do what[ever] we want. In human society, freedom also has its limits. Where others' freedom starts, my freedom ends."[74] Cahid also legitimized the requirement for authorization to assemble by pointing out that the same requirement existed in France. Furthermore, he accused the newspapers of misinterpreting the government's intentions.

Vartkes Serengülian criticized Cahid's take on the issue, saying that the two main principles of the constitution were freedom of publication and freedom of speech. "Freedom of speech is a freedom. When harm comes to one of these [freedoms], the constitution is diminished at its very base."[75] He also commented on Cahid's claim that the right to gather was not guaranteed by the constitution:

> I want to say that freedom appears in assembly. . . . The way that there is freedom of speech there is also freedom of assembly. . . . Why should we be afraid? Why should the newspapers not publish their thoughts in their columns and the people not express their thoughts in open spaces? . . . Why are we taking France as an example? France is a bureaucratic country. . . . It is not like England, where there is more freedom. . . . Why cannot we take England as an example? And as much freedom as there is in England, nothing is happening [to threaten security]. . . . Does this mean that the people of England are more civilized than those of France?[76]

Ismail Bey (Gümülcine) spoke next, supporting the government's claim that these measures were necessary to guarantee public order:

> We should trust the government and leave it free in its actions . . . and then if something happens, we cannot put the responsibility on the government. We should evaluate the government's prediction before it takes place . . . and upon this we should wait for the results from the government. . . . We are not with the people who, under the guise of corrupt ideas, want to implement freedom.[77]

Bosho Efendi, the author of the first interpellation, responded, warning the deputies in the Parliament not to use the supposedly "reliable intelligence" claims that had been used by the ancien régime.[78] Bosho again asked upon what the government had based its assessment of the threat:

> Why should well-intentioned gatherings be canceled because of other ill-intentioned assemblies? Why does not the government catch the bad people? . . . What is this reliable intelligence that the government is basing its claim on in banning illegal gatherings? . . . What is this reliable intelligence?[79]

The Armenian deputy of Tekfurdağ, Hagop Babigian, took a middle path. On the one hand, he supported his fellow Armenians' stance, saying that the right to assembly was a natural right, belonging to all Ottomans. When the constitution was written, he claimed, its authors did not see any reason to include a section on the right to assembly. On the other hand, he also agreed with the deputies who supported the government's right to require prior permission and argued in favor of clear limitations: "In these discussions, the right to assembly is found for all Ottomans. However, how is it going to be formed? There is no law for this. Everyone is not entitled to the right of speaking whenever he wants."[80] Babigian explained that assemblies in the streets might endanger public order, because there was no way of telling who was assembling there. The right to assembly should be discussed within the context of constitutional reforms. He supported the government's stance, saying that it was within the government's authority to take such a measure. Babigian's position is a manifestation of his dual obligation as a CUP deputy who was ethnically Armenian.

After this initial phase, the debate about restrictions on public assemblies concentrated on what sort of official document the government would give those wishing to assemble. Haladjian, for example, argued that since the government did have a right to know who was assembling so it could preserve public order, regulation was unobjectionable so long as the document was given to everyone who requested it. He argued, though, that this official document should not be a license, since that would imply that the government had the right to forbid certain events. For him public assembly constitutes the most important basis of the constitution, and freedom "to threaten this is beyond the authority of the executive authority." He argued that the government's proclamation was vague and suspicious, and Parliament was therefore obligated to ask for clarification.[81]

Kozmidi Efendi supported Haladjian, arguing that the right to assembly is one of the basic natural rights of human beings and that the deputies had the right to ask for clarifications from the government. Furthermore, he claimed that if the official document permitting public gatherings were a license, that would open a direct path to despotism.[82]

Responses to this turn in the debate were wide ranging. Mustafa Asim Efendi (Istanbul), despite agreeing that the right to assembly was a natural right, argued that the government's action was beneficial, so there was no need to ask for any clarification. Hampartsum Boyadjian (Kozan) noted that all deputies, whether they supported or opposed the government's position, agreed on the freedom to assembly but that there was disagreement concerning the license to assembly. He agreed that the police were obligated to maintain order during public assemblies but argued that the license issue was not clearly addressed by the government's proclamation, so clarification was necessary.[83]

Emrullah Efendi (Kırkilise) supported the government's action, declaring that people could not simply be allowed to assemble anytime or anywhere they wished. He also minimized other deputies' concerns about the license, saying it was just a piece of white paper.[84]

Zohrab agreed that the government had the right and obligation to prevent disruption to public order, "but the thinking point is the following: Is banning or restricting the right to gather an effective solution?" Moreover, he felt that the debate was obfuscating the real issue. Parliament, he believed, should consider whether the actions of Hilmi Paşa's government had caused unrest. Other deputies asked Zohrab to retreat from this position, but he continued: "The wisdom of abusing this concept of assembling is known. We [Ottomans] are a nation who had been repressed for thirty years under this concept of assembling." At the end of his long speech, Zohrab stated that summoning the prime minister to Parliament to provide clarification on the government's communiqué was an absolute constitutional right. Arif Ismet Bey (Biga) retorted that Zohrab's statements were not made for the sake of truth but rather "for his own benefit." Zohrab immediately responded: "Let him explain; we are all Ottomans here; we are not pursuing private benefits. [Interruption: uproar, uproar.] We are Ottoman deputies; we are not anything else, I think."[85]

At this point, the president of Parliament, Ahmed Rıza came to Zohrab's defense, ordering Arif Bey to either clarify his words or take them back. Arif's answer to the president demonstrates the tension that existed in Parliament concerning the right to assemble. He said that Zohrab was a member of the Liberal Party (Ahrar Fırkası). Hence, his comments regarding the right to assemble were not truly his own. "On the contrary," argued Arif, "it comes from the Ahrar Party's take on assemblies without restrictions or condition, which appears in its program."[86]

At the end of the long debate, many motions were put to a vote. They were divided into two categories: those that urged for an interpellation against the government's proclamation and those that saw the government's action as an attempt to preserve public order. In the end, a motion forwarded by Ömer Lütfi Bey (Dersim) passed. It stated that the mandatory document affording police permission to gather was not a license but simply a requirement to inform the government about gatherings. Therefore, the motion declared that there was no need to ask the grand vizier for clarification.[87] The motion received 130 votes in favor and 50 opposed. Most of the Armenian deputies voted against the motion.[88]

Conclusion

In the first year of the parliamentary debates, Arab deputies were not as active as might be expected, given their numbers. Although some did voice their opposition to major issues pertaining to their geographic areas, such as the railway concessions, they did not participate in the other critical issues that were high on Parliament's agenda. This mainly stemmed from the lack of an Arab parliamentary bloc and a lack of fluency in the Ottoman Turkish language among the Arab deputies. Other reasons were the nonexistence of a major national concern pertaining to the Arabs or the Arab provinces, whereas such issues were evident among Armenians, Greeks, and Bulgarians. After all, not until 1911 did Zionism and its projects in Palestine attract the criticism of many Arab deputies. In general, the orientation of Arab deputies within Parliament seems to have been toward uniformity and support for the CUP bloc.

In contrast, the Armenians, though comparatively few in number, were able to raise major issues in Parliament because of efforts of the Armenian bloc, which acted unanimously on issues that pertained to their ethnic group. The situation of the Anatolian provinces was very critical and occupied a central position in the parliamentary activities of the Armenian deputies. After their effort to support Kâmil Paşa's bill to send an inspection committee to Anatolia failed, they shifted their support to the interpellation motion presented by sixty deputies asking the minister of the interior to account for the absence of public order within the empire. The CUP members, led by Hüssein Cahid, fervidly attacked the motion, arguing that there was no need for an interpellation, and they succeeded in obstructing it. As evident from their extensive involvement, the issue of public assembly was also very important to the Armenian deputies. They, like the Liberal deputies, saw the restriction of assembly as a threat targeting their political activities. Indeed, this may be regarded as the beginning of the CUP's policies of eliminating opposition threats by restricting political activism of opponent groups. This would become more evident in the period following the Counterrevolution, when they would ban the formation of political groups organized on a national basis.

6 THE COUNTERREVOLUTION AND THE "SECOND REVOLUTION"

DURING THE FIRST YEAR of the constitutional regime, tension among the different political forces within the empire reached its apex with the assassination of Hasan Fehmi, editor of *Serbesti*, one of the dominant opposition papers. The event became a catalyst for the crystallization of the Counterrevolution, which, in turn, shaped the history of the Second Constitutional Period, along with CUP domestic policy in general and its attitude toward other ethnic groups in particular. In short, the Counterrevolution led to the demise of the Ottoman dream that the Revolution had promised to fulfill. It was also cited as justification for the drastic measures that the CUP would take in the name of preserving the empire.

Unsurprisingly, feelings about the Counterrevolution varied widely among the empire's ethnic groups. Most of the nondominant groups were concerned that the Counterrevolution would throw them back into the abyss of absolutism and the ancien régime. Other groups, such as the notables, who lost power as a result of the Revolution, viewed this moment as an opportunity to regain power. Similarly, conservative groups who had benefited from the ancien régime viewed this new political moment as the ultimate manifestation of religious victory, in which the Islamic şeriat would replace the "sacred constitution" enacted by the "unfaithful elements" of the empire. The historical record, however, shows that political realities of this period were more complex than these groups anticipated. Like the Revolution, the Counterrevolution was a complex historical event. The discontented groups that took part in the Counterrevolution represented groups with diverse objectives. Despite these differences they had one aim in common: to oust the CUP leadership from the capital. The nondominant groups' role in quelling the Counterrevolution was minimal and mostly symbolic. What was more prominent was their commitment to "shed the last drop of their blood" for the sake of saving the constitution. If one of the important outcomes of the Counterrevolution was a drastic change of CUP policies toward the nondominant groups and the acceleration of that party's authoritarian tendencies, the other was the huge human and material loss suffered by the Armenians as a result of the Adana massacres of 1909, which too often "escapes" the attention of this period's historians.[1]

The deterioration of the situation in the capital began with the assassination of the editor of *Serbesti*, an anti-Unionist daily newspaper owned by the brother of sultan, Reşad Efendi. At the beginning of March 1909, the newspaper published a series of articles against the CUP.[2] On April 6, 1909, Hasan Fehmi was shot on the Galata Bridge while walking with his friend Şakir Bey, a deposed subgovernor. Fehmi died immediately, but Şakir survived his injuries. On April 8, *Serbesti*'s front page appeared with only one sentence in the middle, invoking one of Islam's most cherished prayers: "The first victim of *Serbesti*'s publication: *al-Fātiḥa* for the soul of Hasan Fehmi Bey, who spent his life in exile."[3]

After Fehmi's murder, the situation in the capital deteriorated dramatically. The Liberals accused the CUP of being behind the assassination, while others claimed that the real perpetrator was the palace.[4] Fehmi's funeral, which attracted more than fifty thousand people, turned into a mass rally against the CUP.[5] The ethnic press reacted angrily to the assassination, asserting that the killing had caused much anguish among all the people of Istanbul.[6] The Armenian daily *Zhamanak*, for example, described the incident with the ultimatum: "Either your pen or your life,"[7] implying that free speech could result in a penalty of death.[8] *Zhamanak*'s editorial asserted that people were convinced the CUP had planned the assassination and that Fehmi was paying the price for the harsh language he used against the committee.[9]

On April 7, the Armenian deputy of Istanbul, Krikor Zohrab, submitted an interpellation to Parliament, asking the minister of the interior to explain why Fehmi's killers had not yet been caught. Zohrab argued that the assassination meant more than the death of one man: "The bullets that were fired last night were not fired at the chief editor of *Serbesti*; rather, they were fired at the whole press, at freedom of thinking and conscience in their entirety, and at the whole Ottoman nation."[10] A heated debate took place in Parliament, as Zohrab and his allies insisted that the murder was a political assassination while the CUP members argued that it was a nonpolitical crime. In the end, Zohrab's interpellation was accepted.

During this period, new political groups emerged onto the scene, causing much anxiety among the CUP.[11] One of these organizations would give the CUP particular cause for concern: on April 5, 1909, on the occasion of the Prophet's birthday, Derviși Vahdeti and others officially established the Society of Muhammad (İttihad-ı Muhammedi).[12] Lisān al-Ḥāl noted that about one hundred thousand people participated in the society's inauguration.[13] Aided by public outrage over Fehmi's assassination, the society quickly became the CUP's main competitor.[14] The society published its program, which featured a strongly Islamic anti-Western tone, on March 16, 1909.[15] Through its newspaper, Volkan, the society was able to posture as the defender of bureaucrats, soldiers, lower-ranking officers, students of religion, orphans, the needy, widows, and retired members of the military.[16] Volkan criticized the CUP by claiming that it had removed despotism from the palace only to bring it to Şeref Street, where the CUP headquarters was located.[17] The society through its organ, Volkan, reacted vehemently to the assassination of Hasan Fehmi, even threatening to revolt, and began cooperating with the Liberal Party.[18] The development of partnerships among the Society of Muhammad, the Liberals, and the First Army Corps caused considerable anxiety among CUP circles.

It was in this tense atmosphere that the Counterrevolution took place on March 31, 1909. For decades, Turkish historiography in general and Kemalist historiography in particular labeled the events the "Incident of March 31" (31 Mart Olayı), denying them their proper historical status.[19] Some scholars presented these events as Abdülhamid's attempt to regain power and eliminate the CUP, while others believed that the Liberal opposition provoked them.[20] Still others believed that the CUP instigated these events to recapture Istanbul militarily and depose the sultan.

A recent study by Sohrabi, however, provides a more compelling explanation of why the Counterrevolution took place. Sohrabi argues that the Counterrevolution "brought to light the antagonism—class (economic), cultural, and generational—between the military officers and bureaucrats and their less educated peers and underlings, and also their superiors."[21] The Counterrevolution was not a manifestation of religious fanaticism, as scholars have generally supposed. Although it spoke in the language of religion, it nevertheless was forwarded by diverse groups—the most important of which were lower-ranking soldiers and officers who had opposed the indiscriminate, massive purges initiated by the CUP after the Revolution. When the lower-ranking, populist religious organizations asked for the implementation of the *şeriat*, their aim was not to abolish the constitution but rather to implement the constitution in accordance with the principles of *şeriat*.[22] The Liberals also seized the opportunity to join this opposition movement and score points against the CUP. Thus, like the Revolution, the Counterrevolution was a "multi-actor, multi-vocal event that brought together groups with a variety of interests who finally articulated their demands in the same voice, but this time in the language of religion."[23]

Regarding the instigators of the Counterrevolution, Sohrabi's research demonstrates that none of the CUP's elite competitors—including the palace, the Sublime Porte, the Liberals, or Dervişi Vahdeti—initiated the anti-CUP outburst.[24] Sohrabi's explanation of the Counterrevolution is similar to his explanation of the Revolution: that it was fueled by the conflict between the educated and undereducated officers. The source that best affirms this approach is Krikor Zohrab's motion, signed by many parliamentary deputies, which he submitted to Parliament after the Counterrevolution. In that motion, Zohrab argued that since the proclamation of the constitution, improper perception of the ranker officers (*alaylı*) had been nurtured by the educated officers (*mektepli*), causing a great deal of tension between the two groups.[25] Zohrab asserted that army reforms following the Revolution had resulted in the removal of 85 percent of the ranker officers. Afterward, the small number of officers left in that cadre had been removed, one by one. The introduction of an exam requirement also meant that, generally, only those with a relatively advanced education would pass the exam and be accepted into the army. Zohrab's petition called for reform of the existing situation because "otherwise, huge agitations will rise among the army."[26] The petition contained some suggestions concerning how to address the existing conditions. This institutional conflict played a key role in the Counterrevolution. As Sohrabi argues, "Without this institutional conflict, a Counterrevolution, or for that matter, a revolution, was hard to imagine."[27]

The Counterrevolution Begins

On the night of April 12, the troops of the First Army Corps mutinied and marched toward Ayasofya Square, near Parliament, accompanied by a large number of people in religious garb (*softas*) shouting slogans in favor of the sultan and demanding the restoration of the *şeriat*.[28] This resulted in the resignation of Hilmi Paşa's cabinet, which the sultan promptly accepted. By royal order, on April 14, Tevfik Paşa was appointed grand vizier.[29] Ismail Kemal was elected president of Parliament.[30] This was a huge blow to the CUP, whose members either fled or went into hiding: Ahmed Rıza, Mehmed Cavid, Dr. Bahaeddin Şakir, and Hüssein Cahid all disappeared.[31] Meanwhile, the offices of the CUP's newspapers, Şura-yı Ümmet and Tanin, were destroyed.[32] The deputy of Latakiyya, Muhammad Arslan, was killed, apparently having been mistaken by the counterrevolutionaries for Hüssein Cahid. Although the Counterrevolution shook the CUP's base in the capital, the party still maintained a powerful foothold in Rumelia, where it had the Third Army Corps at its disposal.

In the midst of this crisis, on April 17, the United Ottoman Association (Heyet-i Müttefika-ı Osmaniye) was formed in Istanbul by an initiative of the ARF.[33] On April 18, the new association made the following proclamation: "All the political groups in our country, whose committees and bodies are in danger, have put all differences aside and formed an allied committee under the sublime name of 'Ottoman' in order to maintain peace."[34] The proclamation ended by calling upon all Ottomans to work together to guarantee public order and the safety of the country.[35] The declaration was signed by the CUP Istanbul branch, the Ottoman Liberal Party (Osmanlı Ahrar Fırkası), ARF, Greek Political Committee, Democrats, Albanian Bashkim Central Club, Kurdish Cooperation Club, Circassian Cooperation Club, Bulgarian Club, Mülkiye Graduate Club, Turkish Club of Mutual Assistance, and Ottoman Medical Committee. The United Ottoman Association's aim was to inform the people of the empire that the constitution had been preserved, despite the upheavals of the Counterrevolution. Consequently, it sent special envoys to the provinces to give speeches and published newspaper articles in the capital about loving the homeland.

The CUP also began to act on April 17. The Action Army (Haraket Ordusu) left Salonica and headed to Istanbul to restore public order and discipline among the rebellious troops. It established its headquarters at Aya Stefanos and began negotiations with the new cabinet. After negotiations failed, the Action Army entered Istanbul on April 23 and, after several skirmishes, took control of the city.[36] A few days later, the National Assembly deposed Sultan Abdülhamid II and replaced him with his brother Mehmed Reşad V, putting an end to the Counterrevolution. Members of the Liberal Union's leadership either fled or were arrested. The Counterrevolution forced the army to intervene to guarantee law and order. Although the campaign in Istanbul ended without much bloodshed and tensions in most of the provinces were contained by the CUP, the Counterrevolution would spin violently out of control in the province of Adana.

Reactions of Ethnic Groups to the Counterrevolution

The Counterrevolution was a blow not only to the CUP but also to the other ethnic groups. Nevertheless, most of the ethnic newspapers in Istanbul maintained a neutral stance toward unfolding events. For example, the Armenian newspaper *Zhamanak*'s reaction not only was moderate but actually showed a slight sympathy toward the Counterrevolution, reprinting the prevailing opinion among Muslim intellectuals. During that period, it ran interviews with important figures from the Society of Muhammad and translations from *Volkan*. On April 16, *Zhamanak* ran an interview it had conducted with one of the active members of the society, who explicitly argued that *şeriat* was not inimical to the constitution because even *şeriat* necessitated consultation. He further argued that there was no reason why non-Muslims should not participate in this consultation—that is, Parliament.[37]

This sense of sympathy toward the rankers and the religious elements became even more dominant in the next issue of *Zhamanak*, in which it argued that the soldiers' mutiny targeted neither non-Muslims nor Armenians. On the contrary, the paper's editorials asserted, the soldiers had taken special care not to make an anti-Christian impression and felt an obligation to protect Christians. Furthermore, the editorial noted that the army had reiterated its oath not to endanger the constitution. It was generally expected that threats to the constitution would come from the fanaticism of the religious leaders and *softas* (religious students), but the opposite happened. The religious leaders of Islam affirmed that the constitution was the demand of the *şeriat*. When the Action Army was successful in subduing the Counterrevolution, *Zhamanak* opportunistically shifted its tone by hailing that victory.[38]

The reaction of the Jewish population toward the events of the Counterrevolution was similarly diverse. Most Jewish newspapers in the capital remained neutral, simply reporting events without adding commentary.[39] This could not, however, be said about the Jerusalem-based *Ha-Zvi*, which was extremely critical of the CUP from the first day of the Counterrevolution for bringing the empire to that crisis. The newspaper's editorials argued that CUP policies limiting freedom of speech and freedom of the press had agitated the party's opposition.[40] It particularly censured Grand Vizier Hilmi Paşa, saying that he had been successful in inciting Parliament to give the press a death sentence. His influence, *Ha-Zvi*'s editorial claimed, was so powerful that even two of the Jewish parliamentary deputies—Vital Faradji and Nissim Mazliah—who previously had been staunch supporters of freedom, succumbed to his pressure and became complicit in his policies. Nevertheless, the newspaper insisted that such assault against freedom should not have caused the army to become alarmed and act on its own. The freedom that the CUP sought for millions of Ottomans in the empire became "a game ball in their hands and nothing else." The anger of the general population and the army was directed against both Hilmi Paşa and the CUP.[41] *Ha-Zvi*'s editors accepted the CUP's important role in bringing about a bloodless revolution but argued that the party did not know how to be heroic when it had to fight against an absolutist regime. In closing, the editors called upon the CUP to fulfill its duties, since the entire Ottoman nation had entrusted its hopes to that party.[42]

The Arab response toward the Counterrevolution also varied, though its fluctuations tended to be geographically based, depending upon the composition of the population and the influence of the CUP in different regions. In Lebanon, for example, news of the Counterrevolution shocked the Arab population. The newspapers there expressed extreme pessimism about the situation and called those soldiers who broke into the Parliament "monsters."[43] Nothing, however, stirred the anger and dismay of a local population more than the death of Amir Muhammad Arslan, Arab deputy of Latakiyya.[44] The people of Latakiyya demonstrated in the streets, carrying black flags marked with red crescents and demanding justice for the killing. The newspapers also demanded official condemnation of the heinous act and asked the government to arrest those responsible for it. When Muhammad Arslan's body was brought from the capital to Beirut, a glorified funeral procession took place there.[45] Representatives of all parties, including the CUP, along with a variety of other organizations and communities, participated in the funeral. Members of different ethnic groups, including a member of the Israelite Society (al-Jam'iyyah al-Israi'liyyah), served as pallbearers, and a diverse range of speakers praised the work Arslan had done for the nation.[46]

Suppressing the Counterrevolution

Although representatives of all ethnic groups participated in the Action Army that suppressed the Counterrevolution, the coalition was not decisive in its victory against the counterrevolutionaries. It did, however, demonstrate a common commitment to sacrifice for the sake of freedom and a constitution that had taken thirty years to realize. Among the cases under study, Armenians were among one of the most prominent participants in that movement. This participation took place even at the grassroots level: during the Counterrevolution Armenian youth banded together to protect the Armenian neighborhoods of Istanbul.[47] The official reaction among Armenian leaders was no less notable. Their political parties immediately came to the aid of the Action Army and the CUP in the campaign against reactionary forces.[48] Vahan Papazian, the Dashnak deputy of Van, noted in his memoirs that Istanbul's Responsible Body sent ARF members from Van and Muş to Adapazarı, Izmir, and Rodosto (Tekirdağ) to organize the Armenians for self-defense and enlist them into the Action Army. According to Papazian this was meant to ensure that Armenians did "[their] share in pressuring the anti-constitutionalist movement."[49] The Responsible Body also assisted in the organization of 250 Armenian volunteers in Izmit and Bahçecik, who positioned themselves on the Anatolian Railway to stop passage of deserting soldiers.[50] The most important of these activities, assisting the Action Army's march on Istanbul, was centered in Rodosto. Rupen Der Minassian, one of the Armenian revolutionaries sent to Rodosto, mobilized Armenian volunteers, who received ammunition from the CUP representative in the city.[51]

On April 20, ARF's Western Bureau wrote to the Izmir Committee informing them that the Rumelian army, which included Bulgarian, Greek, Jewish, and Armenian volunteers, were gradually surrounding the capital. The bureau urged the Izmir Committee to mobilize a volunteer battalion of Armenians, Greeks, and Turks, uniting it with the Action Army, which was already advancing on Istanbul. In case that proved to be impossible, the bureau advocated the formation of an Armenian battalion, which would, it asserted, have "great moral importance for the Armenian nation."[52]

When the Salonican army stationed itself in the Üsküdar Selimiye barracks, its captain, Osman Efendi, called upon the Armenian revolutionary groups to join them.[53] In response, ARF and the Hunchaks sent representatives to meet with Osman Efendi, who addressed them:

> As you have taken an oath to defend your homeland, we also have taken the same oath; hence your and our aim are the same. Our troops tonight are scarce and scattered in the barracks; therefore I want to ask you not to spare your help tonight. I know that you are tired of guarding, but I hope that you will continue your selfless dedication tonight.[54]

The leaders of the Armenian revolutionary groups were impressed by this speech and pleased that the Action Army both appreciated their service and gave them official attire. Osman Efendi promised to provide Armenians with ammunition and necessary equipment. As a result of these agreements, the Armenian volunteers began performing their duties as roaming guards. The ARF occupied twelve strategic positions, allocating five guards to each.

In Beyoğlu, Hunchak members enlisted as volunteers in the Action Army. Hunchak and nonpartisan Armenian medical doctors also took on the task of treating the Action Army's wounded. They began this work by transporting wounded soldiers from the battlefront to St. James (Surb Hakob) hospital. About thirty soldiers who fell during the attack on Taşkışla and Taksim were taken to St. James.[55] Nurses from the Armenian Red Cross also joined the doctors to care for the wounded to "demonstrate to our soldier brothers that the Armenian sympathy toward freedom is not through words alone."[56] The Reformed Hunchakian Party in Istanbul sent a delegation to the Action Army indicating their readiness to enlist Armenians. The party emphasized that though it was opposed to the political program of the CUP, it was willing and ready to provide all manner of aid and support for the preservation of the constitution.[57]

In addition to these sources of political and military support, Armenians contributed moral support through the Armenian Patriarchate. On April 27, the locum tenens of the Armenian Patriarchate of Istanbul, Bishop Hovhannes Arsharuni, paid a visit to the three large hospitals in which the Action Army's wounded soldiers were being treated: the Hamidiye Children's Hospital, St. James, and the military hospital of Gümüşsuyu. This gesture seems to have had significant effect on morale and solidarity: an Albanian soldier who was being treated in the Hamidiye hospital kissed the hand of the locum tenens, saying, "I feel recovered now." Bishop Arsharuni answered by addressing all the soldiers: "O Lions of Freedom, your name is going to be carved in gold both in the kingdom of heaven and in our hearts."[58]

In the provinces, Armenians also defended themselves during the Counterrevolution. In Diyarbekir, when flyers were put on Armenian churches promoting the ideas of the Counterrevolution, the ARF placed Armenian guards at the entrances to all the important passages into Armenian neighborhoods. Though there were no major disturbances in Diyarbekir, the same could not be said about the surrounding villages, which witnessed the assaults of Kurdish beys. In Hayne, an Armenian town, the minister of the Armenian Protestants organized the resistance.[59] In Erzurum, the governor and the military commander formed a mixed battalion of Armenians and Turks to protect the Ottoman constitution, and the troops took an oath to shed the last drop of their blood for this cause, if necessary.[60] In Nablus, a group of thirty-two volunteers organized and traveled to Jenin, where they registered at the CUP club in Jenin and volunteered to march on the capital at the first sign from Beirut. Their stated aim was to protect the constitution and the Parliament to save the homeland from despotism.[61]

The Jews of Salonica also took an active part in the Action Army as it moved on the capital.[62] On April 17, the CUP sent a message to the Jewish Club des Intimes in Salonica demanding fidelity to the constitution.[63] Upon receiving this communication, the Jewish community responded that they were "ready to sacrifice for the fatherland."[64] They soon formed a Jewish battalion (Musevi Taburu) and sent it to join the Action Army. Before the men left Salonica, the Jewish community there composed a song for them in Ladino.[65]

The Military March of the Jewish Battalion

Youth from the villages
And many from Salonica
Volunteered to the Army,
Recruited for the battle,

We said, either freedom is achieved
Or our blood will be poured like water
For the love of Turkey.

Turks, Jews, and Christians
All of us Ottomans
We extended a hand each to the other,
Took an oath to be brothers.
To Istanbul we move.
We will fight against the wicked
For the salvation of Turkey.

We closed our shops,
We abandoned our jobs,
We kissed our relatives,
We hugged our friends.
To the army we delivered ourselves,
To the death we went,
For the salvation of Turkey.

Our mothers kissed us
They cried with sorrow
Our fathers pleaded
To God in Heaven
To have mercy on us.
If we sacrifice ourselves,
It is for the salvation of Turkey.

Women and children
Left the city
Without support,
In darkness and hardship.
If they treat them cruelly,
It was for the salvation of liberty:
For the salvation of Turkey.
With the help of God
We set out to the road
We went for long hours,
Forgetting food and drink,
We arrived at Istanbul,
We besieged the city
For the salvation of Turkey.

Niyazi Bey and his party
Many years have gone by
With the help of God,
They have reached their desire.
They brought down the old king,
And in his place they appointed
A just king in Turkey.

The lyrics of this song demonstrate the sacrifice that the Jews of Salonica were willing to make for the sake of the "salvation of Turkey," a theme that also had resonated in the earlier days of the Revolution. The importance of shedding blood for the salvation of Turkey was meant not only to protect and preserve freedom and the constitution but also to reinforce the theme of brotherhood upon which the idea of Ottoman brotherhood was being grafted, albeit in an ambiguous manner.

The approximately seven hundred Jewish volunteers in the Action Army of Şevket Paşa took part in the battles for the capital and the defeat of the sultan, but the army battalion was extremely short-lived. It was established for a specific time only and meant to demonstrate the dedication of Salonica's Jews for protecting the constitution. After the Action Army achieved its goal of liberating the capital from the counterrevolutionary forces, the Jewish battalion was dismantled. Some of the volunteers, however, enrolled in the Ottoman military school.

One of these volunteers was Shemtov Revah, who gave his memoirs to Itzhak Ben Zvi. Based on these memoirs, Ben Zvi argued that the formation of the Jewish battalion was an important precedent for the formation of the Israeli army. According to him most of the Jews who participated in the Jewish battalion were enthusiastic Zionists and nationalists who believed the Young Turk Revolution would open new horizons for the empire's Jews and for Zionism's goal of establishing a Jewish homeland in Palestine.

Shemtov Revah's memoir provides important information about how Jews in Salonica viewed the Counterrevolution and its causes. For example, Revah recounts that there were four major agitators prior to the Counterrevolution: Ali Kemal Bey, editor of İkdam, whom Revah called "a traitor and a British Agent"; the Liberals and the Fener (i.e., the Greek Patriarchate), who were supported by the external powers exerting pressure on the Young Turks; and Dervişi Vahdeti, the main enemy of the CUP, "who attacked the CUP through his newspaper and called for a return to Islam."[66]

During the movement of the Action Army on Istanbul, Revah was given the task of traveling to Kavala, Drama, Seres, Adrianople, and Gallipoli and eventually arrived in Çatalca with 150 Jewish volunteers. When the army began to enter the capital after the siege, the Jewish battalion moved toward Taksim from three directions under the command of Kâzim Bey. During the clashes that followed, twenty-one Jews were killed and twenty-three were injured. After the victory, the survivors were invited to the house of Rabbi Avraham Danon, director of the Jewish Seminary in Kuskuncak.[67] They also paid their respects to Grand Rabbi Haim Nahum in Istanbul.[68]

The Impact of the Counterrevolution on the Provinces

When news of the 1908 Revolution reached the Anatolian and Arab provinces, local authorities received it with reservation and were unwilling to declare the validity of the constitution. The notables and the ulema were also stunned by the news. Some members of these groups began voicing their opposition to the activities of the junior army officers who supported the Revolution. They were afraid that the Revolution and shift of power to the more centralized CUP would endanger their traditional legitimacy.

For this reason, religious officials in the Anatolian provinces joined forces with the *ayan* against the CUP as the Revolution began, causing considerable anxiety in CUP circles. The great rejoicing of the Anatolian non-Muslims—especially the Armenians—at the reinstatement of the constitution alarmed the traditional forces there. The weak public sphere(s) created after the Revolution provided an important medium in which Armenians in the provinces could increase their communal activities. Armenian revolutionary groups, such as the Dashnaks and Hunchaks, once considered dangerous fringe elements by the local and traditional authorities, had suddenly become legitimate and were visibly taking active roles in local politics. The local *hocas* (teachers of religion), *ulema*, and notables were unable to accept the changes that resulted from the Revolution and considered them the abrogation of the Islamic *şeriat*. Thus, they began inciting the public against the CUP and its most important accomplice, the Armenians.

The Society of Muhammad, which was very active in Istanbul, also increased its activities in the provinces after the Counterrevolution, sending emissaries there to preach against the CUP. The society did not confine its recruitment efforts to Anatolia but expanded into the Arab provinces and organized itself in places such as Damascus, Homs, Mosul, and Hama.[69] In Damascus, the society was supported by notables, including 'Abd al-Qadir al-'Ajlani; Amir 'Abdullah, son of 'Abd al-Qadir al-Jaza'iri; and Shaykh Badr al-Din. Their propaganda fell upon willing ears in the provinces, especially among the Bedouins, Circassians, and Kurds. The members of the society were not, however, solely responsible for the disturbances that took place in the provinces during the Counterrevolution. Dissatisfied local elements also provoked chaos, seeing this time of political upheaval as their ultimate opportunity to regain power.

News of the Counterrevolution spread to Anatolia and the Arab provinces quickly. When the news reached Damascus, members of the society and their supporters among the local population, heavily armed, gathered in the city square and threatened to kill members of the CUP who were assembled in the Grand Mosque. For three days this group staged celebrations in honor of the Counterrevolution. A reporter from *Al-Muqtabas* noted that the people of Damascus were so pleased by the Counterrevolution that they occupied the municipality and decorated it,[70] and then they wanted to attack the CUP's

Freedom Club. The reporter claimed that the Damascenes were agitated by five or six local notables who had not been promoted by the constitutional government and had, therefore, become its enemies.[71] Despite these events, there were no major outbreaks in Damascus, because the local military commander threatened military action and induced the crowds to disperse. The counterrevolutionary disturbances in Damascus were organized with one aim in mind: abolishment of the CUP's regime. When the Action Army crushed the Counterrevolution in Istanbul, the Damascene agitations faded and their organizers were sent to Istanbul to be tried by court-martial. In March 1909, as in other Syrian cities, a branch of the society was established in Latakiyya. Many locals, including some notables, joined the society with the aim of eclipsing the CUP and other supporters of the constitution and reinstating the Hamidian regime. The activities of this group attracted the attention of both Christian and Muslim Liberals in Latakiyya, who appealed to the *mutasarrif* Muhammad 'Ali 'Ayni Bey, expressing deep concerns about the society and its actions. The *mutasarrif* immediately contacted the leaders of the anticonstitutional movement and threatened to put them on the gallows if they made a move against the Christians or the CUP.[72]

When news of the Counterrevolution arrived in Jerusalem, everyone—especially members of the CUP branch there—was shocked. The CUP leaders immediately convened a large gathering in the city's garden to protest the appointment of Tevfik Paşa as grand vizier. The event took place on Saturday, April 17. Hundreds of representatives from all the empire's communities came to the city, filling its garden. The governor of Jerusalem, Subhi Bey, read the official telegram from Tevfik Paşa to the crowd.[73] The telegram declared that in accordance with the constitution, the cabinet of Hilmi Paşa had resigned and he had been appointed temporary grand vizier. After this reading, speeches were delivered, all emphasizing the necessity of defending the constitution. Muslims, Christians, and Jews all expressed their opposition to the sudden changes in Istanbul.[74] One Jewish newspaper argued that these speeches were given to "calm the people's spirits and ensure that there [was] no need to fear and that the constitution [was] still in place."[75]

Likewise, in Jaffa on April 19, some ten thousand people gathered in front of the government buildings at the invitation of the CUP. Speeches were delivered against Tevfik Paşa's government. Important figures within the city gave speeches and urged the people to recognize the necessity of preserving the constitution. Afterward, Yusuf Efendi al-'Issa gave a speech suggesting that the crowd should go to the *kaymakam* and inform him that the people did not want to recognize the new government in the capital because it was unconstitutional. At the conclusion of this speech, the crowd roamed the city, carrying Ottoman flags and shouting, "Down with the dictators!" declaring that the people would not accept the new cabinet without the ratification of Parliament.[76]

In most of the other cities of the Arab provinces and the southwestern provinces of Anatolia (Erzurum and Erzincan), the CUP acted similarly, maintaining control, rallying people to its cause, and enlisting volunteers from the local population to join the Action Army. For example, when news of the Counterrevolution and killing of Amir Muhammad Arslan reached Jenin, people there became extremely anxious. CUP officers from Nablus took advantage of this situation, traveling to Jenin to enlist the people in its cause.[77] Local governments in these areas, working in tandem with Young Turk civil and military officers, were able to contain the disturbances without bloodshed. In the southeastern Anatolian province of Adana, however, the disturbances escalated drastically, leading to the massacre of more than twenty thousand Armenians and two thousand Muslims.

Counterrevolution and Violence: The Adana Massacres

The 1909 Adana massacres (April 14–17 / April 25–27) remain a source of contention in the historiography of the Second Constitutional Period. Questions about the factors, motivations, contexts, real culprits, and number of victims remain disputed among historians. Some scholars deny the involvement of local government officials in the massacres, instead blaming the Armenians who revolted as part of a conspiracy to establish the Armenian Kingdom in Cilicia.[78] Other scholars accuse the CUP of acting behind the scenes to destroy the Armenian economic infrastructure in Adana to curb any future political and economic development in the area.[79] A third group of scholars provide more contextualized understanding of the massacres.[80] Of course, it would be impossible to understand the massacres of Adana without putting them in the context of the macro- and microhistorical transformations taking place at the time. Though the history of the Adana massacres will be treated at length by this author in a separate study, a brief overview of events in the context of the Revolution and the Counterrevolution provides the reader with a better understanding of the escalating ethnic tensions and their culmination in the massacres.[81]

As discussed earlier in this book, the Young Turk Revolution caused major changes in the dynamics of power within the provinces, resulting in a great deal of dissatisfaction within some segments of the population. The sudden mushrooming of CUP cells and clubs in the provinces (especially the Anatolian provinces) and the drastic purges that they initiated against the officers of the ancien régime caused extreme anxiety among the notables, the *ulema*, and officers of the previous order. Hence, one cannot understand the changes in Adana after the 1908 Revolution without understanding the waves of regional discontent manifested, especially in the Anatolian provinces. What distinguished Adana from the other cases was its economic and agricultural centrality to Anatolia—which attracted thousands of migrant workers arriving from surrounding regions—and its complex ethnic composition, which was a major catalyst in the deterioration of this ethnic relationship.[82]

As noted earlier, when the constitution was enacted, people in Adana and Mersin began rejoicing.[83] However, these festivities expressed only euphoric feelings and did not reflect the actual attitudes of all sectors of society. Those who benefited from the ancien régime immediately took a hostile position toward the constitution and the CUP. Others immediately took the opportunity to enhance their position within society by claiming to be staunch supporters of the CUP. Ihsan Fikri, a self-proclaimed Young Turk, suddenly became a public figure. With the consent of the Central CUP branch of Salonica, he established a CUP branch in Adana and became the editor of *İtidal* (Moderation), its official organ.[84] As it was for the other CUP branches in the provinces, the first task of the Adana committee was to force the local governor to resign. The governor, Bahri Paşa, duly resigned, and the CUP branch administered the province for a short time until the arrival of the new governor. It also succeeded in removing other important civil and military officials.

Meanwhile, to counter the CUP's influence, Abdülkadir Bağdadizâde, one of the most influential notables of Adana, formed a group called the Agricultural Club (Ziraat Kulübü) composed of Adana notables and religious students.[85] When Cevad Bey was appointed governor, he immediately kowtowed to Bağdadizâde's faction. Hence, after the Revolution, two opposing forces emerged in Adana, one CUP-backed group supporting Fikri and another made of local notables supporting Governor Cevad Bey, Ali Efendi Gergerlizâde, and, most important, Abdülkadir Bağdadizâde.[86] By siding with each camp in turn, the press, led by *İtidal* and *Rehberi İtidal* (Guide to moderation), mirrored this struggle.

After the proclamation of the constitution, the Armenians of Adana took an active part in the celebrations. Their festivities and demonstrations in honor of the constitution were especially striking. The public sphere created after the

1908 Revolution allowed Armenian political parties, especially the Hunchaks and the Dashnaks, to be active in Adana. The physical and verbal manifestations of Armenians in the public sphere—political processions; bearing and selling arms in public;[87] theatrical presentations hailing the Armenian historical past, especially the Armenian Kingdom of Cilicia;[88] and cultural revival through the print media—alarmed the dissatisfied elements, which began using print media to air their own anxieties and discontent concerning the new order.[89]

The historical record is unclear as to what actually was taking place in Adana's Armenian community at this time. American medical missionary Dr. F. D. Shepard of Aintab reflected about the situation by saying that Armenians, "intoxicated with the new wine of liberty, often gave offense by wild talk or arrogant behavior."[90] It is unclear whether these actions by some Armenians testify to their intention to rebel against the government for the sake of achieving independence. American missionary Dr. Thomas D. Christie, who was positioned at Tarsus, argued in an interview with an Armenian newspaper after the massacres that there was no proof that the Armenians, as a whole, desired separation from the Ottoman people or government. He conceded that there were a very "few foolish Armenians" who exasperated the Turks with their boasting and threats. He added, however, that "their acts and words ought not to be taken as justifying in the slightest degree the cruelties that make this recent massacre worse than any that have gone before it."[91]

The relationship in Adana between the Armenian ecclesiastical leadership and the newly formed local government also went downhill. It is noteworthy that the previous governor, Bahri Paşa, had a cordial relationship with the Armenians—especially with the prelate of Adana, Bishop Moushegh Seropian.[92] Seeing the tense situation, Bishop Seropian sent a pastoral letter to the Armenians of Adana, emphasizing the need for harmony among the people.[93] Concomitantly, however, the uncertain situation and rising tension led Bishop Moushegh to encourage Armenians to buy arms:[94]

> We advise the people that, in order to be able to fulfill their duties toward the country and the constitution, every person should be armed more or less according to his ability. That readiness should be at the same time somehow a means for self-defense, against an unfortunate attack, until the constitutional government comes to their aid.[95]

Dr. Christie, in response, criticized the words and deeds of Bishop Moushegh, as well as the young men who were following him. He argued that it was wrong to bring tin boxes of arms and ammunition to Mersin that were addressed to Armenians in Adana.[96] Although Christie would argue later that even such actions do not prove that there was an intention to rebel against the government, it is clear that the local Muslim population felt threatened.[97] In their eyes, Bishop Moushegh became an agitator and the source of tensions for inciting the Armenians against the Turks and encouraging them to establish the Kingdom of Cilicia.[98]

In March 1909, ethnic relations in Adana began to deteriorate dramatically, a trend made evident by sporadic attacks on Armenians. One of these attacks precipitated the first wave of the Adana massacres. On April 9, an Armenian named Hovannes was attacked by a group of Turks led by a man named Isfendiar.[99] During the ensuing fight, Hovannes killed Isfendiar, wounded some of the other attackers, and fled to the Armenian Quarter in Adana. From there he escaped to Cyprus. Isfendiar's funeral attracted not only those angered by the killing but also much of the element dissatisfied with the new order, the constitution, and its Armenian "collaborators."[100] As the situation intensified, the governor of Adana telegrammed Istanbul warning of an imminent threat in Adana. On April 14, Adil Bey, undersecretary of state in the Interior Ministry, responded with a telegram: "The financial institutions along with foreign buildings should be protected, and peace should be preserved."[101] Some of the Armenian sources understood this telegram as an order to massacre them.[102] This sentence is, however, too vague to be definitively interpreted in that way. One thing is certain: when news arrived from Istanbul that the Counterrevolution was underway, the situation in Adana exploded.

In Adana, Tuesdays were market days. Peasants would travel from their villages to Adana in the morning and return in the evening. On Tuesday, April 13, these peasants for some reason did not return to their homes. It is noteworthy that because of seasonal migration, sixty thousand to seventy thousand additional Armenian, Kurdish, and Turkish farmworkers inhabited Adana at the time, further complicating the volatile situation. On April 14, the disturbances began. Armenians opened their shops in the early morning but soon saw groups of Turks, Kurds, Circassians, Başıbozuks,[103] Cretans, and Muslim refugees carrying hatchets, blunt instruments, axes, and swords in their hands, while wearing white bandages around their fezzes,[104] in various quarters of the city.[105] This made the Armenians extremely anxious, and they quickly closed their shops.[106] When the Muslims of the city saw that Armenians were closing their shops early, they also became anxious, and a rumor spread that the Armenians were going to attack them. The mob, consisting of Turks, Kurds, Fellahs, Circassians, Gypsies, and Cretan refugees, began looting and attacking the center of town. Zor Ali, the police superintendent, rallied his troops and besieged the Armenian Quarter of Şabaniye. Meanwhile, Armenians took a defensive position in the Armenian Quarter and fortified themselves in houses.[107]

The first day of the massacres brought sporadic, unorganized attacks. On the first night, the mob began burning the Armenian Quarter.[108] The attacks intensified the next day.[109] The majority of the Armenian population found shelter in Armenian churches and schools, and some others went to foreign missions. By the third day, the mob had grown as Turks arrived from Aleppo and Sivas to take part in the pillage. Since the Armenians were running short of ammunition, they asked the government for protection.[110] In response, the governor organized a reconciliation meeting between Turkish and Armenian notables. By the fourth day, the situation had calmed but only after a great deal of bloodshed. It is impossible to accurately assess the number of casualties. The carnage, looting, and killing were widespread and lasted three days (April 14, 15, and 16). Many Armenians were killed, as were many Muslims, some of them while attacking the Armenian Quarter. Armenian shops, businesses, and institutions suffered immense damage.[111] It seems that the first wave of massacres was, however, minor when compared to what came later in the second wave.

Most of the Armenian and European sources indicate that between the first and second waves, Ihsan Fikri, leader of the CUP in Adana, played an important role in inciting the masses against the Armenians.[112] Through his newspaper, İtidal, he began to verbally attack the Armenians, using extraordinarily violent language to convince the masses that the Armenians had attempted a coup d'état to establish the Kingdom of Cilicia.[113] This provocation played an important role in mobilizing the masses and preparing them for the ensuing massacre.

On April 20, four days after the first incidents, thousands of free copies of İtidal were distributed in the streets of Adana. In this issue, Fikri, along with his colleagues Ismail Sefa Özler and Burhan Nuri, ferociously attacked the Armenians. In an article entitled "Müdhiş bir İsyân" (A horrible uprising), Sefa stated that a wave of boiling rage and independence was destroying the country. He argued that Armenians, like the Turks, had been oppressed for thirty-three years by the despotic regime before uniting with the Turks in their "holy revolution." Sefa claimed, however, that Armenians had betrayed the Revolution, quickly beginning to prepare for an uprising by stockpiling weapons.

According to Sefa, the first signs of agitation began when two Muslim youths were killed in the Armenian Quarter in the Şabaniye neighborhood—the incident of the murder of Isfendiar. Sefa argued that although the governor had assured the Turkish population that he would capture the murderer, thus restoring order, the Armenians defied the rule of law by refusing to turn over the murderer. To Sefa's mind, this was nothing less than an uprising (*isyân*).[114] He concluded with the claim that when the Armenians, "after all this barbarism and crime," saw the profusion of soldiers and people pouring in from the villages, they understood that their revolt was not going to succeed. Hence, they stopped their attacks.

In the same issue, an article by Burhan Nuri pursued the anti-Armenian campaign on more abstract grounds, posing the rhetorical question, "Can the Armenians establish a state?" Burhan answered that only the foolish would believe that Armenians, numbering fewer than two million people scattered throughout the empire, could defeat the Ottoman Empire and be able to establish an independent country. Burhan attacked the European powers in his article, declaring that those powers could not legally impose on the Ottoman Empire the establishment of an Armenian state in Cilicia. Burhan concluded:

> If the Armenians intend to form a state, the land for that state should not be in the Ottoman Empire; rather, they should look for it in the poles, in the desert lands of Africa, and immigrate there. They cannot reach their goal scattered in Istanbul, Adana, Aleppo, Diyarbekir, Bitlis, and Van.[115]

Regardless of whether the claims made by *İtidal* were true, they were vital in shaping public opinion in Adana, particularly the claims regarding the Armenian conspiracy. These articles fomented public opinion in Adana after the first wave of massacres. According to British vice consul in Adana, Charles Doughty-Wyllie, every Turk in the town was fully persuaded at the time that the Armenians had set light to their own houses with the intention of bringing about foreign intervention. Rumors about Armenian atrocities committed against Muslim men and women were also widespread.[116] According to Doughty-Wyllie, the Turks put all the blame for the massacre that would follow on the Armenians. Their claim was that it was clear that the Armenians had set a day on which to rebel against the Turks, both because the Armenians had armed themselves and because delegates of the Hunchak Party, along with preachers like Bishop Moushegh, had urged the Armenians to openly fight the Turks and set up a principality.[117] Although Doughty-Wyllie believed that the Hunchak Party was planning some kind of unrest, he nevertheless argued that they represented just a fraction of the people. He argued that the kind of widespread destruction that would occur in the second wave of the massacre could not have taken place without some "secret preparation on the Turkish side," demonstrating the premeditated nature of the event on the part of the local government and the CUP branch in Adana.[118]

After the first phase of the massacres, Armenians were elated when they heard the news that additional troops would come to Adana from Mersin to help preserve order.[119] On April 25, some 850 soldiers from the Second and Third Regiments—part of the Action Army—arrived from Dede Ağaç. When the regiments set up a camp in Adana, shots were fired at their tents. A rumor immediately spread that the Armenians had opened fire on the troops from a church tower.[120] The military commander of Adana, Mustafa Remzi Paşa, made no attempt to validate these rumors but simply ordered his soldiers to strike back at the Armenians. On Sunday, April 25, at 1:00 p.m., a battalion attacked the Apkarian school, which housed those people injured in the first wave of the massacres. Soldiers poured kerosene on the school and set it on fire with the people still inside.[121]

Regular soldiers, reserve soldiers (redif), and civilian mobs, along with the Başıbozuks, then proceeded to attack the Armenian Quarter. They burned down churches and the schools. The conflagration in the city of Adana continued until Tuesday morning, April 27, and destroyed the entire Armenian residential quarter, along with most of the houses in the outlying districts inhabited by Christians.[122] While the massacres were taking place in Adana, rumors spread throughout the province that Armenians had revolted in Adana, killed all the Muslims, and were going to destroy the villages. This caused extreme anxiety and provoked retaliatory attacks by the Muslims on Armenian villages outside Adana. The second wave of the massacres was, therefore, larger in scale and more ferocious. Thousands of innocent civilians were killed.

The local and international uproar in response to the massacres was overwhelming. The CUP, which had just come back into power after the Counterrevolution, sent investigative commissions to the region and ordered the establishment of military tribunals to try the culprits. The tribunals and investigative commissions sent from Istanbul attested to the fact that the local government officials—including Governor Cevad Bey and the commander of the army, Mustafa Remzi Paşa—were complicit in the Adana massacres.[123] Abdülkadir Bağdadizâde and his faction were also convicted of planning the massacres. The CUP representative in Adana, Ihsan Fikri, was convicted for inciting the masses against the vulnerable Armenian population of Adana.[124]

The reaction of the central government and the CUP toward the real culprits of the atrocities was lenient, as the court-martial's decision indicates.[125] Most of the key architects of the massacres received light sentences. Meanwhile, about fifty Muslims, some of them innocent,[126] and six Armenians were sentenced to death, while many others were sentenced to imprisonment with hard labor.[127] It seems that the CUP, weakened by the Counterrevolution, was hesitant to take drastic measures against the real culprits of the massacres in order to prevent further agitations that would endanger the party's grip over the region. The CUP's lenient reaction to the Adana massacres shook the trust of the Armenians toward them. The Dashnaks were the only Armenian entity that continued to cooperate with the CUP after the trials. Against all criticisms from other Armenian groups and political parties, the Dashnaks decided to make a final attempt to work with the CUP, pursuing land restitution and reform, the two bastions of its collaboration with the Young Turks.[128] The reluctance of the CUP to pursue these goals would, however, prove to be a crippling blow to the ARF-CUP alliance.[129]

The Fall of Abdülhamid II

The fall of Abdülhamid II was hailed by all the ethnic groups in the Ottoman Empire and signified the beginning of a new phase. The victory of the Action Army was thus transformed into a "Second Revolution" for most of the ethnic groups. One of the Armenian political parties equated the victory of the Action Army at Yıldız Palace with the French revolutionaries' victory at the Bastille. For them April 24, 1909, was the day in which the Turkish Bastille was liberated by the army. The newspaper *Dzayn Hayrenyats'*, official organ of the Reformed Hunchak Party, described the Yıldız Palace as the Turkish Bastille, "whose walls have heard thousands of death sentences for thirty-three years."[130] The Dashnak organ called the event a "Second Revolution" and accused the sultan of initiating the agitations and of being the agent behind the Adana massacres.[131] Arab newspapers also hailed the victory of the Action Army and equated April 24, 1909, to July 24, 1908, which "became an important day that brought down despotism" and opened a new page for the empire.[132] *Ha-'Olam*, a Zionist newspaper, viewed April 24 as a victory not only for the empire but also for Zionism, declaring the beginning of an era in which their national objectives would be realized.[133] As evidence for these assertions, the paper argued that the Ottoman

Turkish press and the more influential leaders of the Young Turk movement had demonstrated their sympathy toward the objectives of Zionism.[134]

Despite all the celebrations of the Action Army's victory and the dethronement of the sultan, Armenians, Jews, and to a lesser extent Arabs were cautious about the new situation and critical of the CUP. As a result of the Adana massacres, Armenians were especially critical. The reaction of the Dashnaks, despite their continued cooperation with the CUP after the massacres, is a testament to this mood among the Armenians. In one of the party's first public reactions to the Action Army's victory, published in *Droshak*, its official organ, the Dashnaks accused the CUP of establishing a party dictatorship that had become "the most unfortunate way to reform the empire." The CUP was accused in *Droshak* of embracing "the worst creed of nationalism and . . . aiming at realizing the impossible: and that is to melt all the different [ethnic] elements into Ottomanism, to invent from all the empire not only one, united (state), but also one nation." While admitting that the Dashnaks "knew about these ideas from the beginning," the editorial asserted they "did not expect that [the CUP] would graft [its ideology] so quickly onto their Ottoman reality." It voiced a concern that the CUP wanted to establish a completely centralized system under the hegemony of the Turkish elements—one in which "the Ittihadist Party can say, like Louis XIV, 'I AM THE STATE.'"[135] The editors argued that the CUP had called supporters of decentralization "the wretched" and destroyers of the state.

After criticizing the policies of the CUP, the editorial also lamented the indifference that the CUP had demonstrated toward complaints from the Armenians of the eastern provinces prior to the Counterrevolution. The paper argued that Armenians had demanded that the CUP cleanse the Armenian-populated provinces of the adherents of the ancien régime but to no avail. The editors asserted that the Cilician massacres had been a direct result of this neglect. *Droshak*'s editors nevertheless maintained some hope that the CUP's reaction toward bringing justice in regard to the Cilician massacres would be its litmus test. The article concluded by warning the CUP that if it turned the constitution into a party dictatorship and declared *millet-i hâkime* (the ruling nation), the people of the empire would witness internal agitation, external intervention, and dismemberment of the empire.[136]

The Jerusalem-based Jewish newspaper *Ha-Zvi* also criticized CUP policies and argued that the Counterrevolution demonstrated the failure of their policies. That newspaper's editors argued that it was possible for Turkey to develop to the level of the European countries if the principles of the Revolution were correctly implemented, but when the Young Turks had established their rule, most of them had forgotten their first principles on which they took an oath. The CUP's decision to limit the freedom of the press and sacrifice the freedom of assembly, they argued, had provided a pretext for the Counterrevolution. Furthermore, the editors declared that the CUP should have known that "in the place where there is the idea of freedom and light, there also is the idea of conservatism and darkness." The article concluded by stating that if the Young Turks and the Ottomans wanted to see the empire become a free and developed country, they would have to fight in every way against the conservatives and "all those who suck the blood of the nation."[137]

It is certain that after the Counterrevolution, the CUP pursued illiberal and extraconstitutional policies, including restrictions on freedom of association, freedom of assembly, and freedom of the press, which severely limited the civil liberties achieved by the Revolution. The ethnic groups considered those very liberties to be the foundation of the new Ottoman society, and the resulting dissatisfaction resulted in the Counterrevolution. The Counterrevolution, in turn, became a pretext for the CUP to justify its assumed role as the guardian of the constitution, even if it had to take unconstitutional steps in the name of the constitution. For the ethnic groups, on the other hand, the Counterrevolution and the policies that the CUP pursued afterward were a huge blow. When the ethnic groups were fighting against the Counterrevolution, they were doing so not to save the CUP from the verge of collapse but rather to save the constitution. While they viewed the constitution as the vehicle through which their civil liberties, as well as their national rights and privileges, would be protected, the CUP viewed the constitution as a means to preserve the integrity of the empire. These contradictory aims and the divisions that developed from them would combine with preexisting factionalism to destroy the pan-Ottoman dreams of the Revolution.

CONCLUSION

ON FRIDAY, DECEMBER, 30, 2011, more than one hundred years after the Young Turk Revolution of 1908 and in the wake of the Egyptian Revolution, Sheikh Mazhar Shahin, imam of the 'Umar Makram Mosque in Cairo's Tahrir Square, entered the Anglican Church of Kasr al-Dobara with a delegation of hundreds of Muslims to congratulate the Anglican Christians on the new year. His entrance into the church was accompanied by extensive applause from the Christians. The pastor of the church, Reverend Sameh al-Qasim, welcomed the imam and invited him to the altar to convey his holiday message. Sheikh Shahin rose to the altar amid jubilation and a standing ovation from both Christians and Muslims. After hugging Reverend al-Qasim, Sheikh Mazhar began his speech:

> In the name of God, the Merciful, the Compassionate . . . I am Sheikh Mazhar, the imam of the 'Umar Makram Mosque . . . We have been here in 'Umar Makram approximately since 2005. There is a strong relationship between me and this church. It is an intimate relationship, a relationship of love and a relationship of harmony; an Egyptian relationship, principally. . . . [more people applauding; attendees shouting "one hand, one hand" and "Long live the Crescent with the Cross"] My relationship to this church has been commanded to me by Islam, because Islam orders us to treat our neighbors well. Hence this relationship derives from two spirits: one is the religious spirit, and the other one a patriotic spirit. . . . The pillars of this country were founded with the sweat

of the Egyptians . . . Muslims and Christians [alike]. . . . This church specifically has great significance to the Revolution because . . . it opened its doors from the first day of the Revolution of the 25th of January [2011], as the Mosque of 'Umar Makram did on the first day. And, as Egyptians used to sleep in the Mosque of 'Umar Makram without anyone asking them about their name or their religion during the days of the Revolution, the men and the youth of Egypt also used to sleep here in this church without anyone asking them about their religion and their beliefs. . . . Egypt will remain a safe country, guarded by whoever walks on it, be they Muslims or Christians.[1]

This eloquent speech by Sheikh Mazhar on the theme of brotherhood between Christians and Muslims in postrevolutionary Egypt was neither his first nor his last. These speeches were intended to strengthen the ties between Muslim and Christian Egyptians at a critical juncture in the country's history. These sorts of speeches are very much indicative of the euphoria and optimism that pervades postrevolutionary societies, as we saw in the case of the rhetoric that followed the Young Turk Revolution in 1908. Unfortunately, the political realities often fail to live up to the promise of such stirring oratory, which aims to transcend boundaries of ethnicity and religion to consecrate a new era and create a new citizenry that will live on equal terms in a free, democratic, constitutional republic. In the wake of both the Young Turk Revolution and the Egyptian Revolution, continued tensions between Christians and Muslims quickly became part of the postrevolutionary political milieu.

The self-immolation of the Libyan peddler Mohammad Bouazizi on December 17, 2010, became a catalyst for the Arab Spring, which led to the collapse of authoritarian regimes in Egypt, Libya, Tunisia, and Yemen. Although some regimes, like Syria's, are caught in a disfigured "revolutionary process" that claims hundreds of lives on a daily basis, other regimes, like Jordan's and Morocco's, contained the opposition by initiating reforms, cabinet changes, and greater freedom of speech.

Since the turmoil that began in 2010 continues to play out in the Middle East, it is premature to evaluate the outcomes of the Arab Spring. One of the most popular analyses of these events, however, ascribes the "success" of these revolutions to social media's ability to accelerate the pace of revolution by mobilizing thousands of people through virtual, real-time social networks. It is undeniable that modern technology has played an important role in the Arab Spring, but it would be a fallacy to represent them as the primary factor. Such revolutions are not a new phenomenon in the annals of Middle Eastern history.

More than a century ago, Middle Eastern societies witnessed a similar cycle of uprisings against autocratic regimes in the Ottoman Empire's Young Turk Revolution of 1908 and Iran's Constitutional Revolution of 1905–1911. In a political process that informs events in today's Middle East, these societies began a rudimentary process of democratization by establishing some of the crucial institutions for democracy, including constitutions and parliaments.

The vibrant discourse about justice, legality, constitutionalism, freedom, equality, and fraternity that currently is shaping postrevolutionary societies in the Arab world can be traced back to the 1908 Revolution. Despite having the same lexicon, however, there are some major differences in the discourses of these two historical periods. Whereas revolutionary movements against authoritarian regimes are now taking place within postcolonial nation-states, the Revolution of 1908 took place in an imperial framework. The Revolution seemed to be the last effort of a politically dominant group to preserve the territorial integrity of the Ottoman Empire. This group, the Young Turks as represented by the CUP, was influenced by European ideas of progress, biological materialism, and positivism. As a result, the CUP believed that the application of scientific ideology derived from the ideals of the Enlightenment was the only way to save the Ottoman Empire from collapse. However, the CUP's uncritical adaptation, acceptance, and implementation of constitutionalism became counterproductive when they failed to forge a unified nation. Were they true constitutionalists? Did they really believe that through Parliament and mass politics the Ottoman Empire was going to be able to encounter the epidemics of nationalism? Did they really believe that the different nondominant groups in the empire could be part of a new society à la America's? Were the policies that they pursued after the Revolution the most rational ones given the time, context, and "unrealistic" demands of the disgruntled nondominant groups?

The Revolution and its impact on the nondominant groups within the empire were complex, resulting in microrevolutions among the Armenians and Jews against their own ancien régimes. The Revolution also, however, created new obstacles and problems. The postrevolutionary period was rife with deep, intraethnic tensions among Armenians, Arabs, and Jews, as well as between religious and secular forces, raising serious questions about representation and citizenship. For the Armenians, the Revolution meant a long-awaited end to the lingering injustices that afflicted them in the eastern provinces. They soon realized, however, that the new government was unwilling to find a just solution to these problems. The Adana massacres of 1909 became a turning point during which most Armenians lost their confidence in the Revolution and its architect, the CUP. The Zionists were similarly disappointed: for them, the Revolution was a source of hope that their national project of establishing a Jewish homeland in Palestine would be realized once and for all. Like the Armenians, however, the Zionists soon realized that the CUP was not willing to tolerate such decentralizing projects. In the case of the Anatolian and Arab provinces, the Revolution led to the erosion of social and political stability by disrupting a finely tuned balance that had governed the region for decades. The erosion of stability in the Anatolian provinces had serious implications on future developments in the region, the earliest manifestation of which were the Adana massacres.

By discussing the interplay among nondominant groups from a variety of ethnic backgrounds and regions, I have illustrated that even on the eve of the Revolution, the movement's ideals and principles were ambiguous, not only to its originators, the Young Turks, but also to the other ethnic groups that immediately rushed to harvest the fruits of the Revolution, only to be disappointed. This ambiguity created major tensions throughout the empire. The euphoric feelings endemic to any major political transformations were themselves contradictory, since many ethnic and religious groups discovered that their common joy was based in mutually contradictory aspirations. The CUP, meanwhile, was ready to use any means necessary to preserve the territorial integrity of the Ottoman Empire. Constitutionalism and parliamentarianism, being the common regional and global trend of the time, was apparently the best available means to curb the power of the despotic Ottoman monarchy and save the shrinking empire from the clutches of the European powers. Once the constitutional regime was (re)established, the CUP nonetheless did not shy away from taking extralegal and extraconstitutional measures to preserve and strengthen its grip over the empire and its agitated nondominant groups.

But preserving an empire containing multiple ethnic groups and diverse religions at the beginning of the twentieth century proved to be a daunting task. The empire's nondominant groups, having initially viewed the Revolution as a new page in the formerly dark history of the empire and a chance to live as equal citizens, soon realized the difficulties of reconciling their ethnic identities with the Young Turks' version of Ottomanism. From the perspective of the Muslim masses, granting equal rights and freedoms to non-Muslim groups was a serious violation of both the şeriat and the Ottoman tradition through which they had governed those groups for centuries. In addition, the Young Turks were aware from the beginning that any ideological, political, and/or territorial concessions to the different ethnic groups would have dire consequences for them. Political decentralization, proportional representation, the protection of ethno-religious privileges, policies favoring the use of national languages, freedom, and liberal Ottomanism were the recipe for the dismemberment of the empire. Thus, even prior to the Revolution, these ideals were removed from the CUP's political program and replaced by centralization, universal representation, elimination of ethno-religious privileges, policies favoring the Ottoman Turkish language, restriction of freedom, and a more chauvinistic type of Ottomanism with a fervor for Turkification. This was the major source of contention between the dominant and nondominant groups, damaging the rudimentary democratic process and hampering cooperative political development.

The Young Turk Revolution opened a Pandora's box of ethnic issues that had been kept closed for decades by the Hamidian regime. When these issues became apparent as part of the postrevolutionary political landscape, the CUP was reluctant and/or unable to find a satisfactory remedy to them. Whereas Sultan Abdülhamid II had been able to deal with these problems through repression, the CUP had more difficulty justifying the use of force in an era of constitutionalism. Faced with a choice between maintaining political progressivism and maintaining the empire, however, the CUP gradually hijacked first the legal system and then the executive branch to protect its vital interests. In extreme cases, it resorted to the use of violence to clamp down on opposition groups, including the Liberals, Armenians, Arabs, Albanians, and Greeks. Thus, the CUP's policies toward disgruntled, nondominant groups became one of the factors that prevented a truly democratic process from flourishing in the region during the first decade of the twentieth century.

A year after the Adana massacres, Adom (Harutyun Shahrigian), one of the most important Dashnak intellectuals, wrote a book, *Mer Hawatamk'ĕ Azgayin Harts'in Masin* (Our creed with regard to the national question), in which he severely criticized the Young Turks' policies for handling the postrevolutionary turmoil. In the book's conclusion, Adom explained the Armenian vision of Ottomanism, saying that it was "greater, more sublime, and more perfect than the one comprehended and yearned for by the narrow[-minded], chauvinist Turkish intellectuals." Adom contended that "Ottomanism is not a nationality and does not have an ethnic or ethnographic component; rather, it has a territorial- and state-related [*erkrayin ew pedakan*] definition." For him, Ottomanism is "the collective union of the individual citizens." In his tone, Adom also explicitly despised the CUP's Turkification policies and predicted their down-fall, asserting that even through legal and political pressure, national collective units cannot be fully assimilated, dissolved, or eliminated. For him, "even massacres cannot achieve that aim." Adom predicted that the empire would be saved and the constitution strengthened only through the cooperation of its national groups.[2]

Adom's stance against the Young Turks' vision of Ottomanism was not restricted to the Armenians but extended to the Arabs, Albanians, Greeks, and Zionists, all of whom recognized the gradual metamorphosis of the CUP's policies. That metamorphosis can be explained both as a reactionary movement against the rising tide of ethnic nationalism and agitations by different ethnic groups and as a direct attempt by the CUP to strengthen its grip over the empire. Indeed, on the eve of World War I, the CUP began implementing its most radical version of nationalism: the homogenization of Anatolia, which was transformed from a multicultural society of Armenians, Kurds, Assyrians, and Greeks into the heartland of Turkish nationalism. This transition, influenced by social Darwinism, was implemented through social engineering. The Armenian genocide became the most successful and extreme manifestation of this homogenization process.[3]

The revolutionary dreams of the empire's nondominant groups were shattered not only by the CUP's authoritarian tendencies but also by the contradictory dynamics that highlighted the revolutionary and postrevolutionary political processes. The incompatibility of their dreams with those of the CUP and the asymmetries of power that defined their relationship with the Young Turks ensured these disappointments. From their weak position as nondominant groups, they attempted to pressure the CUP into implementing long-awaited reforms and pushed for decentralization. Once they realized that the democratic process and their political visions had been aborted, these groups resorted to mobilizing international powers to exert pressure on the Ottoman government, a kind of interference that the CUP had despised from the day of its inception. In the end, the revolutionary dreams of all the empire's political and national groups were shattered because, in an era of rising nationalism and increased global communication, the Ottoman Empire, like many others, fell victim to the rise of nation-states.

REFERENCE MATTER

NOTES

Introduction

1. *Al-Muqaṭṭam*, August 31, 1908, no. 5906, 4. *Al-Muqaṭṭam*, which was published in Cairo by Yaʿqub Sarruf, Faris Nimr, and Bishara Taqla, maintained an identification with the British policy in the empire. Others argue that it was financed by the British. The newspaper had a circulation of five thousand. See Ami Ayalon, *Language and Change in the Arab Middle East: The Evolution of Modern Arabic Political Discourse* (New York: Oxford University Press, 1987), 177.

2. *Al-Muqaṭṭam*, September 1, 1908, no. 5907, 4.

3. Ibid., August 31, 1908, no. 5906, 4.

4. See Charles Kurzman, *Democracy Denied, 1905–1915: Intellectuals and the Fate of Democracy* (Cambridge, MA: Harvard University Press, 2008).

5. Nader Sohrabi, *Revolution and Constitutionalism in the Ottoman Empire and Iran* (New York: Cambridge University Press, 2011), 6.

6. Elizabeth Thompson, *Justice Interrupted: The Struggle for Constitutional Government in the Middle East* (Cambridge, MA: Harvard University Press, 2013).

7. For a critique of ethnic nationalism, see James L. Gelvin, *Divided Loyalties: Nationalism and Mass Politics in Syria at the Close of Empire* (Berkeley: University of California Press, 1998), 4–22; Hasan Kayalı, *Arabs and Young Turks: Ottomanism, Arabism, and Islamism in the Ottoman Empire, 1908–1918* (Berkeley: University of California Press, 1997), 1–16; Keith David Watenpaugh, *Being Modern in the Middle East: Revolution, Nationalism, Colonialism, and the Arab Middle Class* (Princeton, NJ: Princeton University Press, 2006), 55–61.

8. According to Michael Ignatieff, civic nationalism maintains that "the nation should be composed of all those—regardless of race, colour, creed, gender, language or ethnicity—who subscribe to the nation's political creed." For him this type of nationalism sees the nation "as a community of equal, rights-bearing, citizens, united in a patriotic attachment to a shared set of political practices and values." See Michael Ignatieff, *Blood and Belonging: Journeys into the New Nationalism* (New York: Farrar, Straus and Giroux, 1994), 6.

9. Sohrabi, *Revolution and Constitutionalism in the Ottoman Empire and Iran*, 26.

10. Aviel Roshwald, *Ethnic Nationalism and the Fall of Empires: Central Europe, the Middle East and Russia, 1914–23* (London: Routledge, 2001), 6.

11. Bent D. Jørgenson, "Ethnic Boundaries and the Margins of the Margin in a Post-colonial and Conflict Resolution Perspective," *Peace and Conflict Studies* 4 (1997), http://www.gmu.edu/programs/icar/pcs/jorgens.html.

12. Fredrik Barth, *Ethnic Groups and Boundaries: The Social Organization of Culture Difference* (Prospect Heights, IL: Waveland Press, 1998), 10.

13. Recent articles gathered in a volume edited by François Georgeon provide innovative research on the Young Turk Revolution. See François Georgeon, ed., *"L'ivresse de la liberté": La Révolution de 1908 dans l'Empire ottoman* (Paris: Peeters, 2012). In addition to the classical work of Şükrü Hanioğlu, *Preparation for a Revolution: The Young Turks, 1902–1908* (New York: Oxford University Press, 2001), and *The Young Turks in Opposition* (New York: Oxford University Press, 1995), see the pathbreaking book of Nader Sohrabi, *Revolution and Constitutionalism in the Ottoman Empire and Iran*. For the latest case study of the impact of the Revolution on the region of Palestine, see Yuval Ben-Bassat and Eyal Ginio, eds., *Late Ottoman Palestine: The Period of Young Turk Rule* (London: I. B. Tauris, 2011). On the same region, see Michelle Campos, *Ottoman Brothers: Muslims, Christians, and Jews in Early Twentieth-Century Palestine* (Stanford, CA: Stanford University Press, 2011); and Abigail Jacobson, *From Empire to Empire: Jerusalem between Ottoman and British Rule* (Syracuse, NY: Syracuse University Press, 2011). For other recent contributions, see Janet Klein, *The Margins of Empire: Kurdish Militias in the Ottoman Tribal Zone* (Stanford, CA: Stanford University Press, 2011); and Doğan Çetinkaya, *The Young Turks and the Boycott Movement: Nationalism, Protest, and the Working Classes in the Formation of Modern Turkey* (London: I. B. Tauris, 2013). On the region of Macedonia, see İpek Yosmaoğlu, *Blood Ties: Religion, Violence, and the Politics of Nationhood in Ottoman Macedonia, 1878–1908* (Ithaca, NY: Cornell University Press, 2013); Julia Phillips Cohen, *Becoming Ottomans: Sephardi Jews and Imperial Citizenship in the Modern Era* (New York: Oxford University Press, 2013); Dikran Mesrob Kaligian, *Armenian Organization and Ideology under Ottoman Rule 1908–1914* (New Brunswick, NJ: Transaction Publishers, 2009); Rashid Khalidi, *Palestinian Identity: The Construction of Modern National Consciousness* (New York: Columbia University Press, 1997); Watenpaugh, *Being Modern in the Middle East*; and Kayalı, *Arabs and Young Turks*.

14. For two excellent comparative studies of the three empires, see Roshwald, *Ethnic Nationalism and the Fall of Empires*; and Karen Barkey and Mark Von Hagen, *After Empire: Multiethnic Societies and Nation-Building: The Soviet Union and the Russian, Ottoman, and Habsburg Empires* (Boulder, CO: Westview Press, 1997).

15. M. Şükrü Hanioğlu, *A Brief History of the Late Ottoman Empire* (Princeton, NJ: Princeton University Press, 2008), 72–108.

16. Kemal H. Karpat, "Millets and Nationality: The Roots of the Incongruity of Nation and State in the Post-Ottoman Era," in *Christians and Jews in the Ottoman Empire: The Functioning of a Plural Society*, ed. Benjamin Braude and Bernard Lewis (New York: Holmes and Meier, 1982), 1:162–163.

17. On the reform period, see Roderic H. Davison, *Reform in the Ottoman Empire, 1856–1876* (Princeton, NJ: Princeton University Press, 1963); Moshe Ma'oz, *Ottoman Reform in Syria and Palestine, 1840–1861: The Impact of the Tanzimat on Politics and Society*

(Oxford: Clarendon Press, 1968); Selim Deringil, *The Well-Protected Domains: Ideology and the Legitimation of Power in the Ottoman Empire, 1876–1909* (London: I. B. Tauris, 1998); Selçuk Akşin Somel, *The Modernization of Public Education in the Ottoman Empire, 1839–1908: Islamization, Autocracy, and Discipline* (Leiden, Netherlands: Brill, 2001); Kemal H. Karpat, *The Politicization of Islam: Reconstructing Identity, State, Faith, and Community in the Late Ottoman State* (New York: Oxford University Press, 2001); Benjamin C. Fortna, *The Imperial Classroom: Islam, the State, and Education in the Late Ottoman Empire* (Oxford: Oxford University Press, 2002); Itzchak Weismann and Fruma Zachs, eds., *Ottoman Reform and Muslim Regeneration* (London: I. B. Tauris, 2005).

18. On the Young Ottomans, see Şerif Mardin, *The Genesis of Young Ottoman Thought: A Study in the Modernization of Turkish Political Ideas* (Syracuse, NY: Syracuse University Press, 2000); and Nazan Çiçek, *The Young Ottomans: Turkish Critics of the Eastern Question in the Late Nineteenth Century* (London: I. B. Tauris, 2010).

19. See Robert Devereux, *The First Ottoman Constitutional Period: A Study of the Midhat Constitution and Parliament* (Baltimore: Johns Hopkins University Press, 1963). For a new analysis of the period, see Aylin Koçunyan, "Negotiating the Ottoman Constitution 1856–1876" (PhD diss., European University Institute, Florence, 2013).

20. On Sultan Abdülhamid, see François Georgeon, *Abdülhamid II: Le sultan calife (1876–1909)* (Paris: Fayard, 2003).

21. Hanioğlu, *Young Turks in Opposition*, 200–212; and idem, "Blueprints for Future Society: Late Ottoman Materialists on Science, Religion, and Art," in *Late Ottoman Society: The Intellectual Legacy*, ed. Elisabeth Özdalga (London: Routledge, Curzon, 2005), 27–116.

22. The bibliography on the Young Turks is extensive; I will mention only the most important studies here: Georgeon, *"L'ivresse de la liberté"*; Sohrabi, *Revolution and Constitutionalism in the Ottoman Empire and Iran*; Hanioğlu, *Preparation for a Revolution*; idem, *Young Turks in Opposition*; Aykut Kansu, *Revolution of 1908 in Turkey* (Leiden, Netherlands: Brill, 1997); idem, *Politics in Post-revolutionary Turkey, 1908–1913* (Boston: Brill, 2000); Erik Jan Zürcher, *Unionist Factor: The Role of the Committee of Union and Progress in the Turkish National Movement, 1905–1926* (Leiden, Netherlands: Brill, 1984); Feroz Ahmad, *The Young Turks: The Committee of Union and Progress in Turkish Politics, 1908–1914* (Oxford: Clarendon Press, 1969); M. Naim Turfan, *Rise of the Young Turks: Politics, the Military and Ottoman Collapse* (London: I. B. Tauris, 2000); and Çetinkaya, *Young Turks and the Boycott Movement*

23. For general information about these transformations, see Razmik Panossian, *The Armenians: From Kings and Priests to Merchants and Commissars* (New York: Columbia University Press, 2006), 128–223.

24. Benjamin Braude, "Foundation Myths of the *Millet* System," in Braude and Lewis, *Christians and Jews in the Ottoman Empire*, 1:69–88; Karpat, "Millets and Nationality," 142.

25. See Biwzand Kʻechʻean, *Patmutʻiwn S. Pʻrkchʻi Hiwandanotsʻin Hayotsʻ i K. Polis* (Istanbul: G. Pagtatlian Press, 1887), 49. For an English study on the Amiras, see Hagop L. Barsumian, "The Armenian Amira Class of Istanbul" (PhD diss., Columbia Uni-

versity, 1908). See also Pascal Carmont, *The Amiras: Lords of Ottoman Armenia*, trans. Marika Blandin (London: Gomidas Institute, 2012).

26. Arab notables were large landowner families in the Arab provinces.

27. See Arshak Alpōyachean, "Azgayin Sahmanadrut'iwně ir Dzagumě ew Kira-rut'iwně," in *Ĕndartsak Ōrats'uyts' Surb P'rkich' Hivandanots'i* (Istanbul: H. Madteosian Press, 1910); Vartan Artinian, *The Armenian Constitution System in the Ottoman Empire 1893–1963: A Study of Its Historical Development* (Istanbul: n.p., 1988).

28. At the end of the eighteenth century, there were about sixty-five Armenian artisans (*esnafs*) in Istanbul. For more information about the Armenian *esnafs*, see Hayk Ghazaryan, *Arewmtahayeri Sots'ial-Tntesakan ew K'aghak'agan Kats'utiwně 1800–1870 t't'* (Yerevan: Haykakan SSH Gitutyunneri Akademiayi Hratkch, 1967), 293–301. On Armenian merchant networks in the Ottoman Empire, see Bedross Der Matossian, "The Armenian Commercial Houses and Merchant Networks in the 19th Century Ottoman Empire," *Turcica* 39 (2007): 147–174.

29. For the French influence on the Armenian intelligentsia, see James Etmekjian, *The French Influence on the Western Armenian Renaissance* (New York: Twayne Publishing, 1964).

30. For the role of the Armenians in the Ottoman bureaucracy in the nineteenth century, see Harut'iwn Mrmērian, *Hin Ōrer u Ayd Ōreru Hay Medzatuneře, 1550–1870* (Venice: St. Lazzaros Press, 1901); Kevkork Pamukjian, *Zamanlar, Mekanlar, Insanlar* (Istanbul: Aras Publication, 2003); Carter Findley, "The Acid Test of Ottomanism: The Acceptance of Non-Muslims in the Late Ottoman Bureaucracy," in Braude and Lewis, *Christians and Jews in the Ottoman Empire*, 1:339–368.

31. *Azgayin Sahmanadrut'iwn Hayots'-Nizamnamēi millēt'i Ērmēnean* (Istanbul: n.p., 1863).

32. See Masayuki Ueno, "'For the Fatherland and the State': Armenians Negotiate the Tanzimat Reforms," *International Journal of Middle East Studies* 45, no. 1 (February 2013): 93–109.

33. Such important newspapers were *Awetaber* (Bearer of good news; 1855–1915), *Meghu* (Bee; 1856–1874), and *Massis* (named after the mountain Ararat; 1852–1908), which played a dominant role in the political discourse of the period.

34. Amalya Kirakosean, *Hay Parberakan Mamuli Matenagrut'iwn, 1794–1967: Ha-mahavak' Ts'ank* (Yerevan: Al. Myasnikyan Public Library, 1970), 480–482.

35. The Mekhitarist Congregation (founded in 1717 and headquartered in Venice and Vienna) played an instrumental role through their press in the Armenian cultural renaissance in the nineteenth century.

36. On Armenians during the First Constitutional Period, see Elke Hartmann, "The 'Loyal Nation' and Its Deputies: The Armenians in the First Ottoman Parliament," in *The First Ottoman Experiment in Democracy*, ed. Christoph Herzog and Malek Sharif (Würzburg, Germany: Ergon in Kommission, 2010).

37. Article 16 of the Treaty of San Stefano (1878) dealt with the Armenians' requiring the Ottoman Empire to implement reforms in the Armenian provinces. These reforms were going to be guaranteed by Russia. See Kh. H. Badalyan, *"Haykakan harts'ě" San-*

Stefanoyi Paymanagrum ev Beṛlini Kongresum, 1878 T' (Yerevan: Erevani Hamalsarani hratarakch'ut'yun, 1955).

38. Osman Nuri, *Abdülhamid-ı Sani ve Devr-i Saltanatı: Hayat-ı Hususiye ve Siyasi-yesi* (1327; repr., Istanbul: Kitabhane-i İslam ve Askeri-Ibrahim Hilmi, 1911), 3:1064.

39. See Richard G. Hovannisian, "The Historical Dimensions of the *Armenian Question, 1878–1923*," in *The Armenian Genocide in Perspective*, ed. Richard G. Hovannisian (New Brunswick, NJ: Transaction Books, 1986), 19–41.

40. Karpat, *Politicization of Islam*, 97; and idem, *Ottoman Population, 1830–1914: Demographic and Social Characteristics* (Madison: University of Wisconsin Press, 1985).

41. See Stephan Astourian, "Silence of the Land: Agrarian Relations, Ethnicity, and Power," in *A Question of Genocide: Armenians and Turks at the End of the Ottoman Empire*, ed. Ronald Grigor Suny, Fatma Müge Göçek, and Norman M. Naimark (Oxford: Oxford University Press, 2011), 55–81.

42. For more information on these and other incidents, see Karō Sasuni, *K'iwrd Azgayin Sharzhumnerĕ ew Hay-K'rtakan Haraberut'iwnnerĕ, 15 Darēn Minchew mer Ōrerĕ* (Beirut: Hamazkayin Publications, 1969), 162–169. For the acts of Mher-Ali, the leader of Hamidiye Kurdish Battalion, in Sivas, see Chahen, "Hamid and Hamidies," *Armenia* 2, no. 7 (April 1906): 33–38. On Armeno-Kurdish relations, see Tessa Hoffman and Gerayer Koutcharian, "The History of Armenian-Kurdish Relations in the Ottoman Empire," *Armenian Review* 39, no. 4 (Winter 1986): 1–45; Janet Klein, "Conflict and Collaboration: Rethinking Kurdish-Armenian Relations in the Hamidian Period (1876–1909)," *International Journal of Turkish Studies* 13, nos. 1–2 (July 2007): 153–166; Garabed K. Moumdjian, "Armenian Kurdish Relations in the Era of Kurdish Nationalism (1830–1930)," *Bazmawēp* 157, nos. 1–4 (1999): 268–347.

43. See the platform of the Armenakan Party in L. Achemean, *Husher Armenak Ekareani 1870–1925* (Cairo: Nor Astgh Press, 1947), 81–86. For more information about the activities of the Armenakan Party, see Artak Darbinean, *Hay Azatagrakan Sharzhman Ōrerēn: Husher 1890ēn 1940* (Paris: Publication of the Armenian National Fund, 1947).

44. On the platform of the party, see "Sōts'ialistakan Dēmokratakan Hnch'akean Kusakts'ut'iwn," in *Tsragir Hnch'akean Kusakts'ut'ean*, 3d ed. (London: Hunchak Press, 1897). For information about the party, see Anahit Ter Minassian, *Nationalism and Socialism in the Armenian Revolutionary Movement* (Cambridge, MA: Zoryan Institute, 1984); and idem, "The Role of the Armenian Community in the Foundation and Development of the Socialist Movement in the Ottoman Empire and Turkey, 1876–1923," in *Socialism and Nationalism in the Ottoman Empire 1876–1923*, ed. Mete Tunçay and Erik Jan Zürcher (London: I. B. Tauris, 1994, in association with the International Institute of Social History, Amsterdam), 109–156.

45. Louis Nalbandian, *The Armenian Revolutionary Movement* (Berkeley: University of California Press, 1963), 108.

46. Manuk G. Chizmēchean, *Patmut'iwn Amerikahay K'aghak'akan Kusakts'ut'eants': 1890–1925* (Fresno, CA: Tpagrut'iwn Nor Ōr-i, 1930), 50–70.

47. *Droshak* was founded in Tbilisi in 1890. After the czarist persecution it moved to Geneva.

48. T'rk'ayastan or Tachkahayastan referred to western (Ottoman) Armenia and was composed of the six vilayets (*vilâyat-ı sitte*) of Erzurum, Van, Bitlis, Diyarbekir, Mamuretülaziz, and Sivas.

49. *Droshak*, August 1894, no. 10, 1–4; and September 1894, no. 11, 1–4.

50. Kum Kapu is the district in which the Armenian Patriarchate is located. The Hunchak Party's pamphlet on the occasion of the Kum Kapu demonstration on July 27, 1890, appears in Hrach' Tasnapetean, *Niwt'er H. H. Dashnakts'ut'ean Patmut'ean Hamar* (Beirut: Publications of the Armenian Revolutionary Federation, Hamskaïne Library, 1984), 1:140–141. On the demonstration, see Nalbandian, *The Armenian Revolutionary Movement*, 118–120.

51. As a result, more than two hundred Armenians were arrested and sent to Angora to be tried. On the Angora trials, see letters and memorandums nos. 97–286, in Correspondence relating to the Asiatic Province of Turkey 1892–93, Turkey No. 3, 1896, presented to both Houses of Parliament by command of Her Majesty, May 1896.

52. The Hamidiye Regiments, also known as the Hamidiye Light Cavalry Regiments (Hamidiye Hafif Süvari Alayları) were created by Sultan Abdülhamid II as irregular militia composed of select Kurdish tribes ordered to protect the empire's eastern border from Russian incursions, suppress Armenian activities, and bring the region into the Ottoman fold. See Klein, *The Margins of Empire*, 1–94.

53. For the answer given to the Sublime Porte on June 3, 1895, see Gabriël Lazean, *Hayastan ew Hay Datě ěst Dashnagreru* (Cairo: Houssaper Press, 1946), 60–61. Sublime Porte is a metonym for the central government of the Ottoman Empire.

54. See the special issue on the Hamidian massacres: Ronald Grigor Suny, ed., *Armenian Review* 47, nos. 1–2 (Summer 2002). Klein provides a very detailed account of the seizure of the Armenian lands in *The Margins of Empire*, 136–152.

55. On the seizure of the bank, see Armēn Karō, *Apruats Ōrer* (Boston: Hayrenik Press, 1948). The book has been translated into English: Armen Garo, *Bank Ottoman: Memoirs of Armen Garo* (Detroit, MI: A. Topouzian, 1990). On the assassination attempt, see Tasnapetean, *Niwt'er H. H. Dashnakts'ut'ean Patmut'ean Hamar*, 1:173. For detailed information regarding the mission, including its methods, alternative plans, tactical information, and type of explosives used, see "Official Report of the Demonstrative Body to the Fourth Congress," in Tasnapetean, *Niwt'er H. H. Dashnakts'ut'ean Patmut'ean Hamar*, 4:194–223.

56. Şeyh-ül İslam was the highest post in the religious establishment of the Ottoman Empire to which a member of the Islamic cleric (*ulema*) class could aspire.

57. *Şura-yı Ümmet*, published in Cairo and Paris from 1902 to 1908, was the main political journal of the Committee of Union and Progress.

58. *Şura-yı Ümmet*, August 16, 1905, no. 80, 1; and September 30, 1905, no. 83, 1–2. For the reaction of the Armenian press, see *Droshak*, August 1905, no. 8 (161), 113; *Armenia* 2, no. 10 (August 1906): 47; *Droshak*, August 1905, no. 8 (161), 1; *Armenia* 1, no. 12 (September 1905): 9; and *Armenia* 2, nos. 2–3 (November–December 1905): 70–71.

59. On relations before and after the Revolution, see Kaligian, *Armenian Organization and Ideology under Ottoman Rule*; A. Asdvadzadrian, "It't'ihat-Dashnakts'akan

Haraberut'iwnnerĕ," *Hayrenik Amsakir* 42, no. 2 (1964): 69–80; idem, "It't'ihat-Dashnakts'akan Haraberut'iwnnerĕ, II," *Hayrenik Amsakir* 43, no. 1 (1965): 68–71; Arsen Avagyan and Gaidz F. Minassian, *Ermeniler ve İttihat ve Terakki: İşbirliğinden Çatışmaya* (Istanbul: Aras Yayıncılık, 2005); Garabed K. Moumdjian, "Struggling for a Constitutional Regime: Armenian–Young Turk Relations in the Era of Abdulhamid II, 1895–1909" (PhD diss., University of California, Los Angeles, 2012). In his major work on the history of the Young Turks, Hanioğlu also provides ample information on the relationship of the Armenians with the Young Turks prior to the 1908 Revolution: Hanioğlu, *Preparation for a Revolution*, 95–104, 191–194. See also Houri Berberian, "Connected Revolutions: Armenians and the Russian, Ottoman, and Iranian Revolutions in the Early Twentieth Century," in Georgeon, *"L'ivresse de la liberté,"* 487–510.

60. For a thorough analysis, see Hanioğlu, *Young Turks in Opposition*, 173–199.

61. The organizers of the First Congress of Ottoman Liberals, the two sons of Mahmud Damad Paşa, Prince Sabahaddin and Prince Lutfallah, had sent invitations to the Reformed (Verakazmyal) Hunchakian Party, to the editors of the Armenian Revolutionary Federation organ *Droshak*, and to the editors of the newspaper *Hunch'ak*. Whereas the Hunchaks did not answer the invitation, the editors of *Droshak* and the central committee of the Reformed Hunchakian Party each sent three delegates to participate in the congress. See *Droshak*, February 1902, no. 2 (122), 23.

62. For *Droshak's* reaction to the First Congress, see ibid., March 1902, no. 3 (123), 33–35.

63. For the Young Turks' criticism of the congresses and activities of the Armenian groups in Europe, see *Şura-yı Ümmet*, May 9, 1902, no. 3, 2–3; August 20, 1902, no. 10, 2; December 1, 1902, no. 17, 1; and August 29, 1904, no. 56, 2. For their criticism of Armenian revolutionary activities within the empire, see *Şura-yı Ümmet*, April 17, 1904, no. 51, 1; August 13, 1904, no. 57, 1–2; and September 30, 1905, no. 83, 2.

64. For ARF's calls for harmony and cooperation, see *Droshak*, October 1906, no. 10 (176), 146; November 1906, no. 11 (177), 161–163; February 1907, no. 2 (180), 19; and March 1907, no. 3 (181), 33–34.

65. The issue of cooperation with the other ethnic elements in the empire (Turks, Kurds, and Assyrians) arose in the 29th session of the congress and was raised once more during the 99th session on April 23, 1907. The minutes of the 99th session of the Fourth Congress appear in Tasnapetean, *Niwt'er H. H. Dashnakts'ut'ean Patmut'ean Hamar*, 3:247.

66. For the decision, see *Haytagir Ōsmanean Ēndimadir Dareru Kongrēin* (Geneva: Droshak Press, 1907).

67. For the activities in Erzurum, see *Droshak*, November 1906, no. 11 (177), 164–165. See also *Şura-yı Ümmet*, July 15, 1907, no. 118, 1; and September 1, 1907, nos. 120–121.

68. On the impact of the Tanzimat reforms on the Jews of the empire, see Daniel J. Schroeter, "The Changing Relationship between the Jews of the Arab Middle East and the Ottoman State in the Nineteenth Century," in *Jews, Turks, Ottomans: A Shared History, Fifteenth through the Twentieth Century*, ed. Avigdor Levy (Syracuse, NY: Syracuse University Press, 2002), 88–107.

69. For the earlier period in the empire's Jewish history, see Moise Franco, *Essai sur*

l'histoire des Israélites de l'Empire ottoman depuis les origines jusqu'à nos jours (Paris: Librairie A. Durlacher, 1897); Abraham Galanté, *Histoire des Juifs de Turquie*, 9 vols. (Istanbul: Isis, 1985); and Salomon Rosanes, *Divre yeme Yiśrael be-Torgamah: 'Al-pi Meḳorot Rishonim*, 6 vols. (Tel Aviv: Devir, 1930–1938).

70. There is debate concerning whether the Jewish community or the state appointed Abraham Levi. Avigdor Levy argues that Levi's appointment as chief rabbi represents the first official Ottoman attempt to improve and strengthen the Jewish position within the empire. Avigdor Levy, "Millet Politics: The Appointment of a Chief Rabbi in 1835," in *The Jews of the Ottoman Empire*, ed. Avigdor Levy (Princeton, NJ: Darwin Press, 1994), 425–438.

71. Aron Rodrigue, "The Beginning of Westernization and Community Reform among Istanbul's Jewry, 1854–65," in Levy, *Jews of the Ottoman Empire*, 439–456. See also Avigdor Levy, *The Sephardim in the Ottoman Empire* (Princeton, NJ: Darwin Press, 1992), 98–124.

72. See *Ḳonsoṭiṭusyon parah lah Nasyon Yiśra'elitah de lah Ṭurḳiyah* (Istanbul: Eṣtampari'ah del G'ornal Yiśra'elit, 1865).

73. On the history of the *Haskalah*, see Shmuel Feiner, *Haśkalah ye-Hiṣṭoryah: Toldoteha shel Hakarat-'Avar Yehudit Modernit* (Jerusalem: Zalman Shazar Center for the History of Israel, 1995).

74. The term "Jewish Eastern Question" was coined by Ludwig Phillipson in 1854. See *Allgemeine Zeitung des Judenthums*, March 27, 1854, no. 13, 151–155. On the ideological premises of the emergence of this perception, see Aron Rodrigue, *French Jews, Turkish Jews: The Alliance Israélite Universelle and the Politics of Jewish Schooling in Turkey, 1860–1925* (Bloomington: Indiana University Press, 1990), 8–17.

75. See Franco, *Essai sur l'histoire des Israélites de l'Empire ottoman*, 158–159; Jonathan Frankel, *The Damascus Affair: "Ritual Murder," Politics and the Jews in 1840* (New York: Cambridge University Press, 1997). See also Mary Wilson, "The Damascus Affair and the Beginning of France's Empire in the Middle East," in *Histories of the Modern Middle East: New Directions*, ed. Israel Gershoni, Hakan Erdem, and Ursula Woköck (Boulder, CO: Lynne Rienner Publishers, 2002).

76. Between 1835 and 1849, some eighteen Jewish newspapers were published. Between 1841 and 1846, their number rose to fifty-three, with thirteen in five European countries.

77. For the history of the Francos, see Abraham Galanté, *Histoire des Juifs d'Istanbul* (Istanbul: Impr. Husnutabiat, 1942), 2:223–226.

78. Ibid., 1:251.

79. Rodrigue, *French Jews, Turkish Jews*, 101–102.

80. For the election of the *meclis-i umumi*, see chapter 3 of the constitution, "Mode d'élection des membres du medjlis-I Oumoumi et leurs attributions," in *Documents officiels turcs concernant les Juifs de Turquie*, by Abraham Galanté (Istanbul: Haim, Rozio, 1931), 16–18.

81. The person would temporarily fulfill the duties of the chief rabbi until the election of a new one.

82. Galanté, *Histoire des Juifs d'Istanbul*, 1:258–259.

83. The two classical studies on the alliance are André Chouraqui, *Alliance Israélite Universelle et la renaissance juive contemporaine, 1860–1960: Cent ans d'histoire* (Paris: Presses Universitaires de France, 1965); and Aran Rodrigue, *Images of Sephardi and Eastern Jewries in Transition: The Teachers of the Alliance Israélite Universelle, 1860–1939* (Seattle: University of Washington Press, 1993). See also idem, *French Jews, Turkish Jews*; Esther Benbassa and Aron Rodrigue, "L'artisanat juif en Turquie à la fin du XIX siècle: L'Alliance israélite universelle et ses oeuvres d'apprentissage," *Turcica* 17 (1985): 113–126.

84. For the different projects, see Franco, *Essai sur l'histoire des Israélites de l'Empire ottoman*, 250–258.

85. Hasan Kayalı, "Jewish Representation in the Ottoman Parliaments," in Levy, *Jews of the Ottoman Empire*, 519–526.

86. M. Şükrü Hanioğlu, "Jews in the Young Turk Movement to the 1908 Revolution," in Levy, *Jews of the Ottoman Empire*, 507–511.

87. For a general history of Zionism, see Waltar Laqueur, *History of Zionism* (New York: Holt, Rinehart and Winston, 1972).

88. Not to be confused with the Jewish Eastern Question mentioned earlier, the Jewish Question referred to the expansive debate in European society in the nineteenth century about the appropriate status of the Jews within their societies. Thus, the idea was created by non-Jews to characterize the Jews as an "existing problem." For an in-depth analysis of the Jewish Question and its different usages by the Jews and the non-Jews alike, see Alex Bein, *The Jewish Question: Biography of a World Problem* (Rutherford, NJ: Fairleigh Dickinson University Press, 1990), 18–31.

89. Theodor Herzl, *Der Judenstaat: Versuch einer Modernen Lösung der Judenfrage* (Leipzig: M. Beitenstein, 1896).

90. Herzl's deal was that he would influence in a positive way European public opinion about the sultan's aggression against the Armenians in the eastern provinces in exchange for supporting the Zionist project in Palestine. See Raphael Patai, ed., *The Complete Diaries of Theodor Herzl* (New York: Herzl Press, 1960), 1:344–350, 370; Marwan R. Buheiry, "Theodor Herzl and the Armenian Question," *Journal of Palestine Studies* 7, no. 1 (Autumn 1977): 75–97.

91. The Jewish Colonial Trust was the first Zionist bank founded at the Second Zionist Congress in 1898 in Basel, Switzerland, as the financial instrument of the Zionist Organization for the realization of the Zionist goal in Palestine. For a contemporary source on the bank, see H. Fram, *The Jewish Colonial Trust (Juedische Colonial Bank), Limited: Its Importance and Possibilities* (Los Angeles: The Young Zionists' Association, 1905).

92. Heiko Haumann, ed., *The First Zionist Congress in 1897: Causes, Significance, Topicality* (New York: Karger, 1997), 22.

93. For more information about the importance of these two conflicts, see Khalidi, *Palestinian Identity*, 99–104. On land disputes, see Neville J. Mandel, *The Arabs and Zionism before World War I* (Berkeley: University of California Press, 1976). See also Yuval Ben-Bassat, *Petitioning the Sultan: Justice and Protest in Late Ottoman Palestine* (London: I. B. Tauris, 2013); and idem, "Rural Reactions to Zionist Activity in Palestine

before and after the Young Turk Revolution of 1908 as Reflected in Petitions to Istanbul," *Middle Eastern Studies* 49, no. 3 (Spring 2013): 349–364.

94. Khalidi, *Palestinian Identity*, 59.

95. See Alex Bein, *Toldot ha-Hityashvut ha-Tsiyonit mi-Tekufat Hertsl ye-'ad Yamenu* (Ramat Gan, Israel: Masadah Press, 1970), 47.

96. Sati' al-Husri indicates that the Tanzimat reforms were implemented in the Arab provinces in piecemeal fashion. They were first implemented in the provinces of Syria, Beirut, and Aleppo and later in Baghdad and Basra. He also asserts that centralization harmed the Arab provinces but did not have the same effect on non-Muslims. Sāti' al-Ḥuṣrī, *Al-Bilād al-'Arabīyah wa-al-Dawlah al-'Uthmānīyah* (Beirut: Dar al-Ilm lil-Malayin, 1960), 93–96.

97. See Moshe Ma'oz, "Changing Relations between Jews, Muslims, and Christians during the Nineteenth Century, with Special Reference to Ottoman Syria and Palestine," in Levy, *Jews, Turks, Ottomans*, 108–118.

98. Fruma Zachs, *The Making of Syrian Identity: Intellectuals and Merchants in Nineteenth Century Beirut* (Leiden, Netherlands: Brill, 2005), 88.

99. Leila Tarazi Fawaz, *An Occasion for War: Lebanon and Damascus in 1860* (Berkeley: University of California Press, 1995).

100. For more information about the life and work of the first governor of Lebanon, see Ep'rem Pōghosean, *Karapet Art'in P'asha Tawutean, Kusakal ew Ěndhanur Kaṛavarich' Libanani, 1816–1873: Keank'n ew gortsunēut'iwně* (Vienna: Mkhitarian Press, 1949). For the *mutasarrifiyyah* of Mount Lebanon, see Engin Deniz Akarlı, *The Long Peace: Ottoman Lebanon 1861–1920* (Berkeley: University of California Press, 1993), 78.

101. After the 1860 massacres, al-Bustani began publishing *Nafir Suriyyah* (Clarion of Syria), a weekly paper that called for the Syrian people to unite against the Ottoman regime. See Butrus Abu Manneh, "The Christians between Ottomanism and Syrian Nationalism: The Ideas of Butrus al-Bustani," *International Journal of Middle East Studies* 2 (1980): 287–304.

102. Albert Hourani, *Arabic Thought in the Liberal Age, 1798–1939* (Cambridge: Cambridge University Press, 1983), 107.

103. See Robert Haddad, *Syrian Christians in Muslim Society: An Interpretation* (Princeton, NJ: Princeton University Press, 1970).

104. *Al-Manār* 9, no. 12 (February 13, 1907): 951.

105. See Tufan S. Buzpinar, "Abdulhamid II, Islam and the Arabs: The Cases of Syria and the Hijaz, 1878–1882" (PhD diss., University of Manchester, 1991), 84–120.

106. Tawfiq Barrū, *Al-'Arab wa-al-Turk fi al-'Ahd al-Dustūrī al-'Uthmānī, 1908–1914* (Damascus: Talas Press, 1991), 34–36.

107. Engin Deniz Akarlı, "Abdülhamid II's Attempt to Integrate Arabs into the Ottoman System," in *Palestine in the Late Ottoman Period: Political, Social, and Economic Transformation*, ed. David Kushner (Jerusalem: Yad Izhak Ben-Zvi, 1986), 77.

108. Their role in the palace clique was also severely criticized by the most important Young Turk historian of the period. See Nuri, *Abdülhamid-i Sani ve Devr-i Saltanatı*, 537–563. See also *Şura-yı Ümmet*, October 10, 1904, no. 61, 2.

109. Philip S. Khoury, *Urban Notables and Arab Nationalism: The Politics of Damascus, 1860–1920* (Cambridge: Cambridge University Press, 2003), 35.

Chapter 1

1. *Levant Herald and Eastern Express*, July 27, 1908, 1. The *Levant Herald and Eastern Express*, a daily published in English and French, was established in 1856 in Istanbul.

2. *Biwzandion*, July 25, 1908, no. 3587, 2. *Biwzandion* (after the first name of the editor) was an afternoon Armenian daily edited by Puzant (Biwzand) Kechian and published in Istanbul (1896–1918). It had a circulation of seven to eight thousand.

3. Mr. G. Barclay to Sir Edward Grey (received July 27), Constantinople, July 26, 1908, in "Correspondence respecting the Constitutional Movement in Turkey, 1908," *Parliamentary Papers*, 1909, 13.

4. For a detailed list of all the dignitaries who attended the meeting, see *Biwzandion*, August 13, 1908, no. 3602, 3, and August 14, 1908, no. 3603, 2; *Arewelk'*, August 14, 1908, no. 6863, 2–3. *Arewelk'* (Orient) was an Armenian newspaper founded in Istanbul in 1884 by Arpiar Arpiarian in cooperation with other Armenian intellectuals. It was a national, political, and literary newspaper with democratic tendencies. A detailed account of the event also appeared in *İkdam*, August 14, 1908, no. 5108, 2. *İkdam* (Perseverance) was a daily newspaper founded by journalist Ahmed Cevdet in 1894. It lasted until 1928 and was one of the most widely read newspapers in Istanbul. After the Revolution *İkdam* became the newspaper of the Liberals and opposed the CUP. See also *Pro Armenia*, August 20, 1908, no. 188, 1. *Pro Armenia*, edited by Pierre Quillard (1864–1912) in 1900, was considered among the influential ARF newspapers in Europe; *Levant Herald and Eastern Express*, August 14, 1908, 1; *Tanin*, August 14, 1908, no. 14, 4. *Tanin* (Echo) was a daily political newspaper published after the Revolution that lasted until 1925. It was edited by Hüssein Cahid Yalçın and became the mouthpiece of the CUP.

5. For a complete biography of Patriarch Tourian, see T'orgom Gushakean, *Eghishē Patriark' Durean* (Jerusalem: Sts. James Press, 1932).

6. For the manifestations of the Revolution in the provinces based on the Ottoman press, see Kudret Emiroğlu, *Anadolu'da Devrim Günleri: II. Meşrutiyet'in İlanı, Temmuz-Ağustos* (Ankara: İmge Kitabevi, 1999).

7. On cultural history, see Peter Burke, *Varieties of Cultural History* (Ithaca, NY: Cornell University Press, 1997).

8. For a general review of the literature on parades and festivities and their relationship to the public sphere, see John L. Brooke, "Reason and Passion in the Public Sphere: Habermas and the Cultural Historians," *Journal of Interdisciplinary History* 29, no. 1 (Summer 1998): 43–67.

9. Susan G. Davis, *Parades and Power: Street Theatre in Nineteenth-Century Philadelphia* (Philadelphia: Temple University Press, 1986), 6.

10. The two major Ottoman periodicals of the period, *Tanin* (CUP) and *İkdam* (Liberals), did not often cover the issue of the revolutionary rituals; the Armenian, Arabic, Hebrew, and Ladino press provided extensive coverage of the festivities.

11. Simon Newman, *Parades and the Politics of the Street* (Philadelphia: University of Pennsylvania Press, 1997), 8.

12. David Kertzer, *Ritual, Politics, and Power* (New Haven, CT: Yale University Press, 1988), 153.

13. Mona Ozouf, *Festivals and the French Revolution* (Cambridge, MA: Harvard University Press, 1988), 22.

14. On the celebrations in Adana, see Hakop T'ērzean, *Atanayi Keankĕ* (Istanbul: Zareh Pērpērean Press, 1909), 33–35.

15. *Lisān al-Ḥāl*, August 19, 1908, no. 5793, 3. *Lisān al-Ḥāl* (Voice of the present), established by Khalil Sarkis in 1877, was published in Beirut. It is considered the most pro-CUP organ in the Arab provinces.

16. For detailed information about the event, see *Biwzandion*, August 20, 1908, no. 3608, 1; *Lisān al-Ḥāl*, August 19, 1908, no. 5793, 3; *Levant Herald and Eastern Express*, August 13, 1908, 2. On the manifestations of the constitution in Adana, see Emiroğlu, *Anadolu'da Devrim Günleri*, 188–193.

17. *Biwzandion*, September 5, 1908, no. 3621, 1; Sir G. Lowther to Sir Edward Grey (received August 10), Therapia, August 4, 1908, in *Parliamentary Papers*, 45. On the manifestations of the constitution in Van, see Emiroğlu, *Anadolu'da Devrim Günleri*, 207–212.

18. Most of the prisoners released after the Revolution of 1908 had been imprisoned by the ancien régime for their political beliefs and activities.

19. *Biwzandion*, September 26, 1908, no. 3639, 1. Mguerdich Khrimian, nicknamed "Hayrik" (father), was one of the most important figures of the Armenian literary and political revival in the nineteenth century. He was patriarch of Istanbul (1869–1873) and then became the catholicos of all Armenians (1892–1907).

20. *İkdam*, July, 28, 1908, no. 5091, 3.

21. The "Hamidiye March," which was in essence in opposition to the sultan, was composed by Dikran Tchouhadjian, an Armenian. Tchouhadjian, known as the "Offenbach of the East," is considered the first composer to apply harmony and Western musical standards to traditional Ottoman music. Founder of the Oriental Music Organization, Tchouhadjian composed the first Ottoman opera, *Arif's Ruse*. See "Tchouhadjian et l'opéra arménien" and "Tchouhadjian et l'Italie," in *Catalogue de l'exposition Roma-Armenia*, ed. Claude Mutafian (Vatican City: Bibliothèque apostolique du Vatican, 1999).

22. *Levant Herald and Eastern Express*, July 27, 1908, 1.

23. *El Tiempo*, August 7, 1908, no. 92, 1080. *El Tiempo* was a Ladino newspaper published in Istanbul during 1872–1930. During the Second Constitutional Period it was a pro-CUP, anti-Zionist newspaper. Under the editorship of David Fresco it supported Haim Nahum, chief rabbi of the Ottoman Empire.

24. *Levant Herald and Eastern Express*, August 5, 1908, 3.

25. *El Tiempo*, August 7, 1908, no. 92, 1080.

26. *Levant Herald and Eastern Express*, August 7, 1908, 1.

27. Along with Poseidon, Kramer Palace was one of the most famous hotels in Izmir. Today it is located near Republic Square and the Atatürk monument in Izmir.

28. *Arewelk‘*, August 7, 1908, no. 6857, 1.

29. M. Geoffroy, consular agent of France in Latakiyya, to M. Fouques-Duparc, consul general of France in Beirut, Latakiyya, August 12, 1908, in *Documents diplomatiques et consulaires relatifs à l'histoire du Liban et des pays du Proche-Orient du XVII° siècle à nos jours*, documents recueillis sous l'égide de Maurice Chéhab [par] Adel Ismail (Beirut: Editions des œuvres politiques et historiques, 1975).

30. *Lisān al-Ḥāl*, August 1, 1908, no. 5778, 1–2.

31. *Levant Herald and Eastern Express*, August 20, 1908, 1.

32. Ibid.

33. *Al-Muqaṭṭam*, August 6, 1908, no. 5885, 4.

34. *Levant Herald and Eastern Express*, August 20, 1908, 1.

35. Ibid., 2.

36. *Defterdar* is an Ottoman Turkish word meaning "the accountant general of the province."

37. *Al-Muqaṭṭam*, August 22, 1908, no. 5899, 3.

38. Ibid.

39. *Ha-Po'el ha-Tza'ir* 1, no. 10 (July 1908): 18. *Ha-Po'el ha-Tza'ir* (The young worker), published in Jaffa in 1907, was the organ of the Jewish political party Hapo'el Hatza'ir. This socialist-oriented party was founded in 1905 to provide a forum for the newly arriving workers of the Second Aliyah (1904–1914) who were settling in Palestine.

40. *Bedel-i askeri* (military exemption tax for non-Muslims) was a revamped version of the *cizye* adopted as part of the Tanzimat reforms in the nineteenth century. *El Tiempo*, August 21, 1908, no. 98, 1143.

41. *Kışla* was the winter barracks for the Ottoman soldiers. Today it is the main police station in the Old City of Jerusalem near the Armenian Quarter. *Arewelk‘*, August 26, 2006, no. 6873, 1; see also *Ha-Po'el ha-Tza'ir* 1, no. 10 (July 1908): 18.

42. *Habazeleth* (Lily), August 10, 1908, no. 74, 2. *Habazeleth* was a Hebrew newspaper published in Jerusalem in 1863. From 1870 to 1911 it was under the editorship of Israel Dov Frumkin. In its later years, the newspaper had distinctly Jerusalem-Hasidic orientation. See also *Levant Herald and Eastern Express*, August 14, 1908, 1.

43. David Kushner, *Moshel Hayiti bi-Yerushalayim: Ha-'Ir yeha-Maḥoz be-'Enay shel 'Ali Ekrem Bai: 1906–1908* (Jerusalem: Yad Yitsḥak Ben-Tsevi, 1995).

44. *Arewelk‘*, August 26, 2006, no. 6873, 1.

45. *Hashkafa*, August 10, 1908, no. 93, 2. *Hashkafa* (Outlook) was a periodical published in Jerusalem by Eliezer Ben-Yehuda between 1896 and 1908 (with an intermission in 1901). *Hashkafa* was connected to Ben-Yehuda's primary publication, *Ha-Zvi/Ha-Or* (1884–1914).

46. *Habazeleth*, August 10, 1908, no. 74, 2; *Ha-Po'el ha-Tza'ir* 1, no. 10 (July 1908): 18.

47. *El Tiempo*, August 21, 1908, no. 98, 1143.

48. *Hashkafa*, August 10, 1908, no. 93, 2.

49. *El Tiempo*, August 21, 1908, no. 98, 1144.

50. *Habazeleth*, August 10, 1908, no. 74, 2.

51. *Levant Herald and Eastern Express*, August 14, 1908, 1.

52. *El Tiempo*, August 21, 1908, no. 98, 1144.

53. *Arewelkʻ*, August 26, 1908, no. 6873, 1.

54. *Habazeleth*, August 7, 1908, no. 73, 3.

55. Ibid., August 17, 1908, no. 77, 2.

56. *Levant Herald and Eastern Express*, September 3, 1908, 2.

57. For a short biography of Izmirlian, see Simon Gapamachean, *Amenapatiw T. T. Mattʻēos S. Arkʻepiskopos Izmirlean, Bardzrashnorh T. Eghishē S. Arkʻepiskopos Durean: Kensagrutʻiwn* (Istanbul: Z. N. Berberian Press, 1908). On his banishment to Jerusalem, see 21–22.

58. *Habazeleth*, August 24, 1908, no. 80, 3.

59. See, for example, Rev. K. Aslanian to Archbishop Madteos Izmirlian (Istanbul, July 18, 1908), in M. Madenataran, Izmirlian Archives, file 13, doc. 403 (13); Rev. Boghos to Archbishop Madteos Izmirlian (Bethlehem, July 19, 1908), in ibid. (14); Rev. Karekin Khachadurian to Archbishop Madteos Izmirlian (Marash, July 31, 1908), in ibid. (22); Rev. Mesrob Naroyants to Archbishop Madteos Izmirlian (Armash, August 20, 1908), in ibid. (49). In Sandro Behbudian, ed., *Vaveragrer Hay Ekeghetsʻu Patmutʻyan: Girkʻ 8. Mattʻēos II Izmirlean Katʻoghikos Amenayn Hayotsʻ: 1872–1910tʻtʻ* (Yerevan: "Hayastan" Publications, 2001).

60. *Levant Herald and Eastern Express*, September 19, 1908, 1.

61. *Biwzandion*, August 27, 1908, no. 3614, 2.

62. *Habazeleth*, August 17, 1908, no. 77, 2.

63. In Armenian, "Azatutʻian vēh akhoyan-hawerzh Getsʻtsʻē Izmirlian."

64. In Ottoman Turkish, "Yaşasın Asker, Yaşasın Ordu, Yaşasın Izmirlian."

65. Edhem Eldem, *Pride and Privilege: A History of Ottoman Orders, Medals and Decorations* (Istanbul: Ottoman Bank and Archive Research Center, 2004), 368.

66. A canopy (Armenian, *ambhovani*) is a symbol exclusive to high-ranking incumbents, used during processions. It is a fairly large, square, silken canopy resting on four or six poles and held in a horizontal position over the head of the incumbent by four or six prominent persons in the church during a procession. In Izmirlian's case, three of the bearers were non-Christians, indicating the importance of the event and the attempt at a secularization of a sacred ritual.

67. *Biwzandion*, August 27, 1908, no. 3614, 2.

68. *Pro Armenia*, September 5, 1908, no. 189, 1350.

69. *Levant Herald and Eastern Express*, August 28, 1908, 2.

70. *Lisān al-Ḥāl*, August 8, 1908, no. 5784, 2–3; *Times*, September 11, 1908, no. 38749, 6. A large picture of him appeared also in the Hebrew newspaper *Ha-ʻOlam*, September 4, 1908, 464. *Ha-ʻOlam*, which began publication in 1907 and lasted until 1950, was the central organ of the World Zionist Organization established by Nahum Sokolow.

71. *Al-Muqaṭṭam*, August 22, 1908, no. 5899, 3. See also *Levant Herald and Eastern Express*, August 20, 1908, 2.

72. *Lisān al-Ḥāl*, August 7, 1908, no. 5783, 1; British consulate general, Beirut, to Sir G. Lowther, Constantinople, August 8, 1908, FO195/2277 [Foreign Office Archives]; *Arewelkʻ*, August 13, 1908, no. 6862, 2; Fakhrī Bārūdī, *Mudhakkirāt al-Bārūdī* (Damascus: Dar al-Haya Press, 1951), 65–66.

73. *Lisān al-Ḥāl*, August 7, 1908, no. 5783, 2; and August 8, 1908, no. 5784, 2.

74. For the image of Fuad Paşa's arrival in Istanbul, see *Resimli Kitab* (Illustrated book), September 1908, 30.

75. *İkdam*, August 13, 1908, no. 5107, 3.

76. Hanioğlu, *Young Turks in Opposition*, 142–166.

77. The slogan of Prince Sabahaddin, who represented the Liberals, was "decentralization and extension of responsibility/authority" (*adem-i merkeziyet ve tevsi-i mezuniyet*). See M. Sabahaddin, *Teşebbüs-i Şahsi ve Tevsi-i Mezuniyet Hakkında Bir İzah* (Istanbul: Cihan, 1324 [1908]); and idem, *Teşebbüs-i Şahsi ve Tevsi-i Mezuniyet Hakkında İkinci Bir İzah* (Istanbul: Mahmud Bey Matbaası, 1324 [1908]).

78. *Biwzandion*, September 5, 1908, no. 3621, 2. On the event itself, see *İkdam*, September 8, 1908, no. 5128, 1; *Arewelkʿ*, September 3, 1908, no. 6879, 2. Krikor Zohrab also wrote about the event in detail. See *Surhandak* (Courier), September 5, 1908, no. 72, 1; and September 9, 1908, no. 74, 1. *Surhandak* was a weekly founded in 1888 under the editorship of Diran Papazian as a continuation of the journal *Hunchʾak*. See also *El Tiempo*, September 4, 1908, no. 104, 1199–1200.

79. *Biwzandion*, September 1, 1908, no. 3617, 2.

80. For the image of the arrival of the relics of Mahumd Damad Paşa, see *Resimli Kitab*, September 1908, 30.

81. *El Tiempo*, September 4, 1908, no. 104, 1199.

82. For the full address, see *Arewelkʿ*, September 17, 1908, no. 6891, 3.

83. Ozouf, *Festivals and the French Revolution*, 129.

84. Ibid., 135–136. In many Armenian churches the dome rests on four independent pillars.

85. Esther Benbassa, *Ha-Yahadut ha-ʿOtʾmanit ben Hitmaʿarvut le-Tsiyonut, 1908–1920* (Jerusalem: Zalman Shaver Center for the History of Israel, 1996), 30.

86. The idea that real history begins with the act of mourning appeared for the first time in *Yerkir Nayiri*, written by Armenian poet Yeghishe Charents (1897–1937). For an intriguing critique, see Marc Nichanian, *Writers of Disaster: Armenian Literature in the Twentieth Century* (London: Taderon Press, by arrangement with the Gomidas Institute, 2002), 46.

87. *Biwzandion*, September 26, 1908, no. 3639, 1.

88. *Pro Armenia*, October 10, 1908, no. 91, 1369.

89. *Arewelkʿ*, August 29, 1908, no. 6876, 2. A note on the wreath read, "From the CUP of Jerusalem, a sacred memory for their oppressed and innocent Armenian compatriots who fell in the known incidents in Istanbul in 1896." These massacres immediately followed the Ottoman Bank seizure by ARF members on August 26, 1986. For the image of the procession heading to the Şişli Armenian cemetery, see *Resimli Kitab*, October 1908, 176.

90. *Arewelkʿ*, August 29, 1908, no. 6876, 2–3.

91. Clifford Geertz, "Centers, Kings, and Charisma: Reflections on the Symbolics of Power," in *Culture and Its Creators: Essays in Honor of Edward Shils*, ed. Joseph Ben-David and Terry Nichols Clark (Chicago: University of Chicago Press, 1977), 150–171.

92. Lynn Hunt, *Politics, Culture, and Class in the French Revolution* (Berkeley: University of California Press, 1984), 54.

93. Selim Deringil, *The Well-Protected Domains: Ideology and the Legitimation of Power in the Ottoman Empire, 1876–1909* (London: I. B. Tauris, 1998).

94. Kertzer, *Ritual, Politics, and Power*, 9–11.

95. See Roland Barthes, "Rhetoric of the Image," in *Image, Music, Text*, trans. Stephen Heath (New York: Hill and Wang, 1977), 32–51.

96. Kertzer, *Ritual, Politics, and Power*, 23–24.

97. Eldem, *Pride and Privilege*, 366.

98. See Nader Sohrabi, "Global Waves, Local Actors: What the Young Turks Knew about Other Revolutions and Why It Mattered," *Comparative Studies in Society and History* 44, no. 1 (2002): 45–79.

99. *Lisān al-Ḥāl*, July 30, 1908, no. 5776, 1.

100. *Habazeleth*, August 17, 1908, no. 77, 2; and August 10, 1908, no. 74, 2.

101. In Armenian, "Azatut'ean Datin Hamar Nahatakwats T'urk' ew Hay Ōsmants'i Eghpayrnerun Anmah Hishatakin 31 Hulis 1908." *Arewelk'*, August 14, 1908, no. 6863, 2; see also *İkdam*, August 14, 1908, no. 5108, 2.

102. *Levant Herald and Eastern Express*, August 20, 1908, 1.

103. Ottoman Turkish, Armenian, Arabic, French, and Greek were the languages most often used in the speeches we are considering.

104. *Biwzandion*, September 8, 1908, no. 3623, 2.

105. *Al-Muqaṭṭam*, September 1, 1908, no. 5907, 4.

106. In the original article the date is July 26, which seems to be a typo.

107. *Al-Muqaṭṭam*, July 29, 1908, no. 5878, 1. On the event, see also *İkdam*, September 9, 1908, no. 5134, 2. On the impact of the Revolution on Egypt, see *İkdam*, August 5, 1908, no. 5099, 3.

108. *Al-Muqaṭṭam*, July 29, 1908, no. 5878, 2.

109. Ibid., 4.

110. *Biwzandion*, August 27, 1908, no. 3614, 2.

111. Ibid., August 17, 1908, no. 3605, 3.

112. *İkdam*, August 14, 1908, no. 5108, 2. For a complete translation of Zohrab's speech that day, see *Arewelk'*, August 14, 1908, no. 6863, 2–3.

113. *Al-Muqaṭṭam*, August 22, 1908, no. 5899, 3.

Chapter 2

1. The first of these was Ami Ayalon's work on the development of the political lexicon in the Arab Middle East. See Ayalon, *Language and Change in the Arab Middle East: The Evolution of Modern Arabic Political Discourse* (New York: Oxford University Press, 1987); Ofra Bengio, *Saddam's Word: Political Discourse in Iraq* (New York: Oxford University Press, 1998). The only work that covers the political discourse of the Second Constitutional Period to any extent is Palmira Brumett's work on cartoons during the period: *Image and Imperialism in the Ottoman Revolutionary Press, 1908–1911* (Albany: State University of New York Press, 2000).

2. A primary contributor to the proliferation of these discussions was the advancement of the education system during the Hamidian period. See Benjamin C. Fortna, *Imperial Classroom: Islam, the State, and Education in the Late Ottoman Empire* (New York: Oxford University Press, 2002).

3. See Roger Chartier, *The Cultural Use of Print in Early Modern France* (Princeton, NJ: Princeton University Press, 1989); idem, *The Cultural Origins of the French Revolution* (Durham, NC: Duke University Press, 1991); idem, *Culture of Print: Power and the Uses of Print in Early Modern Europe* (Cambridge: Polity Press, 1989); Jack Censer, *Prelude to Power: The Parisian Radical Press, 1789–1791* (Baltimore: Johns Hopkins University Press, 1976); Lynn Hunt, *Politics, Culture, and Class in the French Revolution* (Berkeley: University of California Press, 2004). On China, see David Apter and Tony Saich, *Revolutionary Discourse in Mao's Republic* (Cambridge, MA: Harvard University Press, 1994). On Africa, see Pieter Boele van Hensbroek, *Political Discourses in African Thought: 1860 to the Present* (Westport, CT: Praeger, 1999).

4. George Rudé, *Face of the Crowd: Studies in Revolution, Ideology, and Popular Protest: Selected Essays of George Rudé*, ed. and intro. Harvey J. Kaye (New York: Harvester/Wheatsheaf, 1988), 135–136.

5. Nader Sohrabi, *Revolution and Constitutionalism in the Ottoman Empire and Iran* (New York: Cambridge University Press, 2011), 26.

6. This role of the educator was mostly evident in the Young Turk press. Immediately after the Revolution, *Tanin* began publishing a series of articles under the title "Neler Bilmeliyiz: Öğreniyoruz Öğretmiyoruz" (What should we learn? We are learning and not teaching). The title indicates that the newspaper itself was in a process of learning along with the masses and did not have any intention of imposing its own perceptions on them. In each issue, the title was followed by different subjects dealing with various dimensions of politics. For example, see "Devlet nedir? gâyet nedir?" (What is the state? What is the aim?), *Tanin*, August 22, 1908, no. 22, 1; "Meclis-i Mebusanda Azalarin Mıkdarı" (The number of the members of the House of Deputies), August 16, 1908, no. 16, 2; "Intihabatta Iki Derece" (Two stages in the elections), September 7, 1908, no. 38, 1; "Hürriyet-i Matbuat" (Freedom of press), September 12, 1908, no. 43, 2.

7. *Biwzandion*, July 25, 1908, no. 3587, 2 (uppercase in the original).

8. *Al-Mashriq: Majallah Kāthūlīyah sharqīyah tabhathu fī al-'ilm wa-al-adab wa-al-fann*, 1908, no. 11, 733.

9. *Lisān al-Ḥāl*, August 1, 1908, no. 5778, 1.

10. *Al-Ittiḥād al-'Uthmānī* was edited in Beirut by Shaykh Ahmed Hassan Tabbara. It was a daily newspaper until Ottoman authorities closed it down in 1913. Tabbara participated in the First Arab Congress, held in Paris in June 1913, and was subsequently hanged by the Ottomans for his Arab nationalist activities in 1916.

11. *Al-Ittiḥād al-'Uthmānī*, October 5, 1908, no. 12, 1–2.

12. *Al-Muqaṭṭam*, August 27, 1908, no. 5903, 1.

13. *Ha-Po'el ha-Tza'ir* 1, no. 10 (July 1908): 18.

14. *Ha-Shiloach* was a Hebrew periodical established in Berlin in 1896 by Asher Ginzberg, also known as Ahad Ha-'Am in Berlin. *Ha-Shiloach* is the name of a river

mentioned by Isaiah that became a symbol of Ahad-Ha 'Am's Zionism. Leading Jewish intellectuals, such as Chaim Nahman Bialik and Chaim Weizmann, published their views and articles in the periodical. See Ali Mohammed Abd El-Rahman Attia, *The Hebrew Periodical* ha-Shiloah *(1896–1919): Its Role in the Development of Modern Hebrew Literature* (Jerusalem: Hebrew University Magnes Press, 1991).

15. Ya'kov Rabbinovitz was a practical Zionist and an active member in the "Hibat Zion" Zionist movement. Between 1905 and 1908, he visited Palestine, and between 1908 and 1909, he was a regular contributor to *Hed ha-Zman*.

16. *Ha-Shiloach* 19 (July–December 1908): 280.

17. *Biwzandion*, July 28, 1908, no. 3589, 1.

18. See *Al-Ittiḥād al-'Uthmānī*, October 5, 1908, no. 12, 1; and October 8, 1908, no. 15, 1.

19. *Biwzandion*, July 28, 1908, no. 3589, 2. Talleyrand's maxim, which appears in various forms, was stated in response to young diplomats asking him for the secret of his success after his retirement in old age following a long and brilliant career as France's foreign minister.

20. This theme of drunkenness or euphoric feeling after the Revolution was endemic to all the other newspapers. In an editorial in *El Tiempo* addressed to "Our Brothers in Istanbul," the same call was made to a nation drunk with the feelings of freedom. The editors advised their coreligionists to be patient and calm down. *El Tiempo*, July 31, 1908, no. 90, 1033. See also *Al-Mashriq: Majallah Kāthūlīyah sharqīyah tabḥathu fī al-'ilm wa-al-adab wa-al-fann*, 1908, no. 11, 732.

21. *Biwzandion*, July 28, 1908, no. 3589, 2.

22. *Lisān al-Ḥāl*, August 8, 1908, no. 5784, 1.

23. *Biwzandion*, August 11, 1908, no. 3600, 1.

24. *Zhamanak* was founded in Istanbul on October 8, 1908, by Missag Koçunyan. It is the longest continually running Armenian newspaper in Turkey owned by the Koçunyan family. Its current editor is Ara Koçunyan.

25. *Zhamanak*, October 5, 1908, no. 8, 1.

26. *Biwzandion*, August 1, 1908, no. 3593, 1.

27. Ibid., August 18, 1908, no. 3606, 1.

28. This theme of Turkish-Armenian brotherhood and coexistence was especially propagated by Yervant Sermakeshkhanlian, editor of the newspaper *Arewelk'*. See *Arewelk'*, November 26, 1908, no. 6950, 1; and December 5, 1908, no. 6958, 1.

29. *Tanin*, August 7, 1908, no. 6, 1. See also *Levant Herald and Eastern Express*, August 7, 1908, 1. *Tanin* also published an article from the periodical *Servet-i Fünun* (The wealth of knowledge) that asserted that mutual friendship was evident in Anatolia between the Armenians and the Turks. See *Tanin*, August 9, 1908, no. 8, 4.

30. *Biwzandion*, August 8, 1908, no. 3598, 1. For another article that discusses conscription into the army as vital to equality between the different ethnic groups, see ibid., August 22, 1908, no. 3611, 1.

31. *Tanin*, November 7, 1908, no. 97, 1. See also the article by Hüssein Cahid in *Tanin*, November 10, 1908, no. 100, 1.

32. Ibid., November 7, 1908, no. 97, 1.

33. Yervant Sermakeshkhanlian also wrote a harsh editorial against *Tanin*. See *Arewelk'*, November 9, 1908, no. 6935, 1. See also the editorial about the ruling nation (Armenian, *Dirogh Azgě*; Ottoman, *millet-i hâkime*), in ibid., November 20, 1908, no. 6945, 1.

34. *Zhamanak*, October 11, 1908, no. 13, 1.

35. Ibid.

36. *Lisān al-Ḥāl*, August 14, 1908, no. 5879, 1.

37. *Biwzandion*, September 1, 1908, no. 3617, 1.

38. *Hashkafa*, July 31, 1908, no. 30, 1–2.

39. As mentioned in the previous chapter, this theme of the sultan being deceived by the palace circle runs through most of the ethnic press. See, for example, *Al-Manār* 6, no. 11 (July 28, 1908): 420. This is valid only for the ethnic press in the empire. Outside the empire, the ethnic press was more critical of the sultan. See, for example, *Hayrenik'* 10, no. 15 (182) (September 26, 1908): 1.

40. This was big news in the ethnic press. See, for example, *El Tiempo*, July 31, 1908, no. 90, 1036; *Habazeleth*, August 19, 1908, no. 78, 2, and August 21, 1908, no. 79, 5; and *Levant Herald and Eastern Express*, August 8, 1908, 2. See also *Tanin*, August 4, 1908, no. 3, 3.

41. *Biwzandion*, August 7, 1908, no. 3597, 1. The article mentioned the names of Armenians who "collaborated" with the paşas of the ancien régime.

42. Ibid.

43. *Biwzandion*, August 5, 1908, no. 3595, 1. On Izzet Paşa, see Caesar Farah, "Arab Supporters of Sultan Abdülhamid II: 'Izzet al-'Abid," *Archivum Ottomanicum* 15 (1997): 189–219.

44. *Biwzandion*, August 13, 1908, no. 3602, 1.

45. For the reaction in the Arab provinces to the collapse of the most important figures of the ancien régime, see *Lisān al-Ḥāl*, August 4, 1908, no. 5780, 1–2. This article deals with the anger of the people toward the officials of the ancien régime: for example, Izzet Paşa, Abulhuda, and Salim Paşa Melhame.

46. On the collapse of Izzet Paşa, see *Arewelk'*, July 31, 1908, no. 6852, 1. See also ibid., August 1, 1908, no. 6853, 1.

47. See, for example, *Al-Manār* 11, no. 6 (1909): 420.

48. *Biwzandion*, July 31, 1908, no. 3592, 2.

49. *Arewelk'*, September 17, 1908, no. 6891, 1; September 23, 1908, no. 6896, 3; October 12, 1908, no. 6918, 3; and October 19, 1908, no. 6917, 3.

50. *Biwzandion*, September 2, 1908, no. 3629, 3.

51. *Arewelk'*, October 8, 1908, no. 6908, 1.

52. *Zhamanak*, October 3, 1908, no. 6, 1.

53. *Arewelk'*, October 21, 1908, no. 6919, 1.

54. Ibid., October 27, 1908, no. 6924, 1.

55. Ikdam's article appears in *Arewelk'*. See ibid., October 31, 1908, no. 6928, 1. The Catholicosate of Cilicia was established in 1239 in Sis, the capital of the Armenian Kingdom in Cilicia. From 1441 until the present two catholicosates have existed with-

out interruption, one in Echmiadzin and the other in Cilicia (Sis). After the Armenian genocide of 1915–1923 and the collapse of the Ottoman Empire, the Catholicosate of Sis moved to Antelias (Lebanon). Each was independent and had its own jurisdiction. After the establishment of the Armenian Patriarchate in 1461, the Catholicosate of Cilicia continued to function in Sis. It had more than fifteen dioceses under its jurisdiction, including Adana, Sis, Payas, Marash, Aintab, Antioch, Yozgat, and Cyprus.

56. *Arewelk'*, October 21, 1908, no. 6919, 1. After clarifying the situation with the Ministry of the Interior, *Tanin* also argued that these claims were baseless. See *Tanin*, October 21, 1908, no. 82, 7–8.

57. See also the article by Ismail Hakki (Babanzâde), a *Tanin* columnist who later became deputy of Baghdad in the Ottoman Parliament, in *İkdam*, October 22, 1908, no. 5177, 1. On the Armenian reaction to these articles, see *Arewelk'*, October 28, 1908, no. 6925, 2. *Biwzandion* criticized Hüssein Cahid on his argument that there was no need for Article 61. In reply, Cahid criticized *Biwzandion* for misrepresenting his intentions. See *Tanin*, October 19, 1908, no. 80, 1.

58. For ARF's official statement, see *Hayrenik'* 10, no. 58 (200) (November 20, 1908): 1.

59. *Al-Muqaṭṭam*, August 27, 1908, no. 5903, 1.

60. *Habazeleth*, November 23, 1908, no. 21, 3. For a more detailed report about the attack on the Jews in Baghdad, see *El Tiempo*, November 11, 1908, no. 16, 152; and November 19, 1908, no. 19, 177–178.

61. *Biwzandion*, August 18, 1908, no. 3606, 1.

62. Ibid., August 19, 1908, no. 3607, 1.

63. Ibid., August 22, 1908, no. 3611, 1.

64. Ibid., August 27, 1908, no. 3614, 1.

65. Regarding the declaration, see *Droshak*, August 1908, no. 8 (196), 124; *Hayrenik'* 10, no. 35 (477) (August 25, 1908): 1; *Pro Armenia*, August 20, 1908, 1341.

66. See *Arewelk'*, August 28, 1908, no. 6885, 2.

67. The position of the Reformed Hunchakian Party was reflected in one of its newspapers, *Dzayn Hayrenyats'* (Voice of the homeland), published in Istanbul. See *Dzayn Hayrenyats'*, October 23, 1908, no. 1, 1–3; and October 30, 1908, no. 2, 9–10. For the platform of the party, see ibid., October 23, 1908, no. 1, 4–5.

68. *Biwzandion*, September 12, no. 3627, 1. This is part 1 of Sabah Gulian's speech. For part 2, see ibid., September 14, no. 3628, 1.

69. Ibid., September 14, no. 3628, 1.

70. In Arabic, "Jam'iyat al-Ikhā' al-'Arabī al-'Uthmānī." On the society, see Eliezer Tauber, *The Emergence of the Arab Movements* (London: F. Cass, 1993), chap. 7.

71. *Al-Muqaṭṭam*, September 9, 1908, no. 5914, 4.

72. *Al-Ittiḥād al-'Uthmānī*, September 29, 1908, no. 7, 1–2.

73. *Habazeleth*, August 24, 1908, no. 80, 2.

74. In Palestine, the main newspaper that reflected the Sephardic Zionist point of view was *Ha-Ḥerut* (Liberty), first published in 1909. For more information, see Abigail Jacobson, "Sephardim, Ashkenazim and the 'Arab Question' in Pre–First World War Palestine: A Reading of Three Zionist Newspapers," *Middle Eastern Studies* 39, no. 2 (April 1,

2003): 105–130; and idem, "The Sephardic Jewish Community in Pre–World War I Jerusalem Debates in the Hebrew Press," *Jerusalem Quarterly*, no. 14 (Fall 2001): 23–34.

75. *Ha-Po'el ha-Tza'ir* 1, no. 10 (July 1908): 20–21.

76. *Ha-Shiloach* 19 (July–December 1908): 282, 461, 556, 191–192.

77. *El Tiempo*, August 7, 1908, no. 92, 1078–1079.

78. National privileges refer to centuries-old privileges given by the Ottoman state to ethno-religious groups under the *millet* system. Their autonomy was in the realms of religion, culture, education, and judicial institutions.

79. *Zhamanak*, October 5, 1908, no. 8, 1.

80. *Hashkafa*, September 18, 1908, no. 104, 3.

81. In his propagation of decentralization and private initiative, Prince Sabahaddin was influenced by the social theories of Frédéric Le Play and Edmond Demolins. He considered both approaches as harbingers for the progress of the Ottoman Empire. See Prens Sabahaddin, *Türkiye Nasıl Kurtarılabilir? Meslek-i İçtimai ve Programı* (Istanbul: Kadar Matbaası, 1334 [1918]).

82. *Tanin*, September 4, 1908, no. 35, 1. See also ibid., September 19, 1908, no. 50, 1.

83. *Arewelk'*, September 17, 1908, no. 6891, 3.

84. *Biwzandion*, September 8, 1908, no. 3623, 3.

85. On the extension of responsibility, see Yıldızhan Yayla, *Anayasalarımızda Yönetim İlkeleri: Tevsi-i Mezuniyet ve Tefrik-i Vezaif* (Istanbul: İstanbul Üniversitesi Siyasal Bilgiler Fakültesi, 1984).

86. *Biwzandion*, September 18, 1908, no. 3632, 1.

87. Prince Sabahaddin's speech was translated into many languages and printed in the ethnic press. See *El Tiempo*, September 18, 1908, no. 110, 1257–1258. See also *Arewelk'*, September 17, 1908, no. 6891, 3.

88. *Biwzandion*, September 22, 1908, no. 3635, 1.

89. See *Ha-'Olam*, July 9, 1908, no. 30, 393. The Hebrew is a designation that occurs frequently in Zionist writings referring to Palestine.

90. *Ha-Po'el ha-Tza'ir* 1, no. 10 (July 1908): 19–21.

91. *Ha-Shiloach* 19 (July–December 1908): 221.

92. Uppercase in original.

93. In Hebrew, "Havu Eretz bli 'am l'am bli Eretz." *Ha-Shiloach* 19 (July–December 1908): 293–294. The slogan is wrongly attributed to Israel Zangwill, a British humorist and writer who was an active Zionist until 1905. He wrote a very influential novel, *Children of the Ghetto: A Study of a Peculiar People* (1892). What Zangwill actually wrote in the first year of the twentieth century was "Palestine is a country without a people; the Jews are a people without a country." See Israel Zangwill, "The Return to Palestine," *New Liberal Review*, December 1901, 615. See also Adam M. Garfinkle, "On the Origin, Meaning, Use, and Abuse of a Phrase," *Middle Eastern Studies* 27, no. 4 (October 1991): 539–550.

94. *Ha-'Olam*, September 11, 1908, no. 36, 466.

95. Ibid., August 14, 1908, no. 32, 418.

96. *Al-Muqaṭṭam*, September 30, 1908, no. 5932, 1.

97. Ibid., October 3, 1908, no. 5935, 1.

98. Ibid., August 27, 1908, no. 5903, 1–2.

99. Ibid., August 28, 1908, no. 5904, 7.

100. Ibid., September 1, 1908, no. 5907, 2.

101. Arslan's article on the inclusion of Lebanon in the Parliament appeared in two parts in *Lisān al-Ḥāl* on August 17, 1908, no. 5791, 1; and August 18, 1908, no. 5792, 4.

102. In Arabic, *mamālek maḥrūsah* (protected domains) refers to the Ottoman Empire.

103. *Al-Ittiḥād al-'Uthmānī*, September 25, 1908, no. 4, 1–2.

104. *Biwzandion*, September 22, 1908, no. 3635, 1.

105. *Al-Ittiḥād al-'Uthmānī*, November 7, 1908, no. 38, 1.

106. *Al-Muqtabas*, December 27, 1908, no. 10, 4. *Al-Muqtabas* (The quoter) was founded in Egypt in 1906 by the Syrian scholar, historian, and literary critic Muhammad Kurd 'Ali. In 1909 Kurd 'Ali moved the periodical to Damascus, where it was published until World War I. Kurd 'Ali was a former supporter of the CUP and then became a member of the Arab Revival Society.

107. *El Tiempo*, November 20, 1908, no. 20, 187–188. Moise Cohen, also known as Tekin Alp, was one of the forefathers of Turkish nationalism. For more information about Tekin Alp, see Jacob Landua, *Turkish Patriot, 1883–1961* (Leiden, Netherlands: Historisch-Archaeologisch Instituut te İstanbul, 1984).

108. *Habazeleth*, August 31, 1908, no. 89, 1.

109. *Ha-Shiloach* 19 (July–December 1908): 461.

Chapter 3

1. *Biwzandion*, July 30, 1908, no. 3591, 2.

2. François Georgeon, ed., *"L'ivresse de la liberté": La Révolution de 1908 dans l'Empire ottoman* (Paris: Peeters, 2012); Şükrü Hanioğlu, *Preparation for a Revolution: The Young Turks, 1902–1908* (New York: Oxford University Press, 2001); idem, *The Young Turks in Opposition* (New York: Oxford University Press, 1995); Nader Sohrabi, *Revolution and Constitutionalism in the Ottoman Empire and Iran* (New York: Cambridge University Press, 2011); Aykut Kansu, *Revolution of 1908 in Turkey* (Leiden, Netherlands: Brill, 1997); idem, *Politics in Post-revolutionary Turkey, 1908–1913* (Boston: Brill, 2000); Erik Jan Zürcher, *Unionist Factor: The Role of the Committee of Union and Progress in the Turkish National Movement, 1905–1926* (Leiden, Netherlands: Brill, 1984); and M. Naim Turfan, *Rise of the Young Turks: Politics, the Military and Ottoman Collapse* (London: I. B. Tauris, 2000).

3. See, for example, Feroz Ahmad, "Unionist Relations with the Greek, Armenian, and Jewish Communities of the Ottoman Empire, 1908–1914," in *Christians and Jews in the Ottoman Empire*, ed. Benjamin Braude and Bernard Lewis (New York: Holmes and Meier, 1982), 1:401–436. The essay does not provide a coherent picture regarding how these communities were influenced by the Revolution.

4. Yıldız (Star) Palace was built in 1880 and used by Sultan Abdülhamid II as his residence and court.

5. *Biwzandion*, August 22, 1908, no. 3610, 1.

6. *Droshak*, July 1908, no. 7 (195), 105.

7. Echmiadzin (Armenia) is the center of authority of the Armenian Apostolic Church, and the catholicos is its head archbishop. For an example of such criticism, see A. Grigorean, *P'tut'ean Ōchakhĕ, kam, Ōrmaneani Patriark'ut'iwnĕ* (Boston: Azg Publication, 1908).

8. In his memoirs, Ormanian elaborated on the reasons for his resignation, arguing that it was obvious the time had come for him to leave the political arena. This section of the memoir was written on September 15, 1908. See Maghak'ia Ark'. Ōrmanean, *Hishatakagir Erkotasnamya Patriark'ut'ean*, pt. 2 (Istanbul: V. and H. Der Nersissian Press, 1910), 162.

9. *Arewelk'*, July 29, 1908, no. 6850, 1.

10. *Biwzandion*, July 29, 1908, no. 3589, 3. For Ormanian's resignation letter, see Ōrmanean, *Hishatakagir Erkotasnamya Patriark'ut'ean*, 171.

11. *Biwzandion*, August 11, 1908, no. 3600, 1; *Levant Herald and Eastern Express*, August 8, 1908, 2. See also Sir G. Lowther to Sir Edward Grey (received August 17), Therapia, August 11, 1908, in "Correspondence respecting the Constitutional Movement in Turkey, 1908," *Parliamentary Papers*, 1909, 53. See also the severe criticism of a lawyer named A.K. in *Biwzandion*, August 14, 1908, no. 3603, 1.

12. This section of the memoir was written about five days after the incident. See Ōrmanean, *Hishatakagir Erkotasnamya Patriark'ut'ean*, 178.

13. *Arewelk'*, November 5, 1908, no. 6932, 1; *Azgayin Ĕndhanur Zhoghov* [National General Assembly], Nist E (Session V), October 22, 1908.

14. Sir G. Lowther to Sir Edward Grey (received September 26), Therapia, September 20, 1908, in *Parliamentary Papers*, 88; *Biwzandion*, September 26, 1908, no. 3639, 3.

15. *Arewelk'*, October 7, 1908, no. 6907, 3.

16. Minas Cheraz was a teacher, writer, and important public and political figure of the period. He was part of the delegation headed by Mguerdich Khrimian (1820–1907) that went to the Congress of Berlin in 1878 to represent the Armenians. During the Hamidian period he fled to London, where he published *L'Arménie-Armenia*, a bilingual journal in French and English, to influence European public opinion regarding the Armenian Question. In 1898 he moved from Paris to London and continued publication of *L'Arménie* until 1906. After the Young Turk Revolution, he returned to Istanbul, where he was elected president of the Armenian National Assembly. For his analysis of the Armenian Question, see Minas Ch'eraz, *Haykakan Khndir* (Venetik: Surb-Ghazar, 1917). On the life of Cheraz, see Arshak Alpōyachean, *Minas Ch'eraz: Ir Keankĕ ew Gortsĕ; Ir 60–ameay Hobeleanin Art'iw* (Cairo: Habet-Baghdasar Press, 1927).

17. In Armenian, "dsayn bazmats' dsayn Astudzoy." See *Azgayin Ĕndhanur Zhoghov*, Nist B (Session II), October 10, 1908, 15.

18. On the investigation commission, see *Azgayin Ĕndhanur Zhoghov*, Nist D (Session IV), October 17, 1908–Nist ZhA (XI), December, 12, 1908. It took about two years and thirty sessions for the commission to complete its investigation. See Kostandnupolsoy Patriark'ut'iwn, *Teghekagir Nakhord Patriark' Ōrmanean S.i Dēm*

Eghats Ambastanut'eants' K'nnich' Handznazhoghovi: Matuts'uats Azgayin Zhoghovoy 1909–1910 Tareshrjani (Istanbul: Official Publication of the Armenian Patriarchate, 1910). On March 12, 1909, Ormanian sent a long response to the assembly, rejecting all the accusations against him one by one. See Ōrmanean, *Hishatakagir Erkotasnamya Patriark'ut'ean*, 219–242. On the commission's investigation of him, see ibid., 287–312. On the report pertaining to the financial matters of the Patriarchate from 1897 to 1908, see Maghak'ia Ark'. Ōrmanean, *Npastits' Hants'nazhoghov: Hashwets'uts'ag ew Teghekagir* (Pera: n.p., 1908).

19. The Question of Jerusalem dealt with the dire condition of the Armenian Patriarchate of Jerusalem at the end of the nineteenth century and the beginning of the twentieth in terms of maladministration, corruption, lack of leadership, and embezzlement. In the confines of the Armenian Quarter of Jerusalem, the Revolution brought hope to the disenchanted elements within Sts. James Brotherhood and the members of the Armenian community of the city to reform the condition of the Patriarchate. In this they demanded the assistance of the ANA. On the Question of Jerusalem, see Bedross Der Matossian, "Administrating the Non-Muslims and 'The Question of Jerusalem' after the Young Turk Revolution," in *Late Ottoman Palestine: The Period of Young Turk Rule*, ed. Yuval Ben-Bassat and Eyal Ginio (London: I. B. Tauris, 2011), 211–219.

20. Sir G. Lowther to Sir Edward Grey (received September 7), Therapia, September 1, 1908, in *Parliamentary Papers*, 80.

21. *Arewelk'*, September 30, 1908, no. 6901, 1; October 20, 1908, no. 6918, 3; and November 5, 1908, no. 6932, 2. The letter sent by Sebouh (Arshag Nersissian) from Muş to the Responsible Body of ARF in Istanbul provides important information on the dire situation in Muş four months after the proclamation of the constitution. See "C/697–72/From Sebouh to the Responsible Body of Istanbul, October 13, 1908," in *Niwt'er H. H. Dashnakts'ut'ean Patmut'ean Hamar*, by Eruand P'ampuk'ean (Beirut: Publication of the Armenian Revolutionary Federation, Hamskaïne Library, 2010), 6:328–330.

22. Sir G. Lowther to Sir Edward Grey (received September 26), Therapia, September 20, 1908, in *Parliamentary Papers*, 88.

23. Ibid., 44.

24. See *Azgayin Ĕndhanur Zhoghov*, Nist D (Session IV), October 17, 1908, 49–50. *Tanin* also published these demands. See *Tanin*, November 4, 1908, no. 94, 2.

25. *Arewelk'*, November 5, 1908, no. 6943, 3; and November 6, 1908, no. 6944, 3.

26. See Sir G. Lowther to Sir Edward Grey (received October 19), Therapia, October 9, 1908, in *Parliamentary Papers*, 97.

27. The inclusion of archival documents from the Dashnak Archives housed in Watertown, Massachusetts, would have shed more light on the activities of the ARF in the postrevolutionary period. However, the author was not granted access to this important material after several attempts. It is to be hoped that in the near future all reasonable requests from legitimate scholars to make use of this valuable trove of documents will be approved. On the activities of the ARF in the provinces, see Dikran Kaligian, *Armenian Organization and Ideology under Ottoman Rule, 1908–1914* (New Brunswick, NJ: Transaction Publishers, 2009). On the official declarations of the ARF (Eastern and Western

Bureaus) on the Revolution, see "C/18–91/Eastern Bureau's Circular, July 12 [25], 1908"; and "C/53–147/Western Bureau to the American Central Committee, August 13, 1908," in P'ampuk'ean, *Niwt'er H. H. Dashnakts'ut'ean Patmut'ean Hamar*, 6:244–245.

28. On the ARF platform, see *Arewelk'*, September 18, 1908, no. 6892, 1–2. Part 2 of this document appeared in ibid., September 19, 1908, no. 6893, 1–2.

29. See *Circular of the ARF Responsible Body*, Istanbul (August 3, 1908) sent to all the provinces, in *Droshak*, August 1908, no. 8 (196), 124.

30. *Arewelk'*, August 24, 1908, no. 6871, 3. On Agnuni, see Gabriēl Lazean, *Heghap'okhakan Dēmk'er: Mtavorakanner, Haydukner* (Cairo: Nubar Press, 1947), 131–143.

31. Pierre Quillard (1864–1912) was a French journalist, poet, playwright, and translator. He was an anarchist, a staunch supporter of the Armenian Question, and editor of *Pro Armenia*. For his writings on the Armenian Question, see Pierre Quillard, *Pour l'Arménie: Mémoire et dossier* (Paris: Cahiers de la Quinzaine, 1902). On the Armenophile movement in France during the period, see Edmond Khayadjian, *Archag Tchobanian et le mouvement arménophile en France* (Alfortville, France: SIGEST, 2001).

32. Ṛubēn Tēr Minasean, *Hay Heghap'okhakani mě Hishataknerě*, 2d ed. (Beirut: Hamazkain Press, 1977), 5:40. See also Vahan P'ap'azean, *Im Husherě* (Beirut: Hamazkain Press, 1952), 2:26. This raised the criticism of their opponents; see Artak Darbinean, *Hay Azatagrakan Sharzhman Ōrerēn: Husher 1890ēn 1940* (Paris: Publication of the Armenian National Fund, 1947), 80–181.

33. Tēr Minasean, *Hay Heghap'okhakani mě Hishataknerě*, 56.

34. Der Minassian (1882–1951) was a member of ARF who played an important role during the revolutionary movement in the eastern provinces. His seven-volume memoir, *Hay Heghap'okhakani mě Hishataknerě*, is considered one of the most important sources for the history of the ARF and Armeno-Kurdish relations in Anatolia.

35. Tēr Minasean, *Hay Heghap'okhakani mě Hishataknerě*, 45–57.

36. Arsēn Kitur, *Patmut'iwn S. D. Hnch'akean Kusakts'ut'ean (1887–1962)* (Beirut: Shirak Press, 1962), 1:316. See also Hrach Dasnabedian, "The Hunchakian Party," *Armenian Review* 41, no. 4 (164) (Winter 1988): 17–39.

37. The policy of the Hunchaks toward the Young Turks is laid out by Sabah Gulian, editor of the Hunchak newspaper, in Step'an Sapah-Giwlean, *Eritasard T'urk'ia* (Paris: Publication of the Hunchakian Party, 1908). See also *Biwzandion*, September 12, no. 3627, 1, for part 1 of Sabah Gulian's speech; September 14, no. 3628, 1, for part 2.

38. Step'an Sapah-Giwlean, *Pataskhanatunerě* (Providence, RI: Yeridasart Hayastan Press, 1916), 230–237.

39. Ibid., 279. One needs to be careful while dealing with the Hunchak criticisms of the Dashnaks. The Dashnaks approached the CUP with cautious cooperation and were also very critical of their policy; for example, the telegram sent by ARF to the Central Committee of CUP in Salonica on October 20, 1908. See "C/193–73/Telegram from ARF," in P'ampuk'ean, *Niwt'er H. H. Dashnakts'ut'ean Patmut'ean Hamar*, 6:256. For more information about this intricate relationship, see Kaligian, *Armenian Organization and Ideology under Ottoman Rule*.

40. The party was a conglomeration of two Armenian parties: the Verakazmyal

Hunch'akean Kusakts'ut'iwn and Gaghap'arakts'akan Miwt'iwn, previously the Armenakan and Miwt'enakan organizations. See Darbinean, *Hay Azatagrakan Sharzhman Ōrerēn*, 195. On the official declaration of the Reformed Hunchaks about the Revolution, see "C/2041a-4/Official Declaration of the Reformed Hunchakian Party," in P'ampuk'ean, *Niwt'er H. H. Dashnakts'ut'ean Patmut'ean Hamar*, 6:255.

41. See "The Platform of the Armenian Constitutional Democratic Party," in Darbinean, *Hay Azatagrakan Sharzhman Ōrerēn*, 193–204.

42. On the AIU, see Aron Rodrigue, *French Jews, Turkish Jews: The Alliance Israélite Universelle and the Politics of Jewish Schooling in Turkey, 1860–1925* (Bloomington: Indiana University Press, 1990). On the relation of Haim Nahum to AIU, see Esther Benbassa, "L'Alliance Israélite Universelle et l'élection de Haim Nahum au Grand Rabbinat de l'Empire ottoman (1908–1909)," in *Proceedings of the Ninth World Congress of Jewish Studies*, division B, vol. 3, *The History of the Jewish People (the Modern Times)* (Jerusalem: World Union of Jewish Studies, 1986), 83–90.

43. Born in Manisa in 1873, Rabbi Haim Nahum became one of the most important figures of the Sephardic Jewish community in the empire. With the support of AIU, he studied at the Rabbinical School in Paris and in the École Pratique des Hautes Études. While in Paris, he came into contact with the Young Turks.

44. From J. Bigart to Haim Nahum on the occasion of his election to the post of the chief rabbi of the empire (Paris, January 25, 1909), AAIU, Register of Correspondence, S 219; Esther Benbassa, ed., *Haim Nahum: A Sephardic Chief Rabbi in Politics, 1892–1923* (Tuscaloosa: University of Alabama Press, 1995), 154.

45. See Feroz Ahmad, "The Special Relationship: The Committee of Union and Progress and the Ottoman Jewish Political Elite, 1908–1918," in *Jews, Turks, Ottomans: A Shared History, Fifteenth through the Twentieth Century*, ed. Avigdor Levy (Syracuse, NY: Syracuse University Press, 2002), 212–230.

46. Rodrigue, *French Jews, Turkish Jews*, 123.

47. *El Tiempo*, August 17, 1908, no. 96, 1117.

48. *Jewish Chronicle*, August 28, 1908, no. 2056, 8. The *Jewish Chronicle* had anti-Zionist tendencies. Its correspondent in Istanbul was the son of David Fresco, editor of *El Tiempo*, who was one of the leading anti-Zionists. The elder Fresco wrote a series of articles attacking Zionism, which were later published as a booklet. See David Fresco, *Le sionisme* (Istanbul: Impr. "Fresco," 1909).

49. *El Tiempo*, August 19, 1908, no. 97, 1; and August 21, 1908, no. 99, 1.

50. *El Telegrafo*, published in Istanbul (1886–1925), was the main competitor to *El Tiempo*. Its director and chief editor was Itshak Gabay, and it was pro-AIU. The competition between *El Telegrafo* and *El Tiempo* was also the result of personal animosities between Gabay and Fresco.

51. *El Tiempo*, October 14, 1908, no. 3, 39.

52. In a long letter to Itshak Gabay, David Fresco criticized the approach *El Telegrafo* had taken in covering the elections. *El Tiempo*, September 30, 1908, no. 1, 5–8.

53. "Nahum to J. Bigart (Constantinople, 6 September 1908), AAIU, Turkey, XXX E," in Benbassa, *Haim Nahum*, 147.

54. *El Tiempo*, October 21, 1908, no. 7, 64; *Jewish Chronicle*, October 23, 1908, no. 2064, 11.

55. "Nahum to J. Bigart (Constantinople, 21 December 1908), AAIU, Turkey, XXX E," in Benbassa, *Haim Nahum*, 152.

56. *Jewish Chronicle*, September 4, 1908, no. 2057, 9.

57. *El Tiempo*, September 9, 1908, no. 106, 1217.

58. Ibid., September 11, 1908, no. 107, 1229.

59. For the most comprehensive study on the Maccabi club, see Daniyel Tsiper, *Ha-Degel ha-Tsiyoni me-'al ha-Bosforos: Ha-"Makabi" be-Ḳushṭa ben Tsiyonut le-'Ot'maniyut (1895–1923)* (Jerusalem: Alumni Association of the Zionist in Turkey, 2000).

60. *El Tiempo*, September 30, 1908, no. 1, 1289.

61. Ibid., January 22, 1909, no. 47, 451.

62. Ibid.; *El Liberal*, February 19, 1909, no. 7, 1. *El Liberal* was a Ladino newspaper published in Jerusalem in 1908 by Moshe Azriel and edited by Chaim Ben-Attar. It lasted only three months and was replaced by *Ha-Ḥerut* in 1909 under the editorship of Avraham Elmaliach.

63. Raphael Shimon received nine votes; Moshe Haviv, two; and Avraham Danon, one. For detailed information on the election, see *El Tiempo*, January 23, 1909, no. 48, 461–64; *El Liberal*, January 29, 1909, no. 1, 3–4.

64. *Jewish Chronicle*, January 22, 1909, no. 2077, 8.

65. *El Tiempo*, February 3, 1909, no. 51, 493.

66. The two letters of Rabbi Ya'kov Meir addressed to Haim Nahum and to Avraham Efendi Farhi, president of the Secular Council, appear in *El Tiempo*, February 5, 1909, no. 52, 501.

67. For the imperial *firman*, see *Bulletin semestriel de l'Alliance Israélite Universelle* 34 (1909): 46–49, reprinted in Benbassa, *Haim Nahum*, 156–157; *El Tiempo*, March 3, 1908, no. 63, 607.

68. For the letters sent to the hahambaşı, see HM2 8639; HM2 8640; HM2 8641, in Central Archives for the History of the Jewish People Jerusalem (CAHJP) at the Hebrew University of Jerusalem.

69. On the struggles in Damascus before and after the Revolution, see Yaron Harel, *Ben Tekhakhim le-Mahpekhah: Minui Rabanim Rashiyim ye-Hadaḥatam bi-ḳehilot Bagdad, Dameśeḳ ye-Ḥaleb, 1744–1914* (Jerusalem: Ben-Zvi Institute for the Study of Jewish Communities in the East, 2007), 231–235. On the situation of the Jews in Baghdad after the Revolution, see ibid., 306–327.

70. *El Tiempo*, September 2, 1908, no. 103, 1188.

71. Ibid., September 4, 1908, no. 104, 1194.

72. See Der Matossian, "Administrating the Non-Muslims."

73. *Ha-'Olam*, February 2, 1909, no. 3, 1.

74. On Zionism after 1908, see Isaiah Friedman, *Germany, Turkey, Zionism: 1897–1918* (New Brunswick, NJ: Transaction Publishers, 1998), 120–153; Yosef Katz, "Paths of Zionist Political Action in Turkey, 1882–1914: The Plan for Jewish Settlement in Turkey in the Young Turks Era," *International Journal of Turkish Studies* 4, no. 1 (1987): 115–135;

Esther Benbassa, "Le sionisme dans l'Empire ottoman à l'aube du 20 siècle," *Vingtième siècle: Revue d'histoire*, no. 24 (October–December 1989): 69–80; Robert Olson, "The Young Turks and the Jews," *Turcica* 18 (1986): 219–235; Michelle Campos, *Ottoman Brothers: Muslims, Christians, and Jews in Early Twentieth-Century Palestine* (Stanford, CA: Stanford University Press, 2011).

75. The most important work on David Wolffsohn is Eliav Mordechai, *David Volfson: Ha-Ish u-Zemano: Ha-Tenu'ah ha-Tsiyonit ba-Shanim 1905–1914* (Tel Aviv: Institute for Zionist Research, 1977). See also Abraham Robinson, *David Wolffsohn: Ein Beitrag zur Geschichte des Zionismus* (Berlin: Jüdischer Verlag, 1921); and Emil Bernhard Cohn, *David Wolffsohn, Herzl's Successor* (Philadelphia: Press of the Jewish Publication Society, 1944).

76. Eliav Mordechai, *David Volfson*, 142.

77. See the Contract of the Central Zionist Bureau with Jacobson, Central Zionist Archives (hereafter CZA) Z2/6, July 31, 1908.

78. See CZA Z2/7–12.

79. Wolffsohn to Jacobson (Cologne, August 21, 1908), CZA Z2/7.

80. Emanuel Karasso was an important member of the CUP in Salonica; Nissim Mazliah, deputy of Izmir in the Ottoman Parliament; Nissim Russo, undersecretary of the Interior Ministry and a close friend of Talat Paşa; Issac Fernandez, head of the Regional Committee of AIU in Istanbul; and Vital Faradji, Jewish deputy to the Ottoman Empire from Istanbul.

81. Jacobson to Wolffsohn (Istanbul, September 9, 1908), CZA Z2/7.

82. Jacobson to Wolffsohn (Istanbul, September 10, 1908), CZA Z2/7. The Aid Association of German Jews (Hebrew, Ezra; German, Hilfsverein der Deutschen Juden) was established in 1901 by German Jews mainly to help Jewish communities in eastern Europe that became victim to pogroms and wars. See Isaiah Friedman, "Ḥivrat 'Ezra,' Meśrad ha-Ḥuts ha-Germani ve-ha-Pulmus 'im ha-Tzionim 1901–1918," *Katedra* 20 (July 1981): 97–122.

83. Jacobson to Wolffsohn (Istanbul, September 11, 1908), CZA Z2/7.

84. See the letters of David Wolffsohn and Menahem Ussishkin in *El-Tiempo*, January 29, 1908, no. 49, 471.

85. On the meeting of Jacobson with Mazliah and Russo, see Jacobson to Wolffsohn (Istanbul, January 1, 1909), CZA Z2/7.

86. The letter was written in French. David Wolffsohn to Nissim Mazliah and Nissim Russo (Cologne, January 24, 1909), CZA Z2/7.

87. The phrase "to Turkey" (*nach der Türkei*) in Jacobson's original letter is underlined (most probably by Jacobson himself) to emphasize that fact. Jacobson to Wolffsohn (Istanbul, February 2, 1909), CZA Z2/7.

88. Ibid.

89. Wolffsohn to Jacobson (Cologne, January 3, 1909), CZA Z2/7, cited in Mordechai, *David Volfson*, 157.

90. Wolffsohn to Jacobson (Cologne, February 20, 1909), CZA Z2/7.

91. Jacobson to Wolffsohn (Istanbul, October 21, 1908), CZA Z2/7.

92. The paper was *Jeune Turc* (Young Turk), which Jacobson co-edited with Sami Hochberg.

93. The four newspapers were *Courier d'Orient*, *Tasvir-i Ekfar* (Description of opinions), *Ittihad* (Union), and *Journal de Salonique*.

94. On Salonica after the Revolution, see David Farhi, "Yehudei Śaloniḳa be-Mahpekhat ha-Turkim ha-Tze'irim," *Sefunot* 15 (1981): 135–152. See also Mark Mazower, *Salonica, City of Ghosts: Christians, Muslims, and Jews 1430–1950* (New York: Alfred A. Knopf, 2005), 255–271.

95. To a certain extent the local Jewish community of Salonica rejected Zionism on the premise that the Ottoman authorities might consider it unpatriotic. See Rena Molho, *Salonica and Istanbul: Social, Political, and Cultural Aspects of Jewish Life* (Istanbul: Isis Press, 2005), 170.

96. On Jabotinsky's perception of the Ottoman Jews, see *Ha-'Olam*, February 2, 1909, no. 3, 1. See also his speech given to the General Assembly of the Hovevei Tzion committee in Odessa, February 5, 1912, which appears in *Ze'ev Jabotinsky, Ne'umim* (Jerusalem: n.p., 1947).

97. See, for example, *La Epoka*, October 23, 1908, no. 1725, 1. On Jabotinsky's visit and on Zionism in Salonica, see Letters II and III, entitled "Salonica," that were sent to the Zionist newspaper in Cologne, *Ha-'Olam*, January 13, 1909, no. 2, 12–13.

98. *La Epoka*, January 8, 1909, no. 1758, 1.

99. On Karasso's view of Zionism, see *La Epoka*, January 8, 1909, no. 34, 1. January 8, 1909, no. 1758, p. 1.

100. On the attitude of the Young Turks concerning Jewish immigration to Palestine, see David Farhi, "Documents on the Attitude of the Ottoman Government towards the Jewish Settlement in Palestine after the Revolution of the Young Turks (1908–1909)," in *International Seminar on the History of Palestine and Its Jewish Settlement during the Ottoman Period* (Jerusalem: Yad Yitzhak Ben-Zvi and the Institute of Asian and African Studies, Hebrew University of Jerusalem, 1970).

101. *Die Welt*, January 22, 1909, no. 4, 75–76. The closest translation to the German concept of *heimstätte* is "homestead" or "homeland."

102. Caesar Farah, "Arab Supporters of Sultan Abdulhamid II: 'Izzet al-'Abid," in *Archivum Ottomanicum* 15 (1997): 189–219.

103. Hasan Kayalı, *Arabs and Young Turks: Ottomanism, Arabism, and Islamism in the Ottoman Empire, 1908–1918* (Berkeley: University of California Press, 1997), 61.

104. G. P. Devey, Damascus, to Sir G. Lowther, Constantinople, September 4, 1908, FO195/2277 [Foreign Office Archives, hereafter FO].

105. For the names of the members of the CUP Damascus branch, see Fakhrī Bārūdī, *Mudhakkirāt al-Bārūdī* (Damascus: Dar al-Haya Press, 1951), 63.

106. Sir G. Lowther to Sir Edward Grey (received September 7), Therapia, August 26, 1908, in *Parliamentary Papers*, 73.

107. Taj el-Sir Ahmad Harran, "Syrian Relations in the Ottoman Constitutional Period, 1908–1914" (PhD diss., University of London, 1969), 46; Philip S. Khoury, *Urban*

Notables and Arab Nationalism: The Politics of Damascus, 1860–1920 (Cambridge: Cambridge University Press, 2003), 56.

108. FO 195/2277, file 137, Devey's no. 33, Damascus, August 12, 1908, cited in Elie Kedourie, "The Impact of the Young Turk Revolution on the Arabic-Speaking Provinces of the Ottoman Empire," in *Arabic Political Memoirs and Other Studies* (London: William Clowes and Sons, 1974), 137.

109. *Al-Muqaṭṭam*, October 30, 1908, no. 5956, 4; FO 195/2277, file 137, Devey's no. 33, Damascus, August 12, 1908, cited in Kedourie, "Impact of the Young Turk Revolution," 137.

110. *Al-Manār* 12, no. 11 (January 22, 1909): 944; Bārūdī, *Mudhakkirāt al-Bārūdī*, 70.

111. *Al-Muqaṭṭam*, October 30, 1908, no. 5956, 4.

112. Bārūdī, *Mudhakkirāt al-Bārūdī*, 70.

113. Khoury, *Urban Notables and Arab Nationalism*, 57.

114. *Al-Muqaṭṭam*, September 17, 1908, no. 5920, 1.

115. Yūsuf al-Ḥakīm, *Sūriyah wa-al-'Ahd al-'Uthmānī* (Beirut: Catholic Press, 1966), 60. On the life of Yusuf al-Hakim, see C. Ernest Dawn, "Ottoman Affinities of 20th Century Regimes," in *Palestine in the Late Ottoman Period: Political, Social, and Economic Transformation*, ed. David Kushner (Jerusalem: Yad Izhak Ben-Zvi, 1986), 177–180.

116. *Al-Muqaṭṭam* correspondent in Latakiyya reported that there was a mediator attached to the central body, through whom all negotiations would take place. *Al-Muqaṭṭam*, October 2, 1908, no. 5934, 2.

117. Ibid.

118. M. Geoffroy, consular agent of France in Latakiyya, to M. Fouques-Duparc, consul general of France in Beirut, Latakkiya, August 12, 1908, in *Documents diplomatiques et consulaires relatifs à l'histoire du Liban et des pays du Proche-Orient du XVII siècle à nos jours*, vol. 18, documents recueillis sous l'égide de Maurice Chéhab [par] Adel Ismail (Beirut: Editions des œuvres politiques et historiques, 1975).

119. Al-Ḥakīm, *Sūriyah wa-al-'Ahd al-'Uthmānī*, 162.

120. Muḥammad 'Izzat Darwazah, *Mudhakkirāt Muḥammad 'Izzat Darwazah* (Beirut: Dār al-Gharb al-Islāmī, 1993), 181. Darwazah was a Palestinian Ottoman bureaucrat, politician, and historian from Nablus. He was a CUP member in the early stages of the postrevolutionary period but then withdrew from the party because of its Turkification policies.

121. Muhammad Darwazah, who took an active part in the activities of the CUP, mentions in his memoirs that official rule in Nablus became that of the CUP. See Darwazah, *Mudhakkirāt Muḥammad 'Izzat Darwazah*, 182.

122. *Al-Muqaṭṭam*, October 8, 1908, no. 5939, 3.

123. British consulate general, Beirut, to Sir G. Lowther, Constantinople, August 1, 1908, FO195/2277.

124. Salīm 'Alī Salām, *Mudhakkirāt Salīm 'Alī Salām (1868–1938)*, ed. Hassan Hallaq (Beirut: Dār al-Jāmi'īyyah, 1982), 110. See also Kamal Salibi, "Beirut under the Young Turks: As Depicted in the Political Memoirs of Salim Ali Salam (1868–1938)," in *Les Arabes par leurs archives*, ed. Jacques Berque and Dominique Chevallier (Paris: Editions du Centre National de la Recherche Scientifique, 1976), 193–216.

125. British consulate general, Beirut, to Sir G. Lowther, Constantinople, August 8, 1908, FO195/2277.

126. *Al-Muqaṭṭam*, August 12, 1908, no. 5890, 4.

127. Ibid., August 13, 1908, no. 5891, 4.

128. M. Fouques-Duparc, consul general of France in Beirut, to M. Constans, ambassador of France in Constantinople, Beirut, August 21, 1908, in *Documents diplomatiques*, vol. 18.

129. *Al-Muqaṭṭam*, August 20, 1908, no. 5897, 4.

130. On the relations between the temporal and ecclesiastical authorities, see Engin Deniz Akarlı, *The Long Peace: Ottoman Lebanon 1861–1920* (Berkeley: University of California Press, 1993), 163–173.

131. British consulate general, Beirut, to Sir G. Lowther, Constantinople, August 1, 1908, FO195/2277.

132. Ibid., August 20, 1908, FO195/2277.

133. Dennis Walker, "The Relation of Catholic Maronite Patriarch Ilyas Butrus al-Huwayyik with the Ottoman Turks," *Islamochristiana* 28 (2002): 109–123.

134. British consulate general, Beirut, to Sir G. Lowther, Constantinople, September 9, 1908, FO195/2277.

135. M. Fouques-Duparc, consul general of France in Beirut, to M. Constans, ambassador of France in Constantinople, Beirut, September 5, 1908, annexe à la dépêche nº 73 du 7 septembre 1908, in *Documents diplomatiques*, vol. 18.

136. *Al-Muqaṭṭam*, September 3, 1908, no. 5909, 4; and September 10, 1908, no. 5915, 4.

137. British consulate general, Beirut, to Sir G. Lowther, Constantinople, September 9, 1908, FO195/2277. The "Desiderata," presented on September 12, 1908, by a group of Lebanese to the governor general.

138. Shakīb Amīr Arslān, *Sīrah Dhatīyah* (Beirut: Dār Ṭalīʿah, 1969), 37.

139. Arabic, "ḥādithat Bayt al-Dīn." See Bishārah Khalīl Khūrī, *Haqāʾiq Lubnānīyah* (Beirut: Awrāq Lubnānīyah, 1960), 1:57. In his memoirs, Khoury, who later became president of Lebanon (1943–1952), claims that most members of the delegation went there to ask for offices. His father was one of the chief officers in Bayt al-Din.

140. *Lisān al-Ḥāl*, September 16, 1908, no. 5817, 1; *Al-Muqaṭṭam*, September 17, 1908, no. 5920, 4.

141. British consulate general, Beirut, to Sir G. Lowther, Constantinople, September 18, 1908, FO195/2277.

142. Arslān, *Sīrah Dhatīyah*, 37.

143. British consulate general, Beirut, to Sir G. Lowther, Constantinople, September 18, 1908, FO195/2277.

144. Ibid., September 25, 1908, FO195/2277.

145. Arslān, *Sīrah Dhatīyah*, 37. Patriarch al-Huwayyik sent a delegation of three bishops to Paris to ascertain the intentions of the Quai d'Orsay (Foreign Ministry of France). On October 16, they received unequivocal assurances that France stood behind the status quo. For more information about the policy of France toward the *mutasarrifiyyah* of Lebanon after the Revolution, see John P. Spagnolo, *France and*

Ottoman Lebanon: 1861–1914 (London: Ithaca Press for the Middle Eastern Center, St. Anthony's College, Oxford, 1977), 246–270.

146. Arslān, *Sīrah Dhatīyah*, 41.

147. British consulate general, Beirut, to Sir G. Lowther, Constantinople, October 8, 1908, FO195/2277.

148. M. Fouques-Duparc, consul general of France in Beirut, to M. Pichon, minister of foreign affairs, Beirut, September 20, 1908, Direction des affaires politiques n° 79, in *Documents diplomatiques*, vol. 18.

149. British consulate general, Beirut, to Sir G. Lowther, Constantinople, October 30, 1908, FO195/2277.

150. Būlus Musʿad, *Lubnān wa al-Dustūr al-ʿUthmānī* (Cairo: Maʿārif Press, 1909), 58.

151. Akarlı, *The Long Peace.*

Chapter 4

1. *Biwzandion*, August 22, 1908, no. 3610, 1.

2. Ibid. See also ibid., August 28, 1908, no. 3615, 1.

3. Ibid., September 12, 1908, no. 3627, 3.

4. Hasan Kayalı, "Elections and the Electoral Process in the Ottoman Empire, 1876–1919," *International Journal of Middle East Studies* 27, no. 3 (August 1995): 268–273. The most comprehensive book on the elections is Fevzi Demir, *Osmanlı Devleti'nde II. Meşrutiyet Dönemi Meclis-i Mebusan Seçimleri 1908–1914* (Ankara: İmge Kitabevi, 2007).

5. *Biwzandion*, September 24, 1908, no. 3637, 1.

6. *Zhamanak*, November 26, 1908, no. 26, 1.

7. *Arewelk'*, November 4, 1908, no. 6931, 1. This idea was repeated in *Droshak*, September–October 1908, nos. 9–10 (197), 140.

8. *Lisān al-Ḥāl*, September 17, 1908, no. 5818, 1.

9. *Al-Ittiḥād al-ʿUthmānī*, September 26, 1908, no. 5, 1.

10. *El Tiempo*, August 26, 1908, no. 100, 1137.

11. Ibid., September 4, 1908, no. 104, 1199.

12. Yaʿkov Friman was a Zionist and the *Ha-Zvi* correspondent in Istanbul.

13. *Ha-Zvi*, October 2, 1908, no. 4, 2. *Ha-Zvi* was published in Jerusalem from 1884 to 1914 by Eliezer Ben-Yuhuda, a leading pioneer for the revival of Hebrew as a spoken language.

14. Ibid.

15. *Ha-ʿOlam*, August 21, 1908, no. 33, 440; and August 28, 1908, no. 34, 450.

16. Ibid., August 21, 1908, no. 33, 440.

17. *Tanin*, August 9, 1908, no. 8, 1.

18. On the Greeks in the election, see Caterina Boura, "The Greek Millet in Turkish Politics: Greeks in the Ottoman Parliament (1908–1918)," in *Ottoman Greeks in the Age of Nationalism: Politics, Economy, and Society in the Nineteenth Century*, ed. Dimitri Gondicas and Charles Issawi (Princeton, NJ: Darwin Press, 1999), 192–206.

19. *Tanin*, August 29, 1908, no. 29, 2.

20. Ibid., September 10, 1908, no. 41, 1.

21. Ibid., October 26, 1908, no. 87, 1.

22. *Droshak*, September–October 1908, nos. 9–10 (197), 129–131.

23. *Tanin*, November 4, 1908, no. 94, 1.

24. Ibid. On the Armenian reaction to Cahid's criticisms, see *Arewelkʿ*, November 5, 1908, no. 6931, 2–3. The platform appeared also in *İkdam*, October 1, 1908, no. 5156, 2, and on the front cover of *Al-Muqaṭṭam*. See *Al-Muqaṭṭam*, October 8, 1908, no. 5939, 1.

25. *Şura-yı Ümmet*, October 10, 1908, no. 140 (5), 3. *Droshak* published the CUP platform after publishing its own platform. See *Droshak*, September–October 1908, nos. 9–10 (197), 131–132.

26. Article 108 of the Ottoman Constitution of 1876 indicated that the administration of provinces shall be based on the principle of decentralization. See *Tertip Düstur* (1876), 4:4–20.

27. *Şura-yı Ümmet*, October 6, 1908, 1. A copy of the electoral program appears in Tarık Zafer Tunaya, *Türkiye'de Siyasal Partiler: Cilt I, İkinci Meşrutiyet Dönemi (1908–1918)* (Istanbul: Hürriyet Vakfı Yayınları, 1984), vol. 1.

28. *Tanin*, September 24, 1908, no. 55, 1.

29. Ibid., September 25, 1908, no. 56, 1.

30. Ibid.

31. *Droshak*, September–October 1908, nos. 9–10 (197), 140.

32. See "Ōsmanean Khorherdarani Hay Andamnerun Dzeragirĕ," *Biwzandion*, October 13, 1908, no. 3652, 3.

33. *La Epoka*, September 25, 1908, no. 1710, 1.

34. The first issue of *La Epoka* was published on November 1, 1875. On Halevi's life, see Moshe Atiyash, "Ḥakham Saʿadi ha-Levi," *Ṣaloniḳi: ʿIr va-ʾem be-Yiśraʾel* (Tel Aviv: Center for Research into Salonican Jewry, 1967), 255.

35. Ibid.

36. *Biwzandion*, October 6, 1908, no. 3646, 1.

37. Ibid., October 7, 1908, no. 3647, 1.

38. *Lisān al-Ḥāl*, October 21, 1908, no. 5847, 2.

39. *El Tiempo*, October 30, 1908, no. 11, 102.

40. Haladjian held a doctorate in jurisprudence and political and economic sciences from Paris. He was a member of the CUP and of the general administration of the Public Debt Administration. Haladjian's candidacy was challenged openly by Bedros Hamamdjian, who heavily criticized him in a series of articles. See *Arewelkʿ*, November 16, 1908, no. 6941, 1–2; November 19, 1908, no. 6944, 2; and November 30, 1908, no. 6953, 2.

41. Petros Halachean, *Khorhrdaranakan Dzerakir: Parzetsʿi Hasgiwgh Giragi 14/27 September 1908* (Istanbul: H. Madteosian Press, 1908). The speech also appeared in *Arewelkʿ*, September 29, 1908, no. 6900, 4.

42. Halachean, *Khorhrdaranakan Dzerakir*, 4.

43. Ibid., 8.

44. Ibid., 12, 18.

45. The Armenian community of Izmir, for example, formed a special committee to campaign for the Armenian candidate. See *Arewelkʿ*, September 29, 1908, no. 6900, 3.

46. *Biwzandion*, September 26, 1908, no. 3639, 3.

47. Ibid., September 30, 1908, no. 3641, 3.

48. Ibid., October 9, 1908, no. 3649, 1. Gulian states that heated debates took place between the representatives of the Hunchaks and the Dashnaks during these meetings. While the latter group supported the CUP, the former was vehemently against any cooperation with the CUP. It preferred to cooperate with the Ahrar Fırkası (Liberal Party). Step'an Sapah-Giwlean, *Pataskhanatunerě* (Providence, RI: Yeridasart Hayastan Press, 1916), 290–298.

49. *Arewelk'*, November 6, 1908, no. 6933, 3; and November 9, 1908, no. 6935, 3.

50. Ibid., November 19, 1908, no. 6944, 3.

51. *Times*, December 11, 1908, no. 38827, 7.

52. *Biwzandion*, December 9, 1908, no. 3701, 3.

53. *Zhamanak*, December 10, 1908, no. 38, 3.

54. *Biwzandion*, December 11, 1908, no. 3703, 3.

55. *Zhamanak*, December 11, 1908, no. 39, 3.

56. Colonel Moise Bey Dalmedico was a first dragoman in the Naval Ministry.

57. *El Tiempo*, October 7, 1908, no. 3, 35.

58. Ibid., October 21, 1908, no. 7, 59.

59. *Ha-Zvi*, December 18, 1908, no. 56, 2.

60. *Biwzandion*, September 24, 1908, no. 3637, 1.

61. Ibid., October 9, 1908, no. 3649, 1. On November 27, the *Times* reported that one of the reasons the Christians failed to secure the victory of their candidate was related to compulsory military service, which at the time was required only of Muslims. Christians paid a tax instead of serving, and an annual census was conducted for the sole purpose of estimating recruits and taxes. Some Christians preferred not to be counted in this census to avoid paying the tax, a practice that decreased the number of Christian voters. See the *Times*, November 27, 1908, no. 38815, 12. See also Boura, "The Greek Millet in Turkish Politics," 202.

62. *Biwzandion*, October 9, 1908, no. 3649, 1.

63. Ibid., December 17, 1908, no. 3707, 2.

64. Vahan P'ap'azean, *Im Husherě* (Beirut: Hamazkain Press, 1952), 2:40.

65. L. Achemean, *Husher Armenak Ekareani 1870–1925* (Cairo: Nor Astgh Press, 1947), 155.

66. P'ap'azean, *Im Husherě*, 41–42.

67. In his memoirs, Papazian confessed that he did not consider himself the best candidate because he did not know Ottoman Turkish, but the ARF's Central Committee of Van decided to nominate him. See ibid., 40–41.

68. *Biwzandion*, December 4, 1908, no. 3697, 1.

69. *Arewelk'*, November 4, 1908, no. 6931, 2. The return of confiscated lands was a key issue in the Dashnaks' electoral platform.

70. At the end of the nineteenth century, Palestine was divided into three sancaks: Nablus, Acre, and Jerusalem. Whereas Nablus and Acre were part of the province of Beirut, Jerusalem was an autonomous district whose governor was answerable to Istanbul.

The *mutasarrifiyyah* of Jerusalem consisted of Jerusalem, Jaffa, Gaza, Hebron, and their surroundings.

71. In 1907, David Wolffsohn sent Dr. Arthur Ruppin to Palestine to investigate the situation of the Jewish Yishuv and explore the possibility of developing its agricultural and industrial sectors. By the decision of the Eighth Zionist Congress (1907), Ruppin was sent to live in Palestine permanently to establish the Palestine Bureau in Jaffa to direct the settlement activities of the Zionist movement.

72. CZA Z2/632, Ruppin to Wolffsohn, September 4, 1908, in Mordechai Eliav, *Dayid Volfson: Ha-Ish u-Zemano: Ha-Tenu'ah ha-Tsiyonit ba-Shanim 1905–1914* (Tel Aviv: Institute for Zionist Research; Jerusalem: Publishing House of the World Zionist Organization, 1977), 154.

73. Those dissatisfied with the results of the election argued that the electoral districts were intentionally divided to give Muslims the majority of the vote. It was reported that the authorities had arranged the constituencies so that no district had a Christian majority. *Times*, November 27, 1908, no. 38815, 12.

74. Eliav, *Dayid Volfson*, 155.

75. Ibid.

76. *Lisān al-Ḥāl*, October 28, 1908, no. 5853, 1.

77. *Al-Ittiḥād al-'Uthmānī*, October 31, 1908, no. 31, 1.

78. *Ha-Zvi*, November 17, 1908, no. 33, 2.

79. *Habazeleth*, November 18, 1908, no. 19, 1.

80. *Lisān al-Ḥāl*, September 9, 1908, no. 5811, 1.

81. Ibid., September 17, 1908, no. 5818, 1.

82. Ibid., November 9, 1908, no. 5863, 1; *Al-Muqaṭṭam*, November 12, 1908, no. 5967, 2.

83. Taj el-Sir Ahmad Harran, "Turkish-Syrian Relations in the Ottoman Constitutional Period, 1908–1914" (PhD diss., University of London, 1969), 68, 69.

84. On the backgrounds of the Arab deputies, see Sabine Prätor, *Der arabische Faktor in der jungtürkischen Politik: Eine Studie zum osmanischen Parlament der II. Konstitution (1908–1918)* (Berlin: Klaus Schwarz, 1993), 27–38.

85. Ibid., 73.

86. The five deputies were Shafiq Bey al-Mu'ayyad al 'Azm, 'Abd al-Raḥmann Basha al-Yusuf, Shaykh Muhammad al-'Ajlani, Shaykh Sulayman Jukhdar, and Rashid Bey al-Sham'a. As mentioned earlier, the notables and *ulema* of Damascus played a powerful card: religious sentiments. Philip S. Khoury, *Urban Notables and Arab Nationalism: The Politics of Damascus, 1860–1920* (Cambridge: Cambridge University Press, 2003), 57.

87. On the elections in Salonica, see Consul-General Lamb to Sir G. Lowther, November 9, 1908, in "Correspondence respecting the Constitutional Movement in Turkey, 1908," *Parliamentary Papers*, 1909, 101–102; see also David Farhi, "Yehudei Saloniḳa be-Mahpekhat ha-Turkim ha-Tze'irim," *Sefunot* 15 (1981): 135–152.

88. *El Tiempo*, August 24, 1908, no. 99, 1148. On Karasso, see Dayid A. Reḳanaṭi, ed., *Zikhron Saloniḳi: Gedulatah ye-ḥurbanah shel Yerushalayim de-Balḳan* (Tel Aviv: Committee of Publishing the Book on the Community of Salonica, 1986), 2:456.

89. *El Tiempo*, August 24, 1908, no. 99, 1148.

90. Ibid., September 4, 1908, no. 104, 1198.

91. Ibid., October 21, 1908, no. 7, 63–64.

92. Ibid., November 4, 1908, no. 13, 121.

93. Edward F. Knight, *Turkey: The Awakening of Turkey; The Turkish Revolution of 1908* (London: J. Milne, 1909), 300.

94. Farid Efendi Aseyo was the son of Shabati Aseyo, a notable of the Jewish community and steward in the Naval Ministry. *El Tiempo* stated that Aseyo was a young, learned, and humble man. Before finishing his studies in the Mülkiye school, he was appointed second dragoman in the Naval Ministry. See *El Tiempo*, November 23, 1908, no. 21, 197.

95. *El Tiempo*, December 11, 1908, no. 29, 272.

96. *Zhamanak*, December 10, 1908, no. 38, 3.

97. Ibid., December 11, 1908, no. 39, 3.

98. *Tanin*, September 27, 1908, no. 58, 1.

99. *Levant Herald and Eastern Express*, December 12, 1908, 1; *İkdam*, December 12, 1908, no. 5226, 1.

100. *El Tiempo*, December 16, 1908, no. 31, 295.

101. The Armenian deputies were Armen Garo, Vartkes Serengülian (Erzerum), Kegham Der Garabedian (Muş), and Vahan Papazian (Van). All four were members of ARF. For short biographical sketches of some of these deputies, see Gabriël Lazean, *Heghap'okhakan Dēmk'er: Mtavorakanner, Haydukner* (Cairo: Nubar Press, 1947). Hagop Babikian (Tekirdağ) and Bedros Haladjian (Istanbul) were both CUP members. Krikor Zohrab (Istanbul) was an independent deputy voting with the Liberal Union. Murad Boyadjian (Kozan) was a Hunchak Party member, and Nazareth Daghavarian (Sivas) and Stepan Spartalian (Izmir) were independent.

102. *Biwzandion*, December 15, 1908, no. 3708, 1.

103. Ibid.

104. Ibid.

105. Ibid., December 18, 1908, no. 3709, 1.

106. Ibid.

107. *El Tiempo*, December 18, 1908, no. 32, 305.

108. *Jewish Chronicle*, December 4, 1908, 11.

109. *El Tiempo*, December 14, 1908, no. 30, 282; and December 14, 1908, no. 30, 281.

110. *Ha-Po'el ha-Tza'ir*, July 1909, 10.

111. *Ha-Zvi*, November 20, 1908, no. 36, 2.

112. Ibid.

113. *Al-Muqaṭṭam*, December 9, 1908, no. 5990, 1.

114. *Lisān al-Ḥāl*, November 9, 1908, no. 5863, 1.

115. *Al-Muqaṭṭam*, October 30, 1908, no. 5956, 4.

116. Further research is necessary to examine whether these claims are true. This could be done through a detailed examination of the demographics of the administrative divisions of the empire and the electoral districts that were assigned by the government.

117. See Hüssein Cahid's article in *Tanin*, November 13, 1908, no. 133, 1.

118. Demir, *Osmanlı Devleti'nde II*, 160–161.

119. On the opposition of the Liberals to the CUP, see Ali Birinci, *Hürriyet ve İtilâf Fırkası: II. Meşrutiyet Devrinde İttihat ve Terrakki'ye Karşı Çıkanlar* (Istanbul: Dergâh Yayınları, 1990). See also M. Şükrü Hanioğlu, *A Brief History of the Late Ottoman Empire* (Princeton, NJ: Princeton University Press, 2008), 153.

Chapter 5

1. The analysis in this chapter is based on official transcripts of the fifty-four parliamentary sessions published in *Takvim-i Vekayi* (Calendar of facts) from December 18, 1908, to April 2, 1909. The sessions in Parliament began on December 17 and ended on March 26.

2. Rashid Khalidi, *Palestinian Identity: The Construction of Modern National Consciousness* (New York: Columbia University Press, 1997); Yuval Ben-Bassat and Eyal Ginio, eds., *Late Ottoman Palestine: The Period of Young Turk Rule* (London: I. B. Tauris, 2011); Michelle Campos, *Ottoman Brothers: Muslims, Christians, and Jews in Early Twentieth-Century Palestine* (Stanford, CA: Stanford University Press, 2011); and Neville J. Mandel, *The Arabs and Zionism before World War I* (Berkeley: University of California Press, 1976).

3. For more information about the politics of the period, see Nader Sohrabi, *Revolution and Constitutionalism in the Ottoman Empire and Iran* (New York: Cambridge University Press, 2011); and Aykut Kansu, *Politics in Post-revolutionary Turkey, 1908–1913* (Boston: Brill, 2000).

4. "Meclis-i Mebusanın Zabıt Ceridesidir, Altıncı İctima, 15 Kânunuevvel 1324" (Session 6), *Takvim-i Vekayi*, December 29, 1908 (16 Kânunuevvel 1324), no. 79. In his newspaper, *Tanin*, Hüssein Cahid called for the resignation of Kâmil Paşa because he was chosen by the sultan and not the nation. See *Tanin*, January 11, 1909, no. 160, 1.

5. "Meclis-i Mebusanın Zabıt Ceridesidir, On Birinci İctima, 30 Kânunuevvel 1324" (Session 11), *Takvim-i Vekayi*, January 15, 1909 (2 Kânunusani 1324), no. 92, 1–4.

6. *Volkan* (Volcano), January 14, 1909, no. 20, 1.

7. "Meclis-i Mebusanın Zabıt Ceridesidir, Yirmi Altıncı İctima, 29 Kânunusani 1324" (Session 26), *Takvim-i Vekayi*, February 16, 1909 (3 Şubat 1324), no. 124, 12–13.

8. "Meclis-i Mebusanın Zabıt Ceridesidir, Yirmi Yedinci İctima, 31 Kânunusani 1324" (Session 27), *Takvim-i Vekayi*, February 18, 1909 (5 Şubat 1324), no. 124, 6–7.

9. Emre Sencer, "Balkan Nationalisms in the Ottoman Parliament, 1909," *East European Quarterly* 38, no. 1 (March 2004): 41–64.

10. See İpek Yosmaoğlu, *Blood Ties: Religion, Violence and the Politics of Nationhood in Ottoman Macedonia, 1878–1908* (Ithaca, NY: Cornell University Press, 2013).

11. The Bulgarian Exarchate was founded by a *firman* from Sultan Abdülaziz. The Exarchate was the direct result of the struggle of the Bulgarian Orthodox Church against the domination of the Greek Patriarchate of Constantinople in the 1850s and 1860s. On church strife, see Thomas Meininger, *Ignatiev and the Establishment of the Bulgarian Exarchate, 1864–1872: A Study in Personal Diplomacy* (Madison: University of Wisconsin Press, 1970); Theodore H. Papadopoullos, *Studies and Documents Relating to the History*

of the Greek Church and People under Turkish Domination (Aldershot, UK: Variorum, 1990); "Meclis-i Mebusanın Zabıt Ceridesidir, Yirminci İctima, 17 Kânunusani 1324" (Session 20), *Takvim-i Vekayi*, February 2, 1909 (20 Kânunusani 1324), no. 110, 5–8.

12. The deputy of Prişține, Hasan Bey, spoke on the Vlach and Bulgarian committees' actions; Hristo Dalchef and Dmitri Vlahof, deputy of Salonica, spoke on the lack of peace in Salonica, Kosovo, and Manastir; and Abdullah Azmi Efendi, deputy of Kütahya, spoke on the assaults in Rumelia.

13. Hristo Dalchef was a lawyer and represented Bulgarians from Macedonia in the Ottoman Parliament. He was a member of the People's Federative Party (Bulgarian Section), created by the Internal Macedonian Adrianople Revolutionary Organization (IMARO) after the Young Turk Revolution of 1908.

14. These bands were guerrilla groups classified by the Ottoman secret services as *çetes*.

15. "Meclis-i Mebusanın Zabıt Ceridesidir, Yirminci İctima, 17 Kânunusani 1324" (Session 20), *Takvim-i Vekayi*, February 2, 1909 (20 Kânunusani 1324), no. 110, 10.

16. Ibid., February 3, 1909 (21 Kânunusani 1324), no. 111, 8.

17. Ibid., February 4, 1909 (22 Kânunusani 1324), no. 112, 5.

18. For an in-depth study of Arabs in Parliament during the Second Constitutional Period, see Sabine Prätor, *Der arabische Faktor in der jungtürkischen Politik: Eine Studie zum osmanischen Parlament der II. Konstitution (1908–1918)* (Berlin: Klaus Schwarz, 1993).

19. Taj el-Sir Ahmad Harran, "Turkish-Syrian Relations in the Ottoman Constitutional Period, 1908–1914" (PhD diss., University of London, 1969), 131.

20. *Al-Hilāl*, April 1, 1909, 415.

21. *Al-Muqtabas*, December 31, 1908, no. 14, 1; *Al-Ittiḥād al-'Uthmānī*, February 15, 1909, no. 15, 8.

22. *Al-Ittiḥād al-'Uthmānī*, April 5, 1909, no. 22, 1.

23. Harran, "Turkish-Syrian Relations," 145.

24. "Meclis-i Mebusanın Zabıt Ceridesidir, Üçüncü İctima, 9 Kânunuevvel 1324" (Session 3), *Takvim-i Vekayi*, December 24, 1908 (11 Kânunuevvel 1324), no. 74, 6.

25. "Meclis-i Mebusanın Zabıt Ceridesidir, Dördüncü İctima, 10 Kânunuevvel 1324" (Session 4), *Takvim-i Vekayi*, December 25, 1908 (12 Kânunuevvel 1324), no. 75, 4.

26. On the Syrian Central Committee, see Eliezer Tauber, *The Emergence of the Arab Movements* (London: F. Cass, 1993), chap. 11.

27. *Lisān al-Ḥāl*, February 13, 1909, no. 5943, 1. Mutran was from Ba'albek and moved to Paris during the Hamidian period, where he was preoccupied with commerce. According to Tauber, in early 1909 Mutran was described by *La Liberté*, a newspaper in Beirut, as "one of the more fervent auxiliaries of the Hamidian regime and corruption." See Tauber, *Emergence of the Arab Movements*, chap. 11.

28. "Proclamation du Comité Central Syrien de Paris à l'occasion de la promulgation de la constitution ottomane, Paris, le 25 décembre 1908," in *Documents diplomatiques et consulaires relatifs à l'histoire du Liban et des pays du Proche-Orient du XVII siècle à nos jours*, 18:127–130.

29. "Meclis-i Mebusanın Zabıt Ceridesidir, On Üçüncu İctima, 1 Kânunusani 1324" (Session 13), *Takvim-i Vekayi*, January 18, 1909 (5 Kânunusani 1324), no. 97, 5.

30. *Takvim-i Vekayi*, December 18, 1908 (5 Kânunusani 1324), no. 95, 8.

31. "Meclis-i Mebusanın Zabıt Ceridesidir, On Dördüncü İctima, 5 Kânunusani 1324" (Session 14), *Takvim-i Vekayi*, January 21, 1909 (8 Kânunusani 1324), no. 98, 4.

32. "Meclis-i Mebusanın Zabıt Ceridesidir, Yirmi Altıncı İctima, 29 Kânunusani 1324" (Session 26), *Takvim-i Vekayi*, February 16, 1909 (3 Şubat 1324), no. 124, 3–13; and ibid., February 17, 1909 (4 Şubat 1324), no. 125, 1–11.

33. On concessions and foreign investments, see Necla Geyikdağı, *Foreign Investment in the Ottoman Empire: International Trade and Relations 1854–1914* (London: I. B. Tauris Academic Studies, 2011), 75–99.

34. On an earlier report, see F. R. Maunsell, "The Hejaz Railway," *Geographic Journal* 32, no. 6 (December 1908), 570–585. For other studies about the political and economic implications of the project, see William Ochsenwald, *Hidjaz Railroad* (Charlottesville: University Press of Virginia, 1980); Muḥammad Diqin, *Sikkat Ḥadīd al-Ḥijāz al-Ḥamīdīyah: Dirāsah wathāʾiqīyyah* (Cairo: S. M. al-Diqin, 1985); Murat Özyüksel, *Hidjaz Demiryolu* (Beşiktaş, Istanbul: Türkiye Ekonomik ve Toplumsal Tarih Vakfı, 2000); and James Nicholson, *The Hejaz Railway* (London: Stacey International, 2005).

35. "Meclis-i Mebusanın Zabıt Ceridesidir, On İkinci İctima, 31 Kânunuevvel 1324" (Session 12), *Takvim-i Vekayi*, January 16, 1909 (3 Kânunusani 1324), no. 93, 1.

36. "Meclis-i Mebusanın Zabıt Ceridesidir, On Altıncı İctima, 8 Kânunusani 1324" (Session 16), *Takvim-i Vekayi*, January 25, 1909 (12 Kânunusani 1324), no. 102, 2–3, 3.

37. Ibid., January 26, 1909 (13 Kânunusani 1324), no. 103, 1–2.

38. See Jonathan McMurray, *Distant Ties: Germany, the Ottoman Empire, and the Construction of the Baghdad Railway* (Westport, CT: Praeger, 2001); Paul Rohrbach, *Die Bagdadbahn Berlin* (Berlin: Wiegandt und Grieben, 1911); Gavriʾelah, *Les dessous de l'administration des chemins de fer ottomans d'Anatolie et de Bagdad* (Constantinople: Typographie et lithographe E. Pallamary, 1911); and Luʾay Baḥrī, *Sikkat Ḥadīd Baghdād: Dirāsah fī Taṭawwur wa-Diblūmāsīyat Qaḍīyat Sikkat Ḥadīd Birlīn-Baghdād Ḥattá ʿām 1914* (Baghdad: Sharikat al-Ṭabʿ wa-al-Nashr al-Ahlīyah, 1967).

39. On the Lynch affair, see Mahmoud Haddad, "Iraq before World War I: A Case of Anti-European Arab Ottomanism," in *The Origins of Arab Nationalism*, ed. Rashid Khalidi et al. (New York: Columbia University Press, 1991), 120–150; and Hasan Kayalı, *Arabs and Young Turks: Ottomanism, Arabism, and Islamism in the Ottoman Empire, 1908–1918* (Berkeley: University of California Press, 1997), 100–102.

40. *Al-Ittiḥād al-ʿUthmānī*, March 22, 1909, no. 20, 2–5.

41. "Meclis-i Mebusanın Zabıt Ceridesidir, Yirmi Altıncı İctima, 28 Kânunusani 1324" (Session 26), *Takvim-i Vekayi*, January 26, 1909 (4 Şubat 1324), no. 125, 9.

42. Ibid., 10.

43. "Meclis-i Mebusanın Zabıt Ceridesidir, Otuz Beşinci İctima, 14 Şubat 1324" (Session 35), *Takvim-i Vekayi*, March 2, 1909 (17 Şubat 1324), no. 138, 9–11.

44. Ibid., 11–14; and ibid., March 3, 1909 (18 Şubat 1324), no. 139, 1–5.

45. Ibid., 8.

46. "Meclis-i Mebusanın Zabıt Ceridesidir, Otuz Yedinci İctima, 18 Şubat 1324" (Session 37), *Takvim-i Vekayi*, March 9, 1909 (24 Şubat 1324), no. 125, 9.

47. *Al-Muqtabas*, March 28, 1909, no. 84, 1.

48. *Al-Ittiḥād al-'Uthmānī*, March 15, 1909, no. 21, 2.

49. *Lisān al-Ḥāl*, March 12, 1909, no. 5966, 1. Years later, Hüssein Cahid differentiated between the Arabs of Syria and Iraq and those of Hidjaz and Yemen. He argued that the loudest (*en gürültücü*) deputies came from Syria and Iraq, whereas those from Hidjaz and Yemen were very quiet. He further argued that he was the reason why many Arab deputies left the CUP, because he had greeted them lightly (*hafif selâm vermişim*) and did not pay attention to them. Hüssein Cahit Yalçın, "Osmanlı Meclisinde Arap Mebuslar," *Yakın Tarihimiz: Birinci Meşrutiyetten Zamanımıza Kadar*, no. 9 (April 26, 1962): 265.

50. As discussed in Chapter 3, one of the major issues that the Armenian National Assembly dealt with in the postrevolutionary period was the situation of Armenians in the eastern provinces.

51. "Meclis-i Mebusanın Zabıt Ceridesidir, Yirmi Dördüncü İctima, 26 Kânunusani 1324" (Session 24), *Takvim-i Vekayi*, January 12, 1909 (30 Kânunusani 1324), no. 120, 6.

52. Ibid., 7.

53. Ibid.

54. Ibid., 8.

55. Ibid., 9.

56. Ibid., 10.

57. Ibid., 10–11.

58. Ibid.

59. Ibid., January 13, 1909 (31 Kânunusani 1324), no. 121, 1.

60. Ibid., 4.

61. "Meclis-i Mebusanın Ceridesidir, Yirmi Beşinci İctima, 27 Kânunusani 1324" (Session 25), *Takvim-i Vekayi*, February 15, 1909 (2 Şubat 1324), no. 123, 4.

62. Ibid., 6.

63. In Ottoman Turkish, "eski doktorlar gibi her hastalığa sulfato olmaz ki."

64. "Meclis-i Mebusanın Zabıt Ceridesidir, Yirmi Beşinci İctima, 27 Kânunusani 1324" (Session 25), *Takvim-i Vekayi*, February 15, 1909 (2 Şubat 1324), no. 123, 6.

65. Ibid., 7–8.

66. Ibid., 9.

67. Cahid is referring either to an Armenian newspaper or to the Liberal newspaper *İkdam*.

68. "Meclis-i Mebusanın Zabıt Ceridesidir, Yirmi Beşinci İctima, 27 Kânunusani 1324" (Session 25), *Takvim-i Vekayi*, February 15, 1909 (2 Şubat 1324), no. 123, 9–10.

69. See Roderic H. Davison, "The Armenian Crisis (1912–1914)," *American Historical Review* 8 (April 1948): 481–505; William J. Van Der Dussen, "The Question of Armenian Reforms in 1913–1914," *Armenian Review* 39, no. 1 (Spring 1986): 11–28; Dikran Mesrob Kaligian, *Armenian Organization and Ideology under Ottoman Rule* (New Brunswick, NJ: Transaction Publishers, 2009), 163–226.

70. *Takvim-i Vekayi*, February 26, 1909, no. 134, 1. The CUP organ, *Tanin*, hailed the government's communiqué. See *Tanin*, February 27, 1909, no. 207, 1.

71. Kansu, *Politics in Post-revolutionary Turkey*, 60.

72. "Meclis-i Mebusanın Zabıt Ceridesidir, Otuz Yedinci İctima, 18 Şubat 1324" (Session 37), *Takvim-i Vekayi*, March 6, 1909 (21 Şubat 1325), no. 142, 4–5.

73. Ibid., 5.

74. Ibid.

75. Ibid., 6.

76. Ibid.

77. Ibid., 7.

78. Ibid., 9.

79. Ibid.

80. Ibid.

81. Ibid., 12.

82. Ibid., 13–14.

83. Ibid., 14–15.

84. Ibid., March 7, 1909 (22 Şubat 1325), no. 143, 3.

85. Ibid., 5.

86. Ibid.

87. Ibid., March 8, 1909 (23 Şubat 1325), no. 144, 2.

88. For a list of the participants in the voting, see ibid., 2.

Chapter 6

1. See Bedross Der Matossian, "From Bloodless Revolution to a Bloody Counterrevolution: The Adana Massacres of 1909," *Genocide Studies and Prevention: An International Journal* 6, no. 2 (Summer 2011): 152–173.

2. *Serbesti*, March 18, no. 121, 1; March 19, no. 122, 1; March 20, no. 123, 1–2; March 31, no. 130, 1–2; April 1, no. 135, 1; April 2, no. 136, 1; April 5, no. 139, 1; and April 7, no. 141, 1.

3. Ibid., April 8, 1909, no. 142, 1.

4. According to *Lisān al-Ḥāl*, on April 22, the owner of *Serbesti*, Mevlanzâde Rifat Bey, claimed that the Sublime Porte ordered the murder of Hasan Fehmi. *Al-Ittiḥād al-ʿUthmānī*, May 17, 1909, no. 28, 9–10.

5. *İkdam*, April 14, 1909, no. 5347, 1.

6. *Zhamanak*, April 9, 1909, no. 136, 1–2; *El Tiempo*, April 9, 1908, no. 78, 2; *Lisān al-Ḥāl*, April 16, 1909, no. 5994, 1; *Habazeleth*, April 19, 1909, no. 79, 1; *Ha-Zvi*, April 18, 1909, no. 149, 1.

7. In Armenian, "kiankʿed kam grichʿd."

8. *Zhamanak*, April 9, 1909, no. 136, 1.

9. Ibid. The CUP headquarters and its two newspapers were located on Şeref Street.

10. "Meclis-i Mebusanın Zabıt Ceridesidir, Elli Üçüncü İctima, 25 Mart 1325" (Session 53), *Takvim-i Vekayi*, April 10, 1909 (28 Mart 1325), no. 177, 5–6.

11. David Farhi, "The Şeriat as a Political Slogan: or, The 'Incident of the 31st of Mart,'" *Middle Eastern Studies* 7, no. 3 (1971): 275–299.

12. *Volkan*, April 5, 1909, no. 95, 1–2. It is important to mention that the society was established in February 1909 but remained in hiding until April of the same year. For details, see *Volkan*, February 6, 1909, no. 37, 3. *Volkan* (Volcano) was established by Dervişi Vahdeti and became the main organ of the Society of Muhammad. It was first published on December 11, 1908, and lasted until April 20, 1909.

13. *Lisān al-Ḥāl*, April 15, 1909, no. 5993, 1–2.

14. Nader Sohrabi, *Revolution and Constitutionalism in the Ottoman Empire and Iran* (New York: Cambridge University Press, 2011), 226–236.

15. *Volkan*, March 16, 1909, no. 75, 2–4.

16. Sohrabi, *Revolution and Constitutionalism in the Ottoman Empire and Iran*, 227; Feroz Ahmad, *The Young Turks: The Committee of Union and Progress in Turkish Politics, 1908–1914* (Oxford: Clarendon Press, 1969), 40.

17. *Azatarar Sharzhun Banakin Haght'akan Mutk'n i K. Polis: Liakatar Hawak'atsoy Patkerazard Kensagrakan Tsanot'ut'eambk'* (Istanbul: Tparan ew Gratun H. G. P'alagashean, 1909), 106.

18. *Volkan*, April 8, 1909, no. 98, 1–2.

19. See Talat Fuat, *31 Mart İrtica* (Istanbul: Türk Matbaası, 1911); Sina Akşin, *31 [i.e., Otuz bir] Mart Olayı* (Ankara: Sevinç Matbaası, 1970); Cemal Kutay, *31 Mart ihtilâlinde Abdülhamit* (Istanbul: Cemal Kutay Kitaplığı ve Tarih Sevenler Kulübü, 1977); Ecvet Güresin, *31 Mart Isyanı* (Istanbul: Habora Kitabevi, 1969); Mustafa Baydar, *31 Mart Vak'ası* (Istanbul: Amil Matbaası, 1955); Sadık Albayrak, *31 Mart Gerici bir hareket mi?* (Istanbul: Bilim-Araştırma Yayınları, 1987); Süleyman Kâni İrtem, *31 Mart İsyanı ve Hareket Ordusu: Abdülhamid'in Selânik Sürgünü* (Istanbul: Temel, 2003); Mustafa Eski, *31 Mart Olayının Kastamonu'daki Yankıları* (Ankara: Ayyıldız Matbaası A.S., 1991).

20. See *Azatarar Sharzhun Banakin Haght 'akan Mutk 'n i K. Polis*, 44.

21. Sohrabi, *Revolution and Constitutionalism in the Ottoman Empire and Iran*, 224.

22. In one of the most important sources covering the period, it is indicated that the *hocas* were saying that they were not against the constitution per se but believed that it should be in accordance with the *şeriat*. *Azatarar Sharzhun Banakin Haght'akan Mutk'n i K. Polis*, 6.

23. Sohrabi, *Revolution and Constitutionalism in the Ottoman Empire and Iran*, 225.

24. Ibid.

25. The ranker officers were the traditional officers who were functionally illiterate. They had risen into the ranks without relying on education.

26. *Azatarar Sharzhun Banakin Haght'akan Mutk'n i K. Polis*, 87.

27. Sohrabi, *Revolution and Constitutionalism in the Ottoman Empire and Iran*, 243.

28. Yunus Nadi, *İhtilâl ve İnkilâb-i Osmanî: 31 Mart–14 Nisan 1325: Hadisat, İhtisasat, Hakayik* (Dersaadet [Istanbul]: Matbaayi Cihan, 1909), 35. For another interpretation of the events on that day, see *Volkan*, April 14, 1909, no. 104, 1–2.

29. Nadi, *İhtilâl ve İnkilâb-i Osmanî*, 44–45.

30. *Azatarar Sharzhun Banakin Haght'akan Mutk'n i K. Polis*, 50.

31. Ibid., 38.

32. *Zhamanak*, April 15, 1909, no. 139, 1. A more detailed description can be found in

Azatarar Sharzhun Banakin Haght'akan Mutk'n i K. Polis, 54–59. See also Osman Nuri, *Abdülhamid-i Sani ve Devr-ı Saltanatı: Hayat-ı Hususiye ve Siyasiyesi* (1327; repr., Istanbul: Kitabhane-i İslam ve Askeri-Ibrahim Hilmi, 1911), 3:1186.

33. See "C/193-171/Constantinople Responsible Body to Western Bureau, April 17, 1909," in Hrach' Tasnapetean, *Niwt'er H. H. Dashnakts'ut'ean Patmut'ean Hamar* (Beirut: Publications of the Armenian Revolutionary Federation, Hamskaïne Library, 1984), 6:269–270.

34. *Zhamanak*, April 19, 1909, no. 143, 1. The following newspapers also signed the proclamation: *Mizan* (Scale), *Sabah* (Morning), *İkdam*, *Tercuman-ı Hakikat* (Interpreter of truth), *Saadet* (Happiness), *Yeni Gazete*, *Osmanlı* (Ottoman), and *Serbesti*.

35. Nadi, *İhtilâl ve İnkilâb-i Osmanî*, 74–78; see also *Zhamanak*, April 19, 1909, no. 143, 1; "C/1719k-4/Proclamation du Comité del'union ottomane," in Tasnapetean, *Niwt'er H. H. Dashnakts'ut'ean Patmut'ean Hamar*, 6:260.

36. For a detailed contemporary description about the Action Army's entrance into Istanbul, see *Azatarar Sharzhun Banakin Haght'akan Mutk'n i K. Polis*, 140–170.

37. *Zhamanak*, April 16, 1909, no. 140, 1.

38. Ibid., April 17, 1909, no. 141, 1.

39. *El Tiempo*, April 9, 1909, no. 78; April 15, 1909, no. 79; April 16, 1909, no. 80; and April 19, 1909, no. 81.

40. *Ha-Zvi*, April 15, 1909, no. 147, 1.

41. Ibid., April 18, 1909, no. 149, 1.

42. Ibid., April 23, 1909, no. 154, 1.

43. *Al-Ittiḥād al-'Uthmānī*, April 26, 1909, no. 25, 1.

44. Ibid., 4. See also Shakīb Amīr Arslān, *Sīrah Dhatīyah* (Beirut: Dār Ṭalī'ah, 1969), 55–56, 74–75.

45. *Al-Ittiḥād al-'Uthmānī*, April 26, 1909, no. 25, 8–12.

46. *Lisān al-Ḥāl*, April 26, 1909, no. 6002, 2.

47. *Azatarar Sharzhun Banakin Haght'akan Mutk'n i K. Polis*, 42.

48. *Biwzandion*, April 28, 1909, no. 3813, 1.

49. Vahan P'ap'azean, *Im Husherě* (Beirut: Hamazkain Press, 1952), 2:109–110.

50. See "C/193-80/Constantinople Responsible Body to Western Bureau, April 29, 1909," in Tasnapetean, *Niwt'er H. H. Dashnakts'ut'ean Patmut'ean Hamar*, 6:272–274. Bahçecik (Bardizag in Armenian) was an Armenian borough in Nicomedia.

51. On the activities of the ARF in Rodosto and its cooperation with the Action Army, see Ṛubēn Tēr Minasean, *Hay Heghap'okhakani mě Hishataknerě*, 2d ed. (Beirut: Hamazkain Press, 1977), 261–273. About fifty-five registered volunteers were being trained there. See "C/193-80/Constantinople Responsible Body to Western Bureau, April 29, 1909," in Tasnapetean, *Niwt'er H. H. Dashnakts'ut'ean Patmut'ean Hamar*, 6:272–274.

52. See "C/193-73/From the Western Bureau to the Committee of Izmir, April, 20, 1909," in Tasnapetean, *Niwt'er H. H. Dashnakts'ut'ean Patmut'ean Hamar*, 6:271. The bureau indicated in its letter that in case the Izmir Committee succeeded in mobilizing only Armenians, they should telegram the message "tout seul"; if they were able to get

the other ethnic groups' participation, then telegram "tout ensemble"; and if they could not achieve the mission, they should send a letter with the message "impossible."

53. *Zhamanak*, April 27, 1909, no. 150, 3.

54. *Azatarar Sharzhun Banakin Haght'akan Mutk'n i K. Polis*, 163.

55. *Zhamanak*, April 27, 1909, no. 150, 1–2.

56. *Azatarar Sharzhun Banakin Haght'akan Mutk'n i K. Polis*, 164.

57. *Dzayn Hayrenyats'*, April 23, 1909, nos. 24–25, 248.

58. *Zhamanak*, April 28, 1909, no. 152, 2.

59. Hovannes Yeritsian, "Hay Heghap'okhakan Dashnakts'ut'iwně Tikranakerti Mēch," *Hayrenik' Amsagir* 34 (April 1956): 86.

60. *Zhamanak*, April 20, 1909, no. 144, 2.

61. *Al-Ittiḥād al-'Uthmānī*, April 26, 1909, no. 25, 14–15.

62. *El Tiempo*, April 30, 1909, no. 87, 822–823.

63. The Club des Intimes, a secular club founded by a group of Jewish leaders, was one of the most important Jewish cultural associations in Salonica. It was established in 1873 and closed in 1910. It sought to promote Jewish cultural and philanthropic activities. See D. Gershon Lewental, "Club des Intimes, Salonica," in *Encyclopedia of Jews in the Islamic World*, ed. Norman A. Stillman, BrillOnline Reference Works, 2013, http://www.encquran.brill.nl/entries/encyclopedia-of-jews-in-the-islamic-world/club -des-intimes-salonica-SIM_0005520.

64. *El Tiempo*, April 23, 1909, no. 83, 301–302.

65. Yitzhak Ben Zvi, "Gdud Yehudi be-Mahpekhat ha-Turkim ha-Tze'irim," in *Zikhron Šaloniķi: Gedulatah ye-ḥurbanah shel Yerushalayim de-Balķan*, ed. Dayid A. Reķanaṭi (Tel Aviv: Committee of Publishing the Book on the Community of Salonica, 1986), 2:89–90. Itzhak Ben Zvi (1884–1963) was a historian, leader of the Labor Zionists, and second president of the State of Israel (1952–1963).

66. Ibid., 88.

67. Ibid., 88–89.

68. *El Tiempo*, April 30, 1909, no. 87, 822–823. David Farhi argues that the Third Army Corps captured Istanbul and suppressed the First Army Corps and that the enlistment of Jews to the Action Army served a political rather than a purely military aim. See David Farhi, "Yehudei Šaloniķa be-Mahpekhat ha-Turkim ha-Tze'irim," *Sefunot* 15 (1981): 147. *Ha-Zvi* also testified to the minimal role the Jewish battalion played in ending the Counterrevolution. An article in the paper argued that while all other ethnic groups participated widely in the effort to end the Counterrevolution, the Jews participated only through the Jewish battalion from Salonica. The article heavily criticized the general indifference of the empire's Jews toward the Counterrevolution. See *Ha-Zvi*, May 4, 1909, no. 163, 2.

69. Muhammad Kurd 'Ali estimated the number at seventy thousand, which sounds like an exaggeration. See Muḥammad Kurd 'Alī, *Khiṭaṭ al-Shām* (Beirut: Dar al-'Ilm lil-Malayin, 1969–1971), 3:120. According to another report, the Society of Muhammad had around ten thousand members when it was established in Hama. See *Al-Ittiḥād al-'Uthmānī*, March 22, 1909, no. 151, 1.

70. The Arabic newspapers referred to the Counterrevolution as the reaction event (ḥadithah irtijaʿiyyah).

71. Al-Muqtabas, May 30, 1909, no. 138, 3–4.

72. Yusūf al-Ḥakīm, Sūrīyah wa-al-ʿAhd al-ʿUthmānī (Beirut: Catholic Press, 1966), 177–178.

73. El Liberal, April 20, 1909, no. 21, 1.

74. Ha-Zvi, April 19, 1909, no. 150, 1–2.

75. Habazeleth, April 19, 1909, no. 79, 1.

76. Lisān al-Ḥāl, April 30, 1909, no. 6006, 3.

77. Al-Ittiḥād al-ʿUthmānī, April 26, 1909, no. 25, 14–15.

78. Esat Uras, Tarihte Ermeniler ve Ermeni Meselesi (Ankara: Yeni Press, 1950); Salahi Sonyel, İngiliz Gizli Belgelerine Göre Adanaʾda Vuku Bulan Türk-Ermeni Olayları (Temmuz 1908–Aralık 1909) (Ankara: Turk Tarih Kurmum Baismevi, 1988). Even in their memoirs, Ottoman officials involved in the events at the time argue that Armenians were preparing to establish the Cilician Kingdom: Mehmed Asaf (the mutasarrif of Cebel-i Bereket), Ali Münif Bey (Adanaʾs deputy in Parliament), and Cemal Paşa (Adanaʾs governor after the massacres). See Mehmed Asaf, 1909 Adana Ermeni Olayları ve Anılarım, ed. İsmet Parmaksızoğlu (Ankara: Türk Tarih Kurumu, 1982). Asaf wrote his memoirs to exonerate himself from the accusations against him by Bishop Moushegh, the prelate of Adana. See also Ali Münif Bey, Ali Münif Bey'in Hâtıraları, ed. Taha Toros (Istanbul: İsis Yayımcılık, 1996); and Cemal Paşa, Hatıralar, Ittihat-Terakki ve Birinci Dünya Harbı, ed. Behçet Cemal (Istanbul: Selek Yayınları, 1959).

79. Vahakn N. Dadrian, "The Circumstances Surrounding the 1909 Adana Holocaust," Armenian Review 41, no. 4 (1988): 1–16; Raymond H. Kévorkian, with the collaboration of Paul B. Paboudjian, "Les massacres de Cilicie d'avril 1909," in "La Cilicie (1909–1921): Des massacres d'Adana au mandat français," ed. Raymond H. Kévorkian, special issue, Revue d'histoire arménienne contemporaine 3 (Paris: La Bibliotheque Nubar, 1993), 7–248; idem, Le génocide des Arméniens (Paris: Odile Jacob, 2006), 97–150; idem, "The Cilician Massacres, April 1909," in Armenian Cilicia, ed. Richard G. Hovannisian and Simon Payaslian, UCLA Armenian History and Culture Series: Historic Armenian Cities and Provinces, 7 (Costa Mesa, CA: Mazda Publishers, 2008), 339–369. See also Biwzand Eghiayean, Atanayi Hayots' Patmut'iwn: Patmagrakan, Eghernagrakan, Azatagrakan, Mshakut'ayin, Azgagrakan, Vaweragrakan, Zhamanakagrakan (Beirut: The Administration of the Union of Adana Armenians, 1970), 220.

80. Aram Arkun, "Les relations armèno-turques et les massacres de Cilicie de 1909," trans. Catherine Ter-Sarkissian, in L'actualité du génocide des Arméniens, ed. Comité de Défense de la Cause Arménienne (Paris: Edipol, 1999), 57–74; Matthias Bjørnlund, "Adana and Beyond: Revolution and Massacre in the Ottoman Empire Seen through Danish Eyes, 1908/9," Haigazian Armenological Review 30 (2010): 125–156; and Meltem Toksöz, "Adana Ermeleri ve 1909 'iğtişâşı,'" Tarih ve Toplum Yeni Yaklaşımlar 5 (Spring 2007): 147–157.

81. For a more detailed analysis, see Der Matossian, "From Bloodless Revolution to a Bloody Counter-revolution."

82. Meltem Toksöz, *Nomads, Migrants and Cotton in the Eastern Mediterranean: The Making of the Adana-Mersin Region 1850–1908* (Leiden, Netherlands: Brill, 2010).

83. See *Lisān al-Ḥāl*, August 19, 1908, no. 5793, 3. For detailed information about the festivities, see *Biwzandion*, August 20, 1908, no. 3608, 1; *Levant Herald and Eastern Express*, August 13, 1908, 2. On the manifestations of the constitution in Adana, see Kudret Emiroğlu, *Anadolu'da Devrim Günleri: II. Meşrutiyet'in İlanı, Temmuz-Ağustos* (Ankara: İmge Kitabevi, 1999), 188–193.

84. Hakop T'ĕrzean, *Atanayi Keankĕ* (Istanbul: Zareh Pērpērean Press, 1909), 35.

85. Moushegh Serobean, *Atanayi Jardĕ ew Pataskhanatunerĕ: Nakhent'ats' Paraganer* (Gahire: Tparan Ararat-S. Darbinean, 1909), 19.

86. During the reign of Bahri Paşa all three (Ihsan Fikri, Abdülkadir Bağdadizâde, and Gergerlizâde) were exiled. Some returned with the aid of Bahri Paşa. See *Zhamanak*, June 15, 1909, no. 191, 1–2.

87. Armenians, along with the Muslims, began selling arms after the Revolution. Later, when the incidents began, they were accused of preparing a revolt. Karabet Çalyan, *Adana Vak'ası Hakkında Rapor* (Istanbul: n.p., 1327), 19–21.

88. The Armenian Kingdom of Cilicia (1198–1375), located on the northeastern shores of the Mediterranean, was formed in the medieval period.

89. See Henry Charles Woods, *The Danger Zone of Europe: Changes and Problems in the Near East* (Boston: Little, Brown, 1911), 171; *İtidal*, May 12, 1909, no. 39, 2–3. This report also appeared in Arabic in *Al-Ittiḥād al-'Uthmānī*, May 31, 1909, no. 29, 3. See Asaf, *1909 Adana Ermeni Olayları ve Anılarım*, 7–8, 27–28; Helen Davenport (Brown) Gibbons, *The Red Rugs of Tarsus: A Women's Record of the Armenian Massacre of 1909* (New York: Century, 1917), 98.

90. F. D. Shepard, "Personal Experience in Turkish Massacres and Relief Work," *Journal of Race Development* 1 (1910–1911): 327.

91. "An Interview with Dr. Christie of Tarsus" (from an Armenian newspaper), August 13, 1909, 2, American Board of Commissioners for Foreign Missions (hereafter ABCFM) Archives.

92. Çalyan, *Adana Vak'ası Hakkında Rapor*, 3.

93. Serobean, *Atanayi Jardĕ ew Pataskhanatunerĕ*, 26.

94. Thomas D. Christie to Mr. Peet, Tarsus, May 6, 1909, 1, ABCFM Archives. Thomas D. Christie provides one of the most concise accounts of the deterioration of ethnic tensions after the Revolution.

95. Serobean, *Atanayi Jardĕ ew Pataskhanatunerĕ*, 32.

96. "An Interview with Dr. Christie of Tarsus" (from an Armenian newspaper), August 13, 1909, 2, ABCFM Archives.

97. According to the *mutasarrif* of Cebel-i Bereket, the weapons were brought from Cyprus to be distributed to the Armenians of Adana by convincing them that the Turks were going to kill them. Asaf, *1909 Adana Ermeni Olayları ve Anılarım*, 7.

98. The deputy of Adana accused him of agitating the revolutionary activities of the Armenians in Adana. See Ali Münif Bey, *Ali Münif Bey'in Hâtıraları*, 49; see also Asaf, *1909 Adana Ermeni Olayları ve Anılarım*, 5–7. Asaf accused him of being a member of the

Dashnak Party and planning for the establishment of the Kingdom of Cilicia. In his book-let composed of two letters sent to the First Military Tribunal, Artin Arslanian exonerates Bishop Moushegh of all charges, saying that, on the contrary, he appealed for the unity of elements (*ittihad-ı anasır*). The booklet furthermore criticizes the ways in which justice was performed. Arslanian himself was imprisoned by the first Military Court and under torture had confessed that the aim of the Armenian agitation was to establish the Kingdom of Cilicia. Artin Arslanyan, *Adana'da Adalet Nasıl Mahkûm Oldu* (Cairo: n.p., 1909), 11.

99. Hakob T'ērzean, *Kilikioy Aghetě: Akanatesi Nkaragrut'iwnner, Vawerat'ught'er, Pashtonakan Teghekagirner, T'ght'akts'ut'iwnner, Vichakagrut'iwnner, Amenen Karewor Patkernerov* (Istanbul: n.p., 1912), 18–19; Çalyan, *Adana Vak'ası Hakkında Rapor*, 14–16; Asaf, *1909 Adana Ermeni Olayları ve Anılarım*, 10–11.

100. See the letter of Stephen R. Trowbridge to William Peet, April 20, 1909, 1, ABCFM Archives; Çalyan, *Adana Vak'ası Hakkında Rapor*, 25.

101. In Ottoman Turkish, "Müessesât-ı mâliye ile emâkin-i ecnebîyenin muhâfazası ve iâde-i âsâyişe dikkat olunması." Çalyan, *Adana Vak'ası Hakkında Rapor*, 47.

102. Kévorkian, *La Cilicie (1909–1921) de massacres d'Adana*, 139; Çalyan, *Adana Vak'ası Hakkında Rapor*, 47–49. Even during the parliamentary debates in the period following the massacre, Armenian deputies in the Ottoman Parliament understood the telegram sent by Adil Bey as an order to massacre the Armenians. For example, Arme-nian Deputy Krikor Zohrab discussed the issue: "I saw the telegram from the Ministry of the Interior of which complaint has been made, and its purport was in keeping with the traditions of the old regime. It did not say 'Kill the Armenians,' but 'restore order.' The hon. members know that that was the formula used under the despotic regime; for-mulas depend upon their interpretations, and it is certain that the phrase, 'Keep order and protect the foreigners and banks in particular,' would be misunderstood there." Enclosure in no. 84, "Summary of the Debate in the Chamber of Deputies on the Adana Massacres in Sir G. Lowther to Sir Edward Grey (received May 11)," Constantinople, May 4, 1909, FO424/219 (Foreign Office Archives), 87–92.

103. Başıbozuks were literary known as "damaged head," meaning "disorderly." They were irregular soldiers of the Ottoman army.

104. All Muslims who participated in the massacres were wearing a white hatband around their fezzes. See Vice-Consul Doughty-Wyllie to Sir G. Lowther, Adana, May 3, 1909, enclosure 4 in no. 96, FO424/219, 110; Çalyan, *Adana Vak'ası Hakkında Rapor*, 29.

105. Lawson P. Chambers to William Peet, May 4, 1909, 1, ABCFM Archives. Law-son Chambers was the nephew of William Nesbitt Chambers, a Canadian-British sub-ject, head of the American mission in Adana.

106. Herbert Adam Gibbons to Maj. Doughty-Wyllie, Mersina, May 2, 1909, 1, ABCFM Archives. Gibbons provides in the letter a lengthy account of the incidents dur-ing the first wave of massacres.

107. Rigal (P.), "Adana. Les massacres d'Adana," in *Lettres d'Ore, relations d'Orient [confidential review of the Jesuit Missions edited in the Order in Lyons]* (Brussels, No-vember 1909), 359–391; Shepard, "Personal Experience in Turkish Massacres and Relief Work," 328.

108. Ferriman Duckett, *The Young Turks and the Truth about the Holocaust at Adana in Asia Minor, during April, 1909* (London: n.p., 1913), 24.

109. See F. W. Macallum to Dr. J. L. Barton, Adana, April 19, 1909, 2, ABCFM Archives. Macallum provides a detailed report based on the various notes made by Rev. W. N. Chambers.

110. Lawson P. Chambers to William Peet, May 4, 1909, 8, ABCFM Archives.

111. For a detailed account of the damage, see Çalyan, *Adana Vak'ası Hakkında Rapor*, 31.

112. *Zhamanak*, June 1, 1909, no. 179, 1–2. See also the lengthy article by Suren Bartevian about *İtidal* in *Biwzandion*, May 19, 1909, no. 3831, 1; see also Vice-Consul Doughty-Wyllie to Sir G. Lowther, Adana, May 2, 1909, enclosure 2 in no. 96.

113. Ihsan Fikri was tried by the Military Tribunal (Dîvân-i Harb-i Örfî) and sentenced to two years in exile for agitating the public during the massacres. From his exile in Alexandria he wrote to the Ministry of Internal Affairs complaining about the unjust accusations against him and the unfair trial. See his letter to the high commissioner of Egypt, October 21, 1909 (Teşrinievvel 1325), DH.MUİ.23–2/21_4 and DH.MUİ.23–2/21_5, Prime Minister's Ottoman Archives (hereafter BOA), Istanbul, Turkey.

114. *İtidal*, April 20, 1909, no. 33, 1–2.

115. Ibid., April 7, 1909, no. 33, 1–2. Even after the second wave of massacres Ihsan Fikri continued to claim that the main reason for the disturbances was the Armenians of Adana's quest to establish their kingdom. See ibid., May 4, 1909, no. 37, 1–2.

116. See Vice-Consul Doughty-Wyllie to Sir G. Lowther, Adana, May 2, 1909, enclosure 2 in no. 96. See also Çalyan, *Adana Vak'ası Hakkında Rapor*, 10–13.

117. See Vice-Consul Doughty-Wyllie to Sir G. Lowther, Adana, April 21, 1909, enclosure 1 in no. 83, FO424/219, 80–84.

118. Vice-Consul Doughty-Wyllie argued that because the massacres were perpetrated on the same day in distant places, the authorities knew of the intended massacre beforehand. In ibid.

119. T'ërzian, *Kilikioy Aghetě*, 94.

120. See Vice-Consul Doughty-Wyllie to Sir G. Lowther, Adana, May 7, 1909, enclosure 3 in no. 103. The vice-consul argues that some Rumelian soldiers indicated that the shots fired at them and that started the whole affair were fired by Turks, either to bring about dissension between the soldiers or to raise the hope of rushing the hated Armenian Quarter. See also Woods, *The Danger Zone of Europe*, 135.

121. Hampartsoum H. Ashjian, *Atanayi Yegehernĕ ew Goniyayi Husher* (New York: Gochnag Press, 1950), 55. See also Lawson P. Chambers to William Peet, May 4, 1909, 10, ABCFM Archives.

122. Woods, *The Danger Zone of Europe*, 137.

123. On the premeditated nature of the massacres, see DH.MKT, 2854/6, BOA, Istanbul, Turkey. This document includes a copy of a telegram submitted by the governmental and parliamentary investigative commissions sent to Adana. That telegram clearly indicates that the incidents were part of a premeditated plan (*evvelce tertib ve ittihâz edilmiş bir plan*). The report was submitted to the Sublime Porte on June 16, 1909

(3 Haziran 1325). See also "Ministry of Internal Affairs, telegram to the Administration of Adana, 14 July 1909" (Temmuz 1325), DH.MKT, 2875/81, BOA, Istanbul, Turkey.

124. See "Ministry of Internal Affairs, telegram to the Prime Minister, July 12, 1909" (29 Haziran 1325), DH.MKT, 2873/58, BOA, Istanbul, Turkey.

125. Karabet Çalyan was extremely cynical concerning how justice was achieved in Adana. See Çalyan, *Adana Vak'ası Hakkında Rapor*, 36–55. I will discuss the role of the court-martials, military tribunals, and government/parliamentary investigative commissions in a separate study. These trials were conducted in a manner that was unsatisfactory to the Armenians, who were extremely angry when the court's decision was announced. Nine Muslims and six Armenians were subjected to capital punishment in the autumn of 1909. In addition, twenty-five Muslims were hung in December 1909, including the mufti of Bahçe. Armenians condemned the court for hanging six innocent Armenians, and articles and booklets were written to denounce the court's decision. Kassab Missak, one of the Armenians who was hung, became a symbol of injustice for Armenians. Some even represented him as the Armenian Dreyfus. See Arslanian, *Adana'da Adalet Nasıl Mahkûm Oldu*, 13. Armenian sources also indicated that some of the Turkish peasants who were hung were innocent. In addition to the military tribunals, two other official bodies were sent to Adana on May 12 to investigate the massacres. Faiz Bey and Harutyun Mosdichian were sent on behalf of the government by the Ministry of Justice, and Hagop Babigian and Yusuf Kemal Bey were sent on behalf of Parliament. Babigian and Kemal Bay were accompanied by the *mutasarrif* of Mersin. Both groups conducted their investigations in Adana and sent their official reports to their respective bodies. On Babigian's report, see Hakob Papikean, *Atanayi Egherně* (Istanbul: Ardzagang Press, 1919). On Kemal's report, see Yusuf Kemal Tengirşenk, *Vatan Hizmetinde* (Istanbul: Bahar Matbaası, 1967), 110–124.

126. Arslanian, *Adana'da Adalet Nasıl Mahkûm Oldu*, 12.

127. See, for example, "War Ministry, telegram to the Ministry of Internal Affairs, November 23, 1909" (10 Teşrinisani 1325), DH.MUİ, 43-1/32_2, BOA, Istanbul, Turkey. The same orders were sent to Adana on November 25, 1909 (11 Teşrinisani 1325). See DH.MUİ, 43-1/32_1, BOA, Istanbul, Turkey; "War Ministry, telegram to the Ministry of Internal Affairs, November 22, 1909" (9 Teşrinisani 1325), DH.MUİ, 43-1/23_2, BOA, Istanbul, Turkey. The same orders were sent to Adana on November 23, 1909 (10 Teşrinisani, 1325). See DH.MUİ, 43-1/23_1, BOA, Istanbul, Turkey.

128. For the accord between ARF and the CUP, see "C/1719c-13/Circular of the Ittihad-Terakki and the A. R. Federation, August 3, 1909," in Tasnapetean, *Niwt'er H. H. Dashnakts'ut'ean Patmut'ean Hamar*, 6:267. See also A. Asdvadzadrian, "It't'ihat-Dashnakts'akan Haraberut'iwnnerě, II," *Hayrenik' Amsagir* 43, no. 1 (1965): 68–71.

129. Dikran Mesrob Kaligian, *Armenian Organization and Ideology under Ottoman Rule* (New Brunswick, NJ: Transaction Publishers, 2009), 64.

130. *Dzayn Hayrenyats'*, May 5, 1909, nos. 26–27, 241.

131. *Droshak*, April 1909, no. 4 (201), 37.

132. *Lisān al-Ḥāl*, May 1, 1909, no. 6007, 1.

133. See *Ha-'Olam*, May 4, 1909, no. 15, 1.

134. *Ha-'Olam*, May 4, 1909, no. 15, 2.

135. *Droshak*, April 1909, no. 4 (201), 42–43.

136. Ibid., 45.

137. *Ha-Zvi*, April 28, 1909, no. 158, 1–2.

Conclusion

1. Sheikh Mazhar Shahin, "Congratulating the Anglicans for the New Year," You-Tube video, televised by SAT 7, December 30, 2012, posted by SATARABIC, January 6, 2012, http://www.youtube.com/watch?v=IW2MPkWETQU&feature=share.

2. Harut'iwn Shahrikean, *Mer Hawatamk'ĕ Azgayin Harts'in Masin* (Istanbul: Hratarakut'iwn Artsiw Zhoghovrdakan Gravacharanots'i, 1910), 87–88.

3. Uğur Umit Üngör, *The Making of Modern Turkey: Nation and State in Eastern Anatolia, 1913–1950* (Oxford: Oxford University Press, 2011); Taner Akçam, *The Young Turks' Crime against Humanity: The Armenian Genocide and Ethnic Cleansing in the Ottoman Empire* (Princeton, NJ: Princeton University Press, 2012); Raymond Kévorkian, *The Armenian Genocide: A Complete History* (London: I. B. Tauris, 2011).

INDEX

Note: page numbers in italics refer to figures.

İtidal (newspaper), 164, 167–68
Al-I'tidāl Party, 128
Ittihad-ı Muhammedi. *See* Society of
    Mohammad
İttihad ve Terraki. *See* Committee of Union
    and Progress
Izmir (Smyrna): Armenian newspapers
    in, 11; celebrations of Revolution in,
    27, 36, 38; and Counterrevolution, 156,
    223–24n52; elections of 1908 and, 100,
    120; Jewish leadership in, 16; Protestant
    college in, 11
Izmirlian, Madteos II (patriarch of
    Istanbul), 33; on Armenian privileges,
    64; banishment of, 14; celebration of
    return from exile, 33–35, 39–40, 194n66;
    and celebration of Revolution, 31; and
    elections of 1908, 116; on freedom, 34, 47;
    as hero of Revolution, 32–33; Nahum's
    visit to, 82; as patriarch of Istanbul, 75,
    76; on role of ethic groups in Ottoman
    society, 53–54
Izmit: Armenian newspapers in, 11; and
    Counterrevolution, 156
Izzet, Ahmed, 57
Izzet Bek, 138

Jabotinsky, Vladimir "Ze'ev," 84, 86
Jacobson, Avigodr, 84–87
Jacobson, David, 86
Jaffa: celebrations of Revolution in, 31, 34;
    Counterrevolution in, 162–63
al-Jam'iyah al-Israi'liyyah. *See* Israelite
    Society
al-Jam'iyyah al-Wataniyyah. *See* National
    Society
Jam'iyat al-Shūrah al-'Uthmāniyyah. *See*
    Ottoman Consultative Society
al-Jaza'iri, 'Abd al-Qadir, 161
Jenin, Counterrevolution in, 163
Jerusalem: Armenian Patriarchate in, 77,
    204n19; celebrations of Revolution in,
    29–31, 38, 42; Counterrevolution in, 162;
    and elections of 1908, 100–101, 111–12;
    Jewish purging of ancien régime from,
    83; as sancak, 214–15n70
Jerusalem Question, 83

Jewish Chronicle (periodical), 81, 206n48
Jewish Colonial Trust, 18, 189n91
Jewish Committee for Parliamentary
    Elections, 109
Jewish Constitution of 1865, 16, 17
Jewish Eastern Question, European Jews'
    interest in, 16–17
Jewish enlightenment (*Haskalah*), 16
Jewish interest groups, 15
Jewish *millet*: chief rabbi, replacement
    of, 81–83, 85, 87, 94; conflict between
    progressive and traditional elements in,
    16–17, 30, 62–63; education programs,
    16, 17; and elections of 1908, 99, 100–101,
    104; factional tension in, 17; impact
    of Tanzimat reforms in, 15–16; Jewish
    autonomy in, 10, 15–16; leadership of,
    16, 17, 188n70; political upheaval after
    Revolution, 81–83, 87, 94, 175; purging of
    ancien régime from, 81–83
Jewish political agenda, 64
Jewish political associations, formation of,
    62
Jewish political participation: elections
    of 1908 and, 100–101, 104, 109, 111–12,
    113–14, 115–16, 118–19, 120; electoral
    campaign committees, 109–10; in
    First Constitutional Period, 17; Jewish
    officials, lobbying by, 82; in Young Turk
    movement, 17
Jewish press: on ancien régime, lingering
    influence of, 57, 60; on antisemitism in
    Baghdad, 60; on chief rabbi, replacement
    of, 82–83; on Counterrevolution, 154–55,
    162; criticism of CUP, 171–72; on elections
    of 1908, 100–101; on freedom, meaning
    and uses of, 51–52; on Jewish political
    goals, 66–67, 71; on required learning of
    Ottoman Turkish language, 69–70
Jewish progressives, post-Revolution rise
    of, 81–83, 87
Jewish Question: as term, 189n88; Zionist
    calls for solution to, 18
Jewish-Turkish Committee, 27
Jewish Youth Organization, 27, 37
Jews: on Action Army victory, 171;
    celebration of Revolution, 23, 27, 30–31,

by, 175, 178; rise of, 2, 3–4. *See also*
separatism; Zionism
nationalism, Turkish: ethnic fear of, 107, 171;
Turkification policies of CUP, 177, 178.
See also Ottomanism
Nationality Law of 1869, 8
national privileges of ethnic groups:
Armenian views on, 56, 64, 66, 104;
conflict between Ottomanism and, 3,
7, 8, 56, 64, 70, 119, 124, 171, 176–77, 178;
CUP views on, 103, 106–7; defined,
201n78; ethnic schools and, 68–69; as
issue in elections of 1908, 103, 105, 106–7;
for Lebanon, 67–68, 94; as political
issue, 64, 66, 119; removal of, as goal of
Revolution, 7, 56, 64, 66, 177
National Society, 90
Nessimi, Ahmed, 116
newspapers. *See* press
Nihad Bey, 65
Nimr, Faris, 1, 45–46, 46–47
Niyazi Bey, 27, 32
Noradoungian, Kapriel, 75
Nuri, Burhan, 167, 168

Odessa Committee, 87
Ormanian, Maghakia (patriarch of
Istanbul), 14, 73, 74–76, 77, 203n8
Ottoman-Arab Brotherhood Society, 62, 88,
128, 129
Ottoman Army: and Counterrevolution,
151–52, 152–53, 155; as guarantor of
freedom, in public mind, 51; honoring of
in celebrations of Revolution, 27, 28, 29,
30, 31, 34, 41, 42, 44, 45, 47; purges of in
Counterrevolution, 152, 164
Ottoman Constitutional Armenian Body,
108–9, 115, 135–36
Ottoman Constitutional Club, 36
Ottoman Consultative Society, 20
Ottoman Empire, centralized: as goal
inconsistent with ethnic group goals,
3, 6, 7, 176, 178; maintaining, as central
goal of Young Turks, 3, 7, 14, 15, 124, 171,
175, 176–77; 19th century reforms and, 8;
Revolution's disruption of, 6
Ottoman Empire, unified: Armenian

support for, 61, 76–77, 80, 103–4; civic
nationalism as effort to maintain, 24–25;
ethnic group expectations and, 25; ethnic
press efforts toward, 53–56; symbolism of
Revolution celebrations and, 40–48, 45
Ottomanism: Arab perceptions of, 20;
and autonomy of *millets*, efforts to
undermine, 8; conflict between national
privileges of ethnic groups and, 3, 7, 8,
56, 64, 70, 119, 124, 171, 176–77, 178; CUP
and, 171; differing perceptions of, 7, 20,
70, 119; equality as goal of, 56; failure of,
3, 21, 177–78; symbolism of Revolution
celebrations and, 43, 48, 54; Young
Ottomans' critique of, 9
Ottoman-Jewish Association, 112
Ottoman ruling class, Amiras and, 10
Ottoman social structures, Revolution's
disruption of, 6
Ottoman Turkish language: learning of by
ethnic minorities, 62, 69–70; as official
language, 103, 104; as qualification for
ethnic participation in Parliament, 100,
101, 111, 113, 117, 135, 147, 214n67; required
learning of, as issue, 68–70, 102, 103, 106,
177
Ozouf, Mona, 25, 37, 38

Palestine: Arab political movements in,
19; Arabs in, as obstacle to Zionist
ambitions, 63; celebration of Revolution
in, 31; Edict of Reform (1856) and, 19;
education system in, 69–70; elections
of 1908 and, 111–12, 120; and freedom,
as issue, 51–52; Jewish press in, 200n74;
political subdivisions in, 214–15n70;
Zionist goals in, 18, 66–67, 71, 85, 176;
Zionist land purchases in, 18, 63, 66;
Zionists in, 15, 18, 63–64, 215n71
Palestine Bureau (Eretz Yisrael Office), 112
Panigel, Elyahu, 31, 83
Panossian, Alexander, 54
Papazian, Vahan, 110–11, 156, 214n67
Parliament: Arab deputies in, 128–29;
assassination of Fehmi and, 150–51;
autonomy of delegates to, as issue, 109;
conflict with administration, 125; CUP

Printed and bound by CPI Group (UK) Ltd, Croydon, CR0 4YY

07/07/2024

14524519-0002